Medicines of the Soul

Medicines of the Soul

Female Bodies and Sacred Geographies in a Transnational Islam

Fedwa Malti-Douglas

UNIVERSITY OF CALIFORNIA PRESS
Berkeley · Los Angeles · London

University of California Press
Berkeley and Los Angeles, California

University of California Press, Ltd.
London, England

© 2001 by
The Regents of the University of California

Library of Congress Cataloging-in-Publication Data

Malti-Douglas, Fedwa.
    Medicines of the soul : female bodies and sa-
cred geographies in a transnational Islam / Fedwa
Malti-Douglas.
        p.   cm.
    Includes bibliographical references and index.
    ISBN 0-520-21593-1 (cloth : alk. paper).—
ISBN 0-520-22284-9 (pbk. : alk paper)
    1. Women in Islam.   2. Feminism—Religious
aspects—Islam.   3. Sex differentiation—Religious aspects—Islam.   I. Title.
BP173.4 .M35   2001
297'.082—dc21   00-021550
                                           CIP

Manufactured in the United States of America

09 08 07 06 05 04 03 02 01 00

10 9 8 7 6 5 4 3 2 1

To the companions of my life and work

Contents

Illustrations

Preface

I have been living with *Medicines of the Soul* for many years. The book grew out of extended residences in Europe, the Middle East, and North Africa. More correctly, the book grew out of innumerable trips to bookstores, walks along crowded Middle Eastern and North African streets, lined as they are with displays of books and pamphlets, raids on any open kiosks selling printed works, visits to book peddlers outside mosques marketing religious pamphlets, and so on.

Collecting these varied and fascinating materials led to my becoming immersed in the discourses of the contemporary Muslim revival. I was especially intrigued by the cultural aspect of this revival, in particular its literary and artistic production. At the same time, my interests pushed me toward the gender component of the revival and the concomitant articulation of female spirituality.

The first edition of Karîmân Hamza's book sitting in a kiosk near Groppi's in Cairo attracted my attention long before I was even considering writing about her or about the subject of spirituality. I read her autobiography avidly and admired her energy and enthusiasm through her written words. On my trips, I have always made it a habit to search the little-known bookstores, some of them more religiously oriented than others. It was this way that I happened in Rabat upon Leïla Lahlou's work detailing her battle with breast cancer. Her story spoke to me, as I am sure it speaks to all her female readers. And then there were those endless forays in the bookstores up and down the Rue Jean-Pierre-Timbaud in Paris that would lead to Sultana Kouhmane's book. It seemed some-how appropriate that her Francophone tale of a Muslim living in the West published in Belgium should be sold in the French capital.

Yet to write a book about three women from three different geo-graphical backgrounds seemed rather adventurous and unconventional, if not overly bold. After all, here were different languages, different coun-tries, and seemingly different experiences of the holy.

Enter serendipity. Fate found me serving on the Academic Council of the Center for Muslim-Christian Understanding at Georgetown Univer-sity with my long-time friend, James Piscatori. In some stolen moments away from meetings and receptions, I sought my friend's advice as we sat on the steps of a Georgetown building. He convinced me that the proj-ect I envisaged was indeed worth pursuing. That conversation tipped the balance and *Medicines of the Soul* was fully launched.

It was in the summer of 1992 that an absolutely idyllic residence at the Bellagio Study and Conference Center would allow me to begin work on the eventual book. My gratitude goes out to Alberta Arthurs, Susan Garfield, Lynne Szwaja, and Tomás Ybarra-Frausto for making that dream a reality.

The research benefited immensely from the lively audiences with whom I shared my ideas over the years. Many were the friends and col-leagues who honored me with prestigious invitations that facilitated these exchanges. For a lecture at the Harvard University Center for Middle Eastern Studies in 1992, Susan Miller and William Graham are to be thanked. I was appointed the James H. Becker Annual Alumna Lecturer for the College of Arts and Sciences at Cornell University in 1992–1993. My gratitude goes to Ross Brann and David Owen for making this honor even more special. Then came the Kareema Khoury Annual Distinguished Lecture at Georgetown University in 1994. Bar-bara Stowasser, the director of the Center for Contemporary Arab Stud-ies, was instrumental in this invitation. But I am also grateful for the recognition bestowed upon me by the members of Kareema Khoury's family who attended the festivities. In 1995, Juan Cole invited me to de-liver the Annual Women and the Middle East Lecture at the University of Michigan, for which I express my deep appreciation. Then there was Rice University in 1996, where Judith Brown, David Nirenberg, Paula Sanders, and members of the Arab-American Educational Foundation went out of their way to make me feel welcome. Jomana Ghandour knows how grateful I am for all she did for me. The presence of physi-cians in the audience expanded the discussion of illness and spirituality into new domains. The Issam M. Fares Lecture at the Fletcher School of Law and Diplomacy at Tufts University in 1997 was a gift from Leila Fawaz. Her extraordinary generosity and that of Dr. Karim Fawaz went beyond what I could have imagined. In 1998, Janet Smarr facilitated the Annual Comparative Literature Exchange Lecture at the University of Illinois, Champaign-Urbana.

For someone working on Morocco, perhaps the greatest honor was my appointment in 1998 as the special distinguished lecturer by the Moroccan-American Commission for Educational and Cultural Exchange in Rabat. Daoud Casewit and his staff went beyond the call of duty to make that occasion a memorable one. Daoud and his wife Fatima shared their friendship with ᶜAbbâs al-Jirârî and his family, who in turn invited us to an extraordinary evening of Andalusian music by the Majmûᶜat Briouel. Participating in this cultural and artistic event helped me understand the relationship of Andalusian music to Leïla Lahlou's saga.

As it turned out, no better audiences could have been imagined for my work on Leïla Lahlou than those in Fez at Muhammad bin Abdallah University and in Ifrane at al-Akhawayn University. In Fez, Khalid Bekkaoui and Fatima Amrani, along with their colleagues and students, paid me the highest compliment by engaging with my work on Morocco, and particularly with Leïla Lahlou's narrative. In Ifrane, Karima Belkadi displayed exemplary patience with having to take care of my difficult physical requirements. I was also most fortunate to have Abdellatif Bensharifa, Wael and Iman Benjelloun, and Moncef and Wafa Lahlou take me under their wings. Dr. Iman Benjelloun's medical knowledge was a great boon as we debated the cultural, religious, and medical implications of Lahlou's breast cancer. The intellectual hospitality I received in Ifrane was only matched by the physical one.

Just as critical as these professional occasions at which friends and colleagues gathered were the personal contributions and friendships that facilitated my work. Egypt is never what it is without the constant presence of my long-time friend, Gaber Asfour, presently the deputy minister of culture. Although a work like *Medicines of the Soul* might seem to be outside his particular interests, nevertheless his intellectual and physical presence in the Egyptian capital has always been an inspiration. I never would have gotten to know Karîmân Hamza without Hasan Hanafi's intervention. He generously provided me with the phone number of Karîmân Hamza's sister, who in turn put me in touch with Karîmân. And what a pleasure and an honor it was for me to interact directly with

Karîmân Hamza herself. Generous beyond imagination, Karîmân and her husband helped me in more ways than one. They shared books, magazines, information, and most importantly time and friendship. Sitting with them on the Nile in the company of Ahmad ᶜUmar Hâshim, the president of al-Azhar University, was an unparalleled experience. I could not have completed the work without their help.

But a book like *Medicines of the Soul* did not just benefit from friendships forged in and around Egypt. Equally important was the Moroccan contribution. It is fair to say that all my work in Morocco has the same guardian angel, Driss Ouaouicha. Driss facilitated my contacts with Leïla Lahlou's family. Abdelmalek Lahlou was incredibly kind and forthcoming with what were obviously painful details of Leïla Lahlou's battle with cancer. I owe him more than I can easily express in words.

In *Medicines of the Soul,* Morocco goes beyond Leïla Lahlou. And once again, Driss Ouaouicha came to the rescue. How many times did he ignore his commitments as dean to help me out! He has never been stingy with that precious commodity that is always in short supply: time. He drove me to Fez and helped me to navigate through the areas of the old city in which revivalist materials lay hidden. He kindly agreed to accompany me on the same pilgrimage taken by Sultana Kouhmane in the Middle Atlas, even driving the four-wheel-drive vehicle that would allow us to traverse the terrain to the holy site. Dean Ouaouicha is the kind of model scholar-teacher-administrator whose combination of diplomatic skill, intellectual vision, and positive attitude makes good things happen.

Other friends in Morocco have always been generous to a fault: Mohammed and Malika Dahbi, Najia El-Alami, Abdelhamid and Najat Lotfi, Abdallah Malki and Amina Bouchakor, Mohammed and Iman Zroura, Hajja Zakiyya and her family. On my frequent trips to Morocco, these friends have done nothing short of spoiling me, making me feel like an honorary Moroccan as they opened their homes and shared their deep knowledge of Morocco. Other Moroccan friends and colleagues have enlightened me in other ways: Mohamed Laamiri, Hasan Mekouar, Fouzia Ghisasi. Information in Belgium was made accessible through the kindness of Tim Jon Semmerling.

Closer to home, Jim Piscatori continued to be a crucial influence as the project developed. I have benefited greatly from his intellectual generosity, as I have from that of other friends like John Esposito. John's presence, like that of Jean Esposito, goes beyond the merely academic. Lee Fontanella and Jane Marcus know the depth of my affection for them.

But no book can ever exist without an editor. I have been lucky to be able to work with Lynne Withey, the associate director of the University of California Press. I am grateful for her friendship, her exemplary patience, her deep knowledge of the field, and of course, her choice of astute and constructive readers (to whom I also owe my appreciation).

Friends, no matter how close, however, represent only one source of intellectual nourishment and sustenance. A different source of nourishment and sustenance has come from Allen Douglas. I have been thanking him over the years in all my books, no matter what the topic. And each time I come to that pleasurable and yet daunting task, I experience the same sense of inability to express the depth of my gratitude: gratitude for his sacrifice of time, gratitude for his incisive mind, gratitude for his unflinching support in those all-too-common moments of hesitation and doubt. He knows that nothing I do could ever be done without him.

Nor would my intellectual pursuits ever be what they are without my other companions, those in the P.-T. family: S., D., and A. The three of them shepherded the project from the moment the first books and pamphlets on the religious revival entered my library. I could never have completed the research and the writing without their presence. They are always there to inject beauty, calm, comfort, laughter, and inspiration in the otherwise turbulent universe of the academy.

NOTE ON TRANSLATION AND TRANSCRIPTION

All translations in the text are my own, unless otherwise indicated. When English or other European translations are available, these are noted in the first citation of the text.

I have used a simplified transcription system in which the lengtheners on lowercase vowels are indicated with the French circumflex. The *ᶜayn* and the *hamza* are represented by the conventional symbols. Specialists should be able to easily identify the Arabic words. Since many of the names under discussion are already westernized, I have used the western form in the discussions. I have, however, transcribed the names in the notes when referring to Arabic originals.

Transnational Conversations

Ask anyone in the West about Islam or the Islamic revival, and women will enter the subject of the conversation immediately. Whether in Muslim countries or outside them, the women of the Islamic religious revival are much talked about. They have been filmed, they have been demonized by secularists, they have been placed on pedestals by male revivalists and apologists.

But what do the women themselves have to say about this? How does their gender affect their participation in the transnational Islamic religious revival? How do illnesses like AIDS and breast cancer play across religion? Is there a female spirituality in the Islamic revival? How do the women revivalists express their spirituality? What are these women's aspirations with regard to a transnational Islam? What message do they wish to transmit about their body and its relation, if any, to their soul?

Three born-again Muslim women from different parts of the world will help answer these questions. Writing in different languages, these three revivalist women detail their spiritual transformations. Karîmân Hamza hails from Egypt, Leïla Lahlou from Morocco, and Sultana Kouhmane from Belgium.[1]

Natalie Zemon Davis, in her fascinating work *Women on the Margins,* writes about three different women who are geographically and culturally apart but who share the same century, the seventeenth. Davis and the three women hold a conversation that intertextually comments on

and redefines the entire project of the ensuing work.[2] Reading this dialogue between the four women created in me a desire to engage in a similar dialogue with the three women who inhabit *Medicines of the Soul*.

The more I thought about it, the more I realized that I had already
engaged myself in an intense dialogue with the three born-again Muslim
women. But my conversation is different from that carried on by Davis
and the three women she writes about. My interchange is also distinct
from that carried on by Michael M. J. Fischer and Mehdi Abedi in their
provocative book, *Debating Muslims*.[3] Mine was a multilayered involvement that moved from the textual to the geographical.

My exchange with Karîmân Hamza, Leïla Lahlou, and Sultana Kouhmane goes beyond *Medicines of the Soul*. This work exists in a dialectic
with my earlier two books on gender and Middle Eastern women:
*Woman's Body, Woman's Word: Gender and Discourse in Arabo-Islamic
Writing* and *Men, Women, and God(s): Nawal El Saadawi and Arab
Feminist Poetics*.[4] These three books come together to form a triptych,
each of whose panels can be read independently but yet whose three com-
positions function as a whole. The two earlier books intersect with *Medicines of the Soul* just as the three women's spiritual sagas intersect one
with the other. A deep intertextuality permeates my three books, which
themselves carry on an intense dialogue on gender, religion, and discourses of the body in Arabo-Islamic culture. Just as the earlier *Woman's
Body, Woman's Word* stretched the chronological limits of these discourses by tying the medieval to the modern, so *Medicines of the Soul*
will stretch geographical and linguistic limits by bringing together authors from Egypt, Morocco, and Belgium, writing in Arabic and French.
And in the same way that *Men, Women, and God(s)* demonstrated the
relationship between contemporary women's writings and the Arabo-
Islamic classical heritage, so *Medicines of the Soul* will show the three
born-again women struggling with this same heritage that will prove to
be crucial to their spiritual experiences. *Men, Women, and God(s)* carried forward the issues developed in *Woman's Body, Woman's Word* in
the work of the Arab world's most outspoken radical feminist. *Medicines
of the Soul* completes the picture by showing the perhaps equally outspoken women on the other side of the religio-cultural divide.

This intertextuality between my own three works represents only
part of my complicated conversation with the three revivalist women.
Another dialogue takes place willy-nilly between the four of us: the cultural and civilizational dialogue. As I traveled the countries of the
Middle East, North Africa, and Europe in search of these women's nar-

ratives, I engaged other issues with the women writers. This engagement, some of it overt and some of it less overt, finally led to the writing of *Medicines of the Soul*.

When, calling from the United States, I attempted to get Karîmân Hamza's phone number in Cairo, the information operator in Egypt asked me if this was the famous television announcer (*al-mudhîᶜa al-mashhûra*). Yes, I was quick to reply. The operator apologized profusely, informed me that the number was unlisted, and kindly suggested that I contact the official offices of al-Idhâᶜa wal-Tilifizyûn, the government television and radio organization. Anyone who has attempted to dial this number in Cairo knows the impossibility of reaching anyone in this way.

When close friends were able to give me a phone number for Karîmân Hamza's sister in Cairo, a different dialogue took place. Hamza's sister had an answering machine with a recording in Arabic and English, requesting that people leave a message. When I finally reached Karîmân Hamza's sister, she insisted on speaking to me in a fluent English and kindly provided me with Karîmân Hamza's phone number. When I dialed this number, I got an answering machine, this time completely in Arabic with the traditional Muslim greeting: "*al-Salâmu ᶜalaykum wa-Rahmat Allâh wa-Barakâtuh*" (Peace be upon you, and the mercy of God and His blessings). I left a message and eventually reached Karîmân Hamza herself. But when I heard the telephone recording I could not help thinking about the ironies in all of our lives. This is the greeting that both Karîmân and Sultana had to learn in their spiritual autobiographies.

Then when I actually met Hamza in Cairo (she was gracious enough to meet my plane) and spent a great deal of time with her, the conversation took on a different quality once again. Karîmân Hamza the person is a warm, highly energetic, and fascinating individual. I watched people watch her wherever we went: in the airport, in hotel lobbies, on the street, on a floating restaurant on the Nile. Women greeted her and asked her for religious advice. There could be no doubt, I was in the company of a celebrity.

From Egypt to Morocco and from Morocco to Europe, I traveled with these women just as they traveled with me. When browsing in a religious bookstore on the outskirts of the old medina of Fez, I was told by the store owner in a fully vocalized Arabic (and not in the Moroccan dialect!) that I should veil myself. I wondered if this was what Karîmân Hamza felt like throughout her narrative as men told her to cover herself and as she debated the issue of the veil over and over again with herself.

A search for Leïla Lahlou the person revealed her unfortunate demise. But the verbal conversation that might have taken place with her took place instead with her husband. I still cannot see certain place names in Morocco (such as Anfa) without thinking about Leïla Lahlou. Breast cancer touches all women no matter the country or the language or the religion. The conversation with Lahlou that was never to be had made me realize the importance of her text.

Living as I do in the transnational universe in which these women circulate, and more particularly having lived large parts of my life in a bilingual French and Arabic universe and other parts as an Arab minority, I could well understand the cultural tensions experienced by Sultana Kouhmane. But easier than finding the real Sultana was tracing her footsteps. One of these was the pilgrimage that she took to the site of Sidi Slimane in the Middle Atlas. I followed her guidance and visited the site myself.

Much more fundamentally, however, *Medicines of the Soul* is not an anecdotal assessment of these three important female writers of the religious revival. The most intense dialogue I pursue with them is through the analysis of their work. These three texts, the reader will discover, are not isolated phenomena that exist only in Egypt or Morocco or Belgium. They are an important part of the transnational Islamic revival (chapter 1). The gendering of this revival takes place on many levels. Women's complicated relationships to their bodies are not insignificant factors. As the reader watches Karîmân progressively covering herself, the discourse of the body will prove all-important (chapter 2). But the body is first and foremost a conduit to the soul, and Karîmân's spiritual trajectory is imbued with, and defined by, Islamic mysticism (chapter 3).

For the Moroccan Leïla Lahlou, breast cancer is the corporal issue that dominates the spiritual saga, as the narrator pursues medical treatment in Europe. Medical discourses are vital as they intersect with gender (chapter 4). But like the text of her coreligionist Karîmân Hamza, that of Leïla Lahlou is deeply spiritual. She will go to Mecca as Karîmân did, and her eventual cure will be effected by the Prophet himself in a dramatic oneiric intervention (chapter 5).

How interesting it then becomes to see that the Prophet also appears to Sultana in Brussels. Moreover, her journey on the path will also be richly endowed with bodies, most of them diseased or maimed. In an odd way, this brings her close to Leïla Lahlou's text (chapter 6). However, Sultana Kouhmane differs fundamentally from both Karîmân Hamza and Leïla Lahlou, because she lives in the West. This colors her narrative and sheds a special light on gender and the Islamic revival (chapter 7).

Nevertheless, all three women participate in the creation of a female spirituality in a transnational Islam. Be it through the different layers of the sacred and other geographies or through the corporal discourses, the three journeys all exploit an important mystical element, tied to gender and the revival (chapter 8).

Just as Karîmân Hamza, Leïla Lahlou, and Sultana Kouhmane engaged me in these dialogues and conversations, so the analysis of their spiritual journeys will engage discourses on gender, corporality, transnationalism, and religious revival. *Medicines of the Soul* is a voyage through women's spirituality in a transnational Islamic revival. A voyage in which the women themselves are the guides.

CHAPTER ONE

Gender, Culture, and Religious Revival

Egypt, Morocco, and Belgium. Breast cancer, AIDS, and the female body. The veil and actresses. Muslims in Europe. These and other geographical and corporal issues are brought together in contemporary female Islamic revivalist autobiographies. *Medicines of the Soul* will explore these areas in three spiritual sagas penned by three "born-again" Muslim women. The first, Karîmân Hamza, hails from Egypt; the second, Leïla Lahlou, from Morocco; and the third, Sultana Kouhmane, from Belgium. Hamza's saga is written in Arabic, that of Lahlou in Arabic with a translation into French, and that of Kouhmane in French.[1] These three first-person conversion narratives testify not only to the power of a transnational Islamic revival movement but to a shared female spiritual experience that transcends linguistic and geographical boundaries.

Of course, to say "gender," "culture," and "religious revival" is to say a multitude of things in a variety of contexts. The Islamic religious revival is by now a household concept that arouses at once fascination and anger in westerners. Add gender and various images emerge, not the least of which is the patriarchal figure of Khomeini coupled with waves of veiled women. Add literature, and one has an even more explosive mixture in which Salman Rushdie figures prominently.[2]

Even the terminology of the Islamic revival has sprouted luxuriantly. *Fundamentalism* is probably the most common term used today for what are seen as extremist, strict, highly traditional, or politicized religious movements. Applying it to the Muslim world can be misleading because of the term's originally American Protestant referent and because major characteristics of American fundamentalism are useless in the demarcation of religious movements in an Islamic context. *Integrist,* taken from French Catholics who wished an integrally Catholic life and society, at least indicates an essential feature of the religious movements under discussion here. But the other referent to integration, as in racial integration or the full acceptance of minorities, can lead to plays on the meanings of the term when one is dealing with Muslim minorities in Europe.[3] I am using the terms *Islamic revival* and *Muslim revivalists* for those who wish to give religion, specifically Islam, a greater, indeed central, role in their lives and in the organization of society. Islamism, on the pattern of socialism, communism, and so forth, should best be reserved for those who consider Islam as a complete ideology, and not as a religion that might be compatible with secular-based ideologies. Obviously, many Islamic revivalists are also Islamists, but they need not always be so.

The Islamic context, with its fascination with gender and woman's body, is only one discursive layer for *Medicines of the Soul.* Other layers include the larger domain of gender and spirituality, in the way it is investigated, for example, in the provocative work of Elizabeth Alvilda Petroff (with her attention to medieval women) or Paula M. Cooey (with her attention to more modern cultural figures).[4] Despite the fact that the three figures featured in *Medicines of the Soul* are twentieth-century writers, many of their constructs and intellectual discourses hark back to the centuries-old Arabo-Islamic tradition.

Another context will prove of great importance: the bilingual and Francophone one. The linguistic interplays in the works of all three writers, as well as the Francophone layer in both Lahlou and Kouhmane, add another level of complexity to *Medicines of the Soul.*

The transnational nature of the religious revival means that its ideas and advocates know no borders. Books may be printed in Cairo and Beirut, but one is as likely to find them in bookstores in other Middle Eastern as well as European capitals. Even a casual walk down the Rue Jean-Pierre-Timbaud in Paris, with its plethora of Muslim bookstores, will attest to this. Pamphlets printed in French in Belgium and Switzerland wend their way to Paris as well as to Francophone North Africa. Cassettes of the sermons of the colorful blind Egyptian Shaykh ᶜAbd al-Hamîd Kishk, to take but one example, can be had as easily (or perhaps more easily) in Houston, Texas, as in many Arab cities.[5] In Europe, one is exposed to religious cassettes and videotapes in both Middle Eastern and European languages.

Certainly, the Islamic religious revival in the Middle East and elsewhere has escaped neither the eye nor the pen of the political scientist (be he or she eastern or western) or the religious studies specialist.[6] Part of the complexity of the Islamic revival movement derives from its ability to at once transcend and be involved in politics. This movement is not just a question of street demonstrations or sermons in the local mosque. Nor is it simple blind confrontation with the West. John L. Esposito has brilliantly analyzed these political entanglements in *The Islamic Threat: Myth or Reality?*[7] More recently, the work of Samuel P. Huntington on the clash of civilizations has rekindled this debate and cast it in a more global perspective. Even before Huntington's book on this topic appeared, his article in *Foreign Affairs* motivated scholars from different regions of the world and from different ideological perspectives to expose his overly simplified arguments.[8]

Yet, the spiritual sagas of women themselves, their journeys from lives of disbelief to ones of religiosity, are uncharted territory, and this despite the veritable publishing industry that exists on women, gender, and the nation-state in the Middle East.[9] Many of the studies in which the veil looms large often restrict themselves geographically to one country or even to one geographical area within a country. A goal of *Medicines of the Soul* is precisely to move away from a geographically bound analytical construct and demonstrate that women's spirituality in the Islamic revival is a transnational phenomenon and incorporates a spiritual geography.

As with the larger topic of women and Middle Eastern societies, apologists and critics line up to speak about the question of gender and the religious revival.[10] Scientific studies of the veil, its meaning, its importance, and other issues related to modest women's clothing sit side by side with materials generated within the revival movement itself.[11] The fascination with the veil in book titles, with veiled women on book covers, that I discussed in a review article in 1979 seems only to have grown.[12] The western obsession echoes the Islamic revival itself.

These materials, written in a variety of languages, emanate from the entirety of the Muslim world, as well as from outside it. Should a reader wish guidebooks on proper behavior for women or their religious duties, they are there.[13] Should a reader wish exemplary stories, say about holy women in Islam, they are there.[14] Should the reader wish illustrations on what the veil should look like, or guides detailing the exact characteristics of woman's dress (for instance, thickness of clothing), they are there.[15] Shaykhs from all corners of the globe deliver legal opinions, *fatâwâ,* on the status of women. These injunctions are most often couched in sorts of advice columns that may or may not be instigated by correspondence from individuals but always provide religious validation.[16]

Bookstores in Paris and London, bazaars in Istanbul and Fez are flooded with pamphlets serving up a textual smorgasbord of legal, cultural, and religious materials to the hungry reader. Numerous series have been devoted to the proper conduct of a Muslim woman, of which but three will be mentioned. The first series, entitled Silsilat al-Mar'a al-Muslima (Series on the Muslim Woman), is published by the conservative Dâr al-Iᶜtisâm in Cairo. The works in this multivolume collection can be found as easily in London (I purchased some of them there) as in other parts of the world. Their subjects range from feminist movements and their links to imperialism and Zionism to the concept of the mother in the Qur'ân or the multiplicity of the Prophet's wives.[17] The second series is entitled Silsilat Rasâ'il ilâ Ukhtî al-Mu'mina (Series on Epistles/ Letters Addressed to My Sister, the Believer).[18] The third series is produced by Muhammad ᶜAtiyya Khamîs, who will resurface in the context of Karîmân Hamza. In this series, The Guide of the Female Believers, the male author deals with various aspects of a woman's religious duties.[19] These pamphlets on gender and women in Islam have, needless to say, attracted scholarly attention in both the East and the West.[20]

And if these programmatic works were not enough, further advice on proper female behavior can be had from poetry (some of which is addressed directly to the woman), novels, short stories, drama, travel literature, and so on.[21] Women's bodies, women's dress, women's social interactions, women's rights: these and other areas raise endless questions in the much-contested contemporary Islamic discourses on gender. And, of course, these discourses are transnational and multilingual.[22]

Clearly, then, in the international circulation of cultural and religious materials, women play a major role, albeit more often as the subject of the discourses. In fact, woman is far more commonly the subject talked about (if not the problem) than the subject talking. Partly as a consequence, one hears endlessly about woman's role or behavior but all too rarely about woman's spirituality. One hears about how the Islamic revival affects women but far less about women's Islamic revival; that is, about their religiosity, their spiritual voyages. After all, there are as many Muslim women as there are Muslim men. And there could be no

Islamic revival without the participation of women. The discourses investigated here are part of the growing cultural corpus emanating from the Islamic revival movement.

This religious cultural production remains opaque. Part of what makes it a difficult domain for the critic is its enormity, stretching as it does from adult literature to children's literature, from painting to cinema, from music to sermons, from legal tract to novel. Children's literature, to take but one area, spans the entirety of the Islamic world and comprises children's magazines, booklets, pamphlets, and so on. These materials are written in a variety of languages to appeal to a variety of Muslim audiences.[23] No matter what the genre or the language, however, this religious corpus of textual materials does not exist in an ideological vacuum. The contemporary Islamic textual corpus advocates a religious way of life. In fact, statistically, sales of religious books outnumber sales of secular books in the Middle East and North Africa.[24]

These religious texts may be popular among a certain group of readers, but they are far from popular among cultural and literary critics. The occultation of the more literary texts of the Islamic revival comes about because of the unwitting collusion of different academic specialties. On the one hand, most studies of religious movements concern themselves with political and theological questions. It is, therefore, no accident that most western authors of book-length studies on the Islamic revival should not be cultural or literary critics.[25] On the other hand, western specialists in Arabic and other literatures of the Middle East, or the Islamic world, or even the Francophone world, consciously confine themselves to the enormous secularized literary and cultural production of the region, perceived as it is to be artistically serious and, hence, more worthy of study.[26]

Islamic literature, or *adab islâmî* to use its Arabic appellation, is a parallel Islamic literary body that encompasses all the genres hitherto promulgated by more secularly minded intellectuals: plays, novels, short stories, and poetry. As such, it sits alongside the more canonical secular literary tradition and functions in a dialectic with it. This dialectical relationship permits a great deal of permeability between the secular and the more religious materials. Interestingly enough, however, this permeability is more often present in the works of the religiously minded writers than in the works of their more secularly minded colleagues. The religious writer swims in a textual universe in which he or she is surrounded by the more secularized members of the writing profession. The secular corpus functions almost as a gauge against which Islamic literature measures itself. Indeed, secular culture haunts the works of the three women writers under discussion.

This permeability is different from the direct confrontation seen, for example, in the Rushdie case. And Salman Rushdie is, of course, not the only writer whose work has caused him or her to collide with conservative religious mores. Just as the Islamic revival is transnational, so are these ideological collisions. Names of women writers, like those of the Bengali physician Taslima Nasrin or her Egyptian medical colleague Nawal El Saadawi, stand alongside that of the 1988 Nobel laureate, the Egyptian Naguib Mahfouz. And this is not to mention the Algerian activist Khalida Messaoudi or the Egyptian academic Nasr Hâmid Abû Zayd. These are all intellectuals subjected to vigorous attacks when not death threats.[27]

At the same time, the discourse of confrontation is part of the background against which the women's spiritual dramas from Egypt, Morocco, and Belgium unfold. When an Arabic reader encounters the name of the famous blind preacher Shaykh Kishk in Karîmân Hamza's journey, it is difficult for that reader to forget Shaykh Kishk's attack on Mahfouz and his novel, *Awlâd Hâratinâ* (translated as *The Children of Gebelawi*), a novel that earned the ire of many religious Muslims.[28]

To say "Islamic literature" is to call attention to a special kind of relationship between Islam and literature. At the same time, to try to pin this relationship on a specific movement, such as the Islamist movement, would be misleading. After all, Islam and literature have had a coexistence that goes back to the days of the Prophet Muhammad. What is distinctive with the revivalist movement is that literary production with a clear religious agenda has been labeled Islamic literature, differentiating it from its more secularized cousin.

The general literary domain has always been of great interest to more religiously oriented intellectuals. Najîb al-Kîlânî, a physician and a creative writer of Islamic literature, has written some provocative works on Islamism and literature, in one of which he discusses various literary critical schools, finally alighting at Islamic literature (*adab islâmî*).[29] He does not hesitate to choose a short story by Mahfouz or one by Tawfîq al-Hakîm or a play by ʿAlî Ahmad Bâkathîr. These are among the shining stars of the modern Arabic literary canon. Al-Kîlânî realizes, moreover, that his choice of the story by Mahfouz may not be propitious, given the already mentioned hostility of religious thinkers to Mahfouz's novel *The Children of Gebelawi*. Al-Kîlânî justifies the inclusion of one of the Arab world's leading writers by arguing that the "Najîb Mahfûz in *Awlâd Hâratinâ* is other than the Najîb Mahfûz" in other works.[30] Al-Kîlânî's involvement with the literary movement known as *adab is-lâmî* led to his penning a fascinating work, more personal in nature and conceived as a "journey," *My Journey with Islamic Literature*.[31]

Al-Kîlânî clearly has no problems with a definition of Islamic litera-ture that includes works of writers who would otherwise not be consid-ered religiously oriented. Muhammad Qutb, the brother of the famous Islamic activist and thinker Sayyid Qutb, is also concerned with the dis-tinguishing features of "Islamic art," including literature.[32] One of the examples he cites and discusses is a play by the prominent Irish play-wright John Millington Synge, *Riders to the Sea*.[33] Muhammad Qutb's point is that one does not need to be a Muslim to be proficient in this type of literature. For him, Synge's play, with its general recourse to the De-ity, among other elements, has a great deal in common with the proper procedure to follow in the creation of Islamic literature.[34] Muhammad Qutb looks to the future and realizes that "the first signs of Islamic art" are appearing, for example, "in the short story, in poetry. . . ." These signs demonstrate that "we are on the road moving up and that, God willing, we will arrive there."[35] Sayyid Qutb, of course, also wrote nov-els and criticism, but the bulk of these precede his conversion.[36]

The discussions of Islamic artistic production clearly demonstrate the fluidity of what constitutes Islamic literature. If Synge can be included in such a discussion, then the parameters of this religious art are broader than one might suspect. This does not mean that the terms of the debate cannot be clearly laid out. Committed literature (as treated, for example, by Susan Rubin Suleiman) is no longer the prerogative of one group. One must extend it, some argue, to the religiously engaged text.[37]

Islamic literature, with all its genres, is a literature in fluorescence, growing stronger with the increase of religious fervor around the globe. There are now even series dedicated to Islamic literary genres, including poetry, biography, the novel, and the story. One such series, Towards a Universal Islamic Literature, includes children's literature.[38] The entirety of the religiously oriented production demonstrates an attempt to alter the course of cultural production, a production seen as an object whose control must move from that of the more secularized and leftist intellec-tuals to that of their more religiously minded cousins.

That this conception is not merely a cultural accident but an impor-tant marker on the contemporary map of the Middle East can be seen when one looks at some recent developments. The Egyptian Ministry of Culture, for example, awarded its highest literary achievement award

(Jâ'izat al-Dawla al-Taqdîriyya) in 1996 to Mustafâ Mahmûd. (He shared it that year with the woman writer Latîfa al-Zayyât.)[39] A physician and a born-again Muslim, Mahmûd is a prominent writer and a television personality. Mahmûd's textual production ranges from fiction and drama to essays and general programmatic writings.[40] His prize, whether so intended or not, testifies to the growing importance of Islamic literature.

Mahmûd, in a recent interview, stated that he considers himself an intellectual and a thinker and not a writer, as opposed to Naguib Mahfouz, who in Mahmûd's eyes, is more of a writer than a thinker.[41] At the same time, when asked about the two terms *Islamic literature* and *Islamic criticism,* Mahmûd was not terribly enthusiastic, since in his opinion the corpus for this material was still too small to permit such a categorization.[42]

In the introduction to one of his novels, *al-Masîkh al-Dajjâl,* Mahmûd takes a variant, though not contradictory, stance. Noting some readers' reaction to his work, Mahmûd justifies himself as a creative writer: "What I wrote was neither religion nor science. Rather it is art, and imagination, and myth, and enters into the domain of fantasy." Mahmûd considers that he was an "artist" who entered the area of religion, though as he puts it, "not through the door of al-Azhar," that centuries-old bastion of traditional learning in the Islamic world.[43] Nor is Mahmûd, as he did in the interview, averse to comparing himself to more canonical writers like Tawfîq al-Hakîm or even the Arab world's great modernizer, Tâhâ Husayn. His argument is that when these writers and others write on Islamic topics, they are not considered legists nor are they read in the same way that one reads "al-Shâfiᶜî and Ibn Hanbal and Abû Hanîfa. Rather, we read them as artists and thinkers who speak to us about God in a new language."[44] Mahmûd is alluding here to the names of the founders of three of the four canonical legal schools in Islam, al-Shâfiᶜî (d. 204/820), Ibn Hanbal (d. 241/855), and Abû Hanîfa (d. 150/767). The reader may well wonder why the twentieth-century author omitted the name of Mâlik ibn Anas (d. 179/796), the founder of the fourth legal school, but that question can only be of anecdotal interest. Once again, and as he did with al-Azhar, Mahmûd is calling for a different reading of creative writing from an Islamic perspective. The comparisons he makes testify to the permeability between the religious and the secular.

Women also surface in the discourses on Islamic literature. Yahyâ Hâjj Yahyâ has devoted a book to the question of woman in the contemporary Islamic short story. Not surprisingly, his perception of the role of woman in this literature does not differ substantially from her role in the guidebooks that delineate proper behavior for Muslim women. This male critic isolates Lahlou's breast-cancer narrative under the heading of "Woman through Her Personal Experience." His treatment of this work, like his treatment of other works, consists of an extremely brief summary of the major events of the story.[45] More importantly, this short work by Yahyâ is symptomatic of much of the contemporary critical work on Islamic literature, in that its analytical framework is superficial.

The attention that both critics and creative writers devote to Islamic literature remains largely directed to a cultural production that is Arabophone, if one excludes references like that of Muhammad Qutb to non-Muslim western writers. Such an outlook is unduly limited when one is examining the transnational Islamic revival. It is only by including writers in other languages, such as the Francophone Sultana Kouhmane, that one can transcend the local. This does not mean that the local is eliminated, simply that it must be viewed in the larger context of the global.[46]

Novels, poetry, and short stories may flourish in this transnational Islamic literature. But one of the favored contemporary revivalist literary genres is certainly the autobiographical. The major figures of the movement have indulged themselves here: from the popular television preacher Muhammad Mutawallî al-Shaᶜrâwî to the above-mentioned Mustafâ Mahmûd.[47] These spiritual journeys of the self represent a distinct type of autobiographical text. As such, they conform to some of the generic rules that govern autobiography. Philippe Lejeune's "autobiographical pact," in which author, narrator, and central character are identical, certainly functions in these works.[48] In the case of women writers, gender dynamics alter the discourse, a by no means unusual textual strategy when one speaks about women and autobiography, as critics such as Domna C. Stanton and others have shown.[49] And, of course, autobiography is not a new player on the Arabo-Islamic literary stage. It should come as no surprise, then, that the wealth and variety of the centuries-old Arabo-Islamic literary tradition should have given birth to the spiritual testimonial. The classic autobiographical text by al-Ghazâlî (d. 505/1111), al-Munqidh min al-Dalâl, is one such case.[50]

But, as with other autobiographical ventures, the male voice has dominated. For the medieval period, woman's spiritual existence was almost always mediated through male scriptors. This is not to say that women did not participate in the religious and spiritual life of the Muslim community. Far from it. Many are the famous women whose names

populate the male textual tradition. There is ʿAʾisha, one of the wives of
the Prophet Muhammad, who was an influential transmitter of *hadîths*,
the codified normative actions and sayings of the Prophet.[51] There are
women poets. There are women scholars. There are women mystics.
Simply, in the medieval prose tradition, women were not scriptors. Their
experience, spiritual or otherwise, was culled and presented by male
authors.[52]

In the modern period, the situation changes. Women pen stories of
their lives and struggles. Greater access to print for women writers means
that, along with other genres, women share in the creation of their own
literary selves, in the process participating in larger cultural dialogues.[53]
Among the more religiously oriented texts and in the sea of materials
defining the female Muslim religious self perhaps the most eloquent and
passionate works are those written by the women themselves. The best-
known work is undoubtedly that of Zaynab al-Ghazâlî, *Ayyâm min
Hayâtî* (Days from My Life).[54] This classic, which has gone into multiple
printings, predates the current Islamic revivalist wave and functions
as an important antecedent to the proliferating revivalist writings by
women. It is perhaps, then, not a surprise that her name dominates in
much of the western discourse on women's autobiographical texts and
Islam.[55] As a prison memoir, Zaynab al-Ghazâlî's work also joins the
corpus of writings by women on their incarceration experience and
should be seen in relation to those works as well.[56] Zaynab al-Ghazâlî's
now appears as a sponsor and introducer to some of the current texts by
born-again women such as that by Shams al-Bârûdî.[57]

These spiritual journeys by born-again female members of the Islamic
community are now traveling many of the Islamic routes well worn by
their male counterparts from Cairo to London and from Paris to Rabat.
Not only that, but these sagas are penned by some of the female stars of
the movement, such as the Egyptian television personality Karîmân
Hamza, just as the male autobiographies are penned by some of the
most popular names on the contemporary Islamist stage, such as Shaykh
Kishk.[58]

To say "born-again" might strike a reader as highly unusual, if not
downright inappropriate, given its association with Christian baptism.
One could also speak here in terms of conversion, which defines the process of what these spiritual journeys are all about. Of course, these voyages are voyages within Islam, in that their narrators have previously
been nominal Muslims, as in the case of Hamza and Lahlou, or living
in a mixed Muslim-Christian household, as in the case of Kouhmane.

While "converting" might be one way of alluding to this change, another might well be "reverting," in the way it is used by an American Muslim. She speaks of the fact that "I feel that when I was born I was a Muslim and was raised Christian. Now I have reverted—not converted—to the true and straight path."[59]

Valerie J. Hoffman discusses the question of the conversion, the born-again, and the more-observant experiences in her study "Muslim Fundamentalists: Psychosocial Profiles." Some of her observations are fascinating, but the narrators of the journeys analyzed here might have trouble engaging with Hoffman's assessment that "It does not appear that Muslim fundamentalists have dramatic spiritual experiences that impel them to turn toward fundamentalism." She states that dramatic conversions exist essentially among the Sufis: "Sufi conversions are typically mystical, the process taking place in a short space of time, or even suddenly, accompanied by often exhilarating and awe-inspiring revelation of spiritual realities, resulting in a profound moral change and an entirely new perspective on life. Muslim fundamentalists do not speak of their experiences in this way at all."[60] The three female narrators in *Medicines of the Soul* will most certainly question this evaluation. They will help determine the precise articulation of spirituality by the women revivalists, as they perceive it and as they describe it.

Interestingly enough, the notion of born-again is one that emanates from the women themselves and does not function as an import from another culture or religious tradition such as the Christian one. This will be clear from the discussions of the individual works below. More importantly, as one looks at other texts in the Islamic revival by women, one discovers that the women themselves refer to their spiritual awakening as a rebirth or as being born-again. In a provocative pamphlet that purports to be a conversation with a Muslim woman who returns to the fold, the subject of the interview is asked to introduce herself. As she does so, she explains that her experience brought about the birth of a newborn.[61] Munâ Yunûs in the pamphlet *Wajh bi-lâ Mâkiyâj* (A Face without Make-Up) would feel very comfortable with this whole idea of born-again, using it herself to describe her own spiritual transformation.[62] None of this would surprise the famous Sayyid Qutb, in a way the ideological ancestor here, who himself declared that he was born in 1951, the year that he became a member of the Muslim Brotherhood.[63]

The born-again phenomenon among female figures on the contemporary cultural stage goes beyond the three spiritual journeys from Egypt, Morocco, and Belgium. The veiling of famous entertainment figures represents a cultural issue of great importance. The famous screen actress Shams al-Bârûdî, the wife of the equally famous figure from the Arab cinema Hasan Yûsuf, not only veiled herself but even wrote about her spiritual transformation.[64] Other personalities range from the actress and singer Shâdiya to a host of other public figures. Their extremely visible veiling even took on aspects of a civilizational debate in which religious authorities such as the already familiar Shaykh Mutawallî al-Sha°râwî were active participants.[65] The big question was whether or not these entertainers had been financially rewarded for their vestimentary transformation. Whatever the financial motivations, if any, behind the veiling, this visible act permitted these highly public women to enter the transnational discourse on women and veiling in Islam. As one walks down the streets of Istanbul today, one can find pamphlets in Turkish discussing the donning of Islamic dress by these prominent figures of the Arab entertainment industry.[66]

Some of the accounts by actresses and singers of their spiritual transformation share much with the three spiritual journeys under investigation. All of these texts are also drastically different from the more ethnographic accounts such as one finds in Nayra Atiya's *Khul-Khaal: Five Egyptian Women Tell Their Stories.*[67] These types of works, of which Atiya's is but one example, facilitate the narrating of lives by women who would not normally have access to print. These works are, in their own way, a flourishing genre that extends to other countries and regions. The collection by Fatima Mernissi, *Le monde n'est pas un harem: Paroles de femmes du Maroc,* is another such work.[68] The books by Karîmân Hamza, Leïla Lahlou, and Sultana Kouhmane place themselves on another register. True, they recount life stories. But the difference is all in the telling. Hamza, Lahlou, and Kouhmane are not in need of an external ethnographic voice to transmit their sagas. They are the creators of their own tales, in which they star.

Wayne Booth, in his perceptive "The Rhetoric of Fundamentalist Conversion Narratives," sets out some critical observations about how one might examine these types of texts. For example, what about the distance the hero has to travel on the journey, or as Booth puts it, the distance "between Badland and Homeland?"[69] Other issues, such as a "major gain, that of falling into the bosom of a loving community of brothers and sisters,"[70] will be crucial on the analytical voyage. Booth deals with a variety of conversion narratives, including narratives of conversions from one religion to another, such as that of Maryam Jameelah from Judaism to Islam, as well as a narrative such as that of Sayyid Qutb, internal to Islam.[71] Narratives of conversion to Islam by non-Muslims are legion.[72]

The life stories of Karîmân Hamza, Leïla Lahlou, and Sultana Kouhmane are internal to Islam. And they play with different textual materials, permitting their authors to engage with larger civilizational and global dialogues. Furthermore, as stories of spiritual quests, of drastic changes in lifestyle, they function almost as calls to arms, as active religious propaganda.

If one had to choose literary relatives for these spiritual sagas, they would undoubtedly be other texts emanating from the contemporary Muslim revival as well as literary texts by more secularized writers of both genders. These spiritual autobiographies partake of certain textual properties that they share with their close literary cousins by male Islamic writers as well as their distant cousins by the less religiously oriented writers of both genders.

One of the most distinctive narrative properties of these texts is the intertextual use of materials from the *turâth,* the rich centuries-old Arabo-Islamic textual tradition, spanning genres from the literary and the philosophical to the historical and the theological. The intricate textual games played by these twentieth-century revivalist texts involve, among other phenomena, a redefinition and recasting of this highly complex tradition. While most often it is the religious corpus that becomes the subject of this intertextual manipulation, this does not have to be the case. Plenty of otherwise "secular" medieval poetry and anecdotal material finds its way into contemporary Muslim revivalist texts.[73]

Any intertextual project, of course, redefines all of the texts or materials it manipulates. I have had occasion to discuss intertextuality from the *turâth* and how it surfaces in contemporary literary materials elsewhere. Its primary effect is the creation of a type of synchrony in contemporary discourses, a synchrony that telescopes the diachronic, permitting events from the Arabo-Islamic past to comment on the contemporary world and vice versa.[74]

The intertextual exploitation of the medieval textual tradition, the *turâth,* by contemporary women writers is extremely significant. What makes these intertextual games critically important is that they are not played merely by the more religiously oriented women, those whose discourses will be analyzed in *Medicines of the Soul*. The relationship of twentieth-century women writers to their heritage transcends the religious-secular dichotomy. The feminist physician Nawal El Saadawi exploits this *turâth* in her fiction, in an attempt to create an alternate feminist theology.[75] In the case of the spiritual sagas, by contrast, the manipulation of the *turâth* helps to create a narrative whose gender components are different from those in the more secularly oriented writers.

The time travel so critical in the spiritual journeys parallels an equally important geographical displacement. The vagaries of traveling female bodies will help set the parameters for a transnational spirituality. The three female guides lead their readers to different continents and to different manifestations of, and locations for, the holy, in the process mapping sacred geographies. The textual dialogue between the three women writers will also involve larger cultural dialogues with, for example, the situation of Muslims in the West.[76]

The travels with three linguistically different guides should not obscure the commonalities in the journeys. Nor should these travels detract from the centrality of the female contribution. Unlike the three women who populate the work of Natalie Zemon Davis, "women on the margins," these three Muslim women are central to the contemporary development of Islam.[77] Karîmân Hamza, Leïla Lahlou, and Sultana Kouhmane are symptomatic and exemplary cases of the revival movement and the tensions around the question of woman and gender. Their discourses move between the secular and the religious, between East and West, between body and soul. The geographies are not merely those of continents and countries but those of the body and of the spirit. From Egypt to Morocco, from Paris to Saudi Arabia, the three journeys will help define the characteristics of a truly female spiritual component in the contemporary Islamic revival.

CHAPTER TWO

Female Body, Male Gaze

One of the most powerful spokeswomen in the Islamic revivalist movement today is without doubt the Egyptian media personality Karîmân
Hamza. Karîmân Hamza was born in 1942. Arab women do not like to
discuss their age, and Karîmân was rather surprised that I, an Arab
woman like her, would ask for this information. Nevertheless, when I
explained that academics in the West did not feel secure until they had
such data, she laughingly consented to reveal her year of birth. She went
through her spiritual transformation around age twenty. At the time, she
was already married. At age twenty-six, she began her involvement with
television, being committed to the idea that the electronic media represented a crucial tool for spreading the word of Islam.[1]

What makes Karîmân Hamza unique is the range of her intellectual
and activist involvement. Not only does she produce and star in television programs, but she is also a prolific author. Her works range from
children's literature to a novel and a guide for the Muslim woman.[2]
Hamza's spiritual autobiography was written sometime during 1976–
1977. Karîmân Hamza, hesitating between the two years, finally added,
"Say 1977."[3] This conversion saga, *Rihlatî min al-Sufûr ilâ al-Hijâb*
(My Journey from Unveiling to Veiling), is most important. Religious
salvation is no simple matter, one discovers, crossing corporal and geographical boundaries, and delimiting patriarchal redefinition of the
female.

The reader of the spiritual saga quickly comes to the realization that Karîmân's life could have been the dream of any young Egyptian secularized woman her age.[4] A family that is quite well to do, living in Heliopolis, a reasonably bourgeois suburb of Cairo. A father who is a professor of journalism at Cairo University and is a successful teacher and writer. Marriage at age sixteen to an army officer. Children. And to all this, add a university degree.

Yet, something is missing: the element that is always missing in a story of conversion, religion. *My Journey from Unveiling to Veiling* is Karîmân Hamza's spiritual quest.[5] Its primary goal is not to provide the life of its protagonist, but only one aspect of her life, the spiritual saga. Perhaps its closest neighbor in the literature of the contemporary Muslim revival is written by a man: Mustafâ Mahmûd's *Rihlatî min al-Shakk ilâ al-Imân* (My Journey from Doubt to Belief).[6] But the two stories differ. Gender dynamics alter the text, perhaps from its very inception, as the differences in the title show so eloquently. Both titles express the idea of a journey, particularly "My Journey" (*Rihlatî*). And both are journeys from one point (*min*) to another (*ilâ*). (The two points are not necessary for the titles to function quite eloquently in the Arabic—the "ilâ," to, would suffice.) But it is the points at which the journeys begin and end that are so divergent. Mustafâ Mahmûd moves from doubt to belief, Karîmân Hamza, from unveiling to veiling. He draws his reader to the mental aspects of his journey, she, to the vestimentary. Indeed, for a spiritual autobiography, Karîmân Hamza's text speaks less of the soul than of the body. And more striking in the work of a woman, it shows this body as defined by and for men.

Karîmân enters the text as a university student, married, and reasonably happy. She ends the text as a highly visible public persona, involved in the media, particularly television. How is her full assimilation into the religious way accomplished? What does this assimilation entail? Who are the major catalysts spurring her forward? This born-again testimony will elucidate these questions and more. Its goal is to provide the saga of a woman who should serve as exemplar to female Muslims the world around.

The actual story of Karîmân's conversion is embedded and hidden behind textual doors (dare one say veils?) which the reader must traverse before entering the life that will unfold. The book is introduced by Muhammad ᶜAtiyya Khamîs, the head of the Jamᶜiyyat Shabâb Sayyidinâ Muhammad, a group that split from the Muslim Brotherhood in January 1940.[7] After this lengthy presentation, Karîmân Hamza introduces her own journey in a short preface-like introduction.[8] For the second edition, the table of contents in the back of the book is followed by some words on Karîmân Hamza by the religious leader Shaykh Muhammad al-Ghazâlî.

Men introducing women's work is certainly not a new phenomenon in modern Arabic letters, be they of the more religious or of the more secular sort. A man's voice validates that of a woman.[9] What is unusual here is the double presence of the male voice, both preceding and following that of the female. One would certainly have sufficed for normal endorsement purposes. In fact, the two male voices function as stamps of approval and of authenticity, testifying to the veracity of the saga.

More importantly, these male voices are acting as protective mechanisms against any criticism that might be leveled against the author Karîmân Hamza. After all, does not Khamîs' introduction address the conversion and compare Karîmân Hamza to great Muslim women of centuries past?[10] Her historical role is clear: she is an exemplar. Al-Ghazâlî's approach is more complex. In his portrayal, Karîmân Hamza becomes the victim of two opposing forces, being attacked at once by both. On the one hand, she is criticized for leaving her face uncovered; on the other, for being a representative of Islam and hence subject to aggression and hatred. The first group would like to silence her voice, to imprison her at home. But no, Shaykh Muhammad al-Ghazâlî argues, Karîmân Hamza's voice should not be silenced.

Though he does call attention to her covered body, what Shaykh Muhammad al-Ghazâlî does not explore is the complexity of Karîmân's voice. Karîmân recounts her journey in the first-person singular. But this is not a simple diachronic saga in which the conversion seals the narrative. Hers is a highly complicated account in which her own travails are intertextually defined and recast by intricate weavings of quotations from classical sources, in particular the Qur'ân and the *hadîth,* as well as generous sections from the works of her spiritual mentor, ʿAbd al-Halîm Mahmûd. Even the first-person pronoun is not terribly stable: Karîmân's narration is enriched by the use of the first-person plural at critical points in the text when she speaks in a more collective and global voice.

And what a story Karîmân will tell! "Worried . . . Worried . . ." Thus does her saga begin. Karîmân is worried about her father's health. In ill health (he has a heart condition), he is still performing his teaching duties at Cairo University. She is afraid of losing him someday. The father's lecture comes to an end and his daughter will accompany him to Heliopolis, where she lives next door to him. Instead of heading to this area of Cairo, however, her father instructs the driver to go to the Institute of Islamic Studies, where Karîmân will deliver some books to ᶜAbd Allâh al-ᶜArabî. The car stops in front of the religious institute. She runs inside quickly with the intention of coming out just as quickly. But things are not so simple. A surprise awaits her.

> The young men of the Institute look at me with an eye that is all astonishment. As though I were from another star that fell by accident on the Institute . . . My clothes are very short, my hair descending, hanging down wild behind my back, and my small dog is in one of my hands, with the other one carrying the books. . . . Concerned, I ask about Dr. ᶜAbd Allâh al-ᶜArabî, but no one answers me. All stare at this strange creature. . . . Me.[11]

This entrance into the Institute of Islamic Studies in Cairo will change Karîmân's life. But, at the moment, neither she nor the reader knows that. What both know is that the young woman is woefully out of place in this religious institution. And this for a simple reason: her external grooming is not what it should be. Her clothing is inappropriate, being too short. Her hair hangs loosely behind her back. The small dog is but an unfortunate victim of this episode. This pet is at first glance a sign that the female hero is a westernized young woman who parades her animal companion around the city with her. But the dog represents much more than this.[12] Karîmân's inquiries remain unanswered. She is turned into a strange object, to be stared at in disbelief, as one might stare at a creature from outer space.

What the narrator has not mentioned to the reader—perhaps because her narration is still in its preconversion period and, hence, she could be considered still not yet cognizant of this information—is that if one wishes to consider her dress and exterior demeanor improper, one should also consider the behavior of the young men improper. As Muslim males, and one would have to assume they are for the story to function, they should avert their gaze from the female. This is a Qurᵓânic injunction that is still alive and well today and that will prove important in later episodes of *Rihlatî*.[13] But, of course, the young men do not avert their gaze, provoking in Karîmân the feeling that she is an alien creature.

This state of alterity, of strangeness, with which the spiritual journey begins is all important, defining the parameters of the problem. Karîmân, as the reader first sets eyes on her—after all that transpires as she provides her own corporal description—is a being apart. The reader has up till now only met Karîmân Hamza through the introductory material, first that of Khamîs and then her own. And her two-page prefatory remarks do not really introduce her. After the proper invocation, she modestly disclaims any pretense of writing "about Dr. ᶜAbd al-Halîm Mahmûd Shaykh al-Azhar al-Sharîf, that giant who made a school and founded an army of the righteous."[14] Who is she, after all, she continues, to write about him and his books? She will, however, establish something, her own personal experience.

This modesty and disclaimer are striking. The first-person narrator is potentially removing herself as object of the discourse. When I asked Karîmân Hamza about the history of the book, she informed me that she had initially planned to write it about Mahmûd and not about herself. The publisher, however, dissuaded her from that and redirected the manuscript so that it would be about the young woman. Along the way, the title of the work also underwent a transformation from being about the learned man to being about Karîmân's spiritual journey. The original title, al-Shaykh ᶜAbd al-Halîm Mahmûd: ᶜAlim Sâra fînâ Fadluhu (Shaykh ᶜAbd al-Halîm Mahmûd: A Learned Man Whose Grace Ran Through Us), was changed to the title the work presently displays.[15]

Be it because of the redirection of the work or simply out of modesty, Karîmân Hamza, in her signed introduction, does not really take the occasion to introduce herself to her reader. That will await the first page of the rihla.

Hence, when that first-person narrator reappears as the central protagonist of the spiritual journey, it is to set herself apart. She stands out from the crowd, but in a negative manner. And this crowd is male. It is the male gaze that defines her, a scopic activity that begins and closes the episode. Does she possess any spirituality? Is she religious? These seem to be almost irrelevant questions. The external determines the internal. This initial state of lack with which Rihlatî min al-Sufûr ilâ al-Hijâb begins will dominate the discourse. Its rectification will be the goal of the journey.

As Karîmân is standing, dog in hand, a shaykh suddenly appears. He is tall, extremely venerable, with features that bring together the modesty of the learned with "something I had not seen before. But I feel it and do not know how to express it." She quickly tries to approach this figure, but the students are faster than she is. They surround him and she is almost unable to see him. Eventually, the entire group finds itself in a lecture hall.

> And there is the venerable shaykh beginning the lecture. And there I am standing, confused, in the middle of this group. Looks of disapproval surround me from every side. . . . The ultimate transgression!! I sat so that I could protect myself from the glances of the students. I held my breath and

the breath of my small dog, and placed the books on my knees, to protect myself with them from the disapproving, furtive glances.[16]

The section introduced by this incident is entitled "al-Liqâ' al-Awwal" (The First Meeting). Karîmân and her dog have entered a forbidden territory, initially dominated by the visual and the scopic. The shaykh enters and the narrator describes his physical appearance. As she walks quickly toward him, the other students surround him and she is unable to see him. Inside the lecture room she herself is surrounded by disapproving glances. When she sits, it is to protect herself from these stares. It is the same protective urge to get away from the gaze that drives her to hold her breath and that of her pet, and then to place the books on her knees.

The male gaze meets the female gaze. It is as if the narrator has seen something she should not have. After all, do not the male students surround the shaykh in such a way that it is difficult for her to see him? Their physical act of surrounding the venerable figure and their scopic surrounding of the narrator are expressed by verbs emanating from the same Arabic triliteral root (h-w-t). But physically isolating and surrounding the shaykh is a protective act, whereas scopically isolating and surrounding the narrator is a hostile one. No one protects her. She must protect herself with her father's books. The privilege of scopic domination belongs to the men, not to the female hero.

No sooner is the domain of the visual abandoned than one enters the domain of the oral/aural. The shaykh begins his lecture with Islamic religious formulae, something alien to the university student. This linguistic issue will resurface momentarily. Then he continues with two exemplary stories of important medieval male mystics, the famous al-Fudayl ibn ʿIyâd (d. 187/803) and the equally famous Ibrâhîm ibn Adham (d. 161/777–78). Al-Fudayl and Ibrâhîm will return below as guides on Karîmân's mystical path.[17]

This lecture that Karîmân stumbles upon inadvertently signals the beginning of her spiritual path, a path that is at once corporal and spiritual.[18] She confides her worries to the reader, going so far as to admit that she had spoken to her mother of her wish to die.[19] The initial anxiety with which the narrative opens has been redefined. To the distress over the physical ill health of the father has been added the concern over the mental ill health of the daughter. "But the words of the shaykh were like the finger of the professional physician, when he places his hand on an illness and prescribes the medication."[20] The spiritual malaise has been turned into a physical one, concretizing it and making possible its cure.

Should it come as a surprise then that, in the morning, Karîmân should accidentally hear that same voice while tuning to her favorite radio program on the Qur'ân? That voice is once again telling the story of a male mystic, this time of Sahl ibn ᶜAbd Allâh al-Tustarî (d. 283/896).[21] The identity of the voice is made when the announcer thanks him: Dr. ᶜAbd al-Halîm Mahmûd. Karîmân calls her father to share her great discovery.

The father's response? He will perform the afternoon prayer with his daughter. "I returned to my bed. Happy, happy. As though I had found a treasure I had lost long ago." [22] The identification of the mystery voice is obviously crucial. The two words, "Happy, happy," stand in opposition to the two words that opened the journey: "Worried. . . . Worried." Happiness has replaced worry.

The father appears that afternoon carrying books by ᶜAbd al-Halîm Mahmûd. He performs the prayer with his daughter and enjoins her to read the books. It will be their last meeting, as he will die soon after. Karîmân does read the books. "I read. I read. As though I were reading myself." Everything the shaykh says is her. "I, exactly. I, despite my descending, wild hair, and despite my naked provocative clothes, despite my laughter and my lightheartedness, despite my being drowned in secular culture and colors and music . . . I discovered myself. . . . Every word this shaykh says agrees exactly with my nature." [23] Karîmân has discovered herself. But the characteristics she calls attention to, the attributes that define her, begin with her external appearance: her hair, her clothes. These were, after all, the properties that set her apart as an alien creature when she first entered the Institute of Islamic Studies. The other elements will also prove important as she treads the spiritual path. But they will never be as crucial as the hair and the clothing.

Like her medieval male predecessors, she has heard the voice. But her path is not so easy. She needs an intermediary between herself and the male Deity, a need that will be analyzed in greater detail below.[24] Suffice it to say that the gender dynamics that perhaps necessitate the creation of this intermediary between the Deity and a female will certainly complicate Karîmân's spiritual journey. It is not simply the Deity who must be satisfied. She must placate the upholders of the Islamic tradition. These, we come to discover, are males.

The father here performs a significant function. He and the shaykh play paradigmatic roles in Karîmân's spiritual development. The father is there first as a professor and lecturer at Cairo University, a secular university. The shaykh is there first as a lecturer at the Institute of Islamic Studies, a religious institution. The father's health is waning from the first page of the book, and he dies as his daughter discovers the identity of Shaykh ʿAbd al-Halîm Mahmûd. The father's last act before dying is to enjoin his daughter to read the books of the shaykh he himself has just purchased for her. The father, after his death, leaves a book that is incomplete. Karîmân and her sister decide to see the book through to publication. And who should write the introduction to that book but ʿAbd al-Halîm Mahmûd? It should not be a surprise that this was Karîmân's idea. By this act, the shaykh has textually inserted himself into the father's book. His transition into the role of substitute father, which is not completed until near the end of the text, is facilitated.

The switch from the biological father to the spiritual one is an eloquent reminder that Karîmân will always be a daughter. By setting her on the right track, the father is also, in a sense, giving her over to a new male authority. The shaykh is not cognizant of this, but he is placed in that role willy-nilly. His mere presence will function as a catalyst that will set Karîmân on the right track and assure that her spiritual journey is complete.

For Karîmân, becoming the "spiritual daughter" of the shaykh, as she puts it, will involve some difficult transitions.[25] She calls ʿAbd al-Halîm Mahmûd to ask him if he would agree to write the introduction to her father's book.[26] When he answers the telephone, he does so with the Muslim greeting: "Peace and the mercy of God be upon you" (al-salâmu ʿalaykum wa-rahmat Allâh). She replies: "Hello. And upon you peace" (âlû. wa-ʿalaykum al-salâm). She marvels at the type of person who answers the telephone in this way. Nevertheless, when she calls him back, she answers his fuller Muslim greeting with the appropriate Muslim answer, and without the "Hello."

> "Peace be upon you, and the mercy of God and His blessings" (al-salâmu ʿalaykum wa-rahmat Allâh wa-barakâtuh).
> "And upon you be peace, and the mercy of God and His blessings" (wa-ʿalaykum al-salâm wa-rahmat Allâh wa-barakâtuh).[27]

The first step, seemingly a small and minor one, has been taken. But more hides behind this first-personal contact than merely a telephone exchange. It is oral/aural, reinforcing the orality/aurality encountered first in the public lecture and then on the radio.

The shaykh was kind enough to write the introduction. Now Karîmân must pick it up from his office in the administrative building of the

Azhar, in the area of al-Sayyidunâ Husayn. Her husband will accompany her. This is fortunate, indeed, because the office employees ignore her request, and it is only the husband's intercession that gets them access to ᶜAbd al-Halîm Mahmûd.[28] How similar is the silence of the office employees to the silence of the young men in the Institute of Islamic Studies! There is progress, however. Karîmân does not feel here like an alien creature.

Yet, what is surprising in this instance is not so much how Karîmân feels but rather the asides she makes on the location of the religious headquarters. These asides function as a geographical manifestation of a much larger and more inclusive discourse in the journey: that on the religious and the secular.[29]

When Shaykh ᶜAbd al-Halîm Mahmûd informs Karîmân that he has indeed written the introduction to her father's book, he requests that she come to the Azhar administrative offices and pick it up. The young woman is ecstatic and informs her husband that she must do this the same day.

> And he has to take me there because I do not know where it is.
> "It is at Sayyidunâ al-Husayn."
> "And where is Sayyidunâ al-Husayn?!! I do not know!!"[30]

The last response by Karîmân would strike anyone who has ever lived in Cairo as strange to say the least. Al-Husayn, as it is known for short, is one of the liveliest areas in Cairo, representing the old city of medieval Cairo. It is at once the area where the centuries-old Azhar is located, boasting a mosque-university complex as well as administrative offices. The district is also where one finds the mosque of al-Husayn, a popular religious site. To all this, add the fact that al-Husayn is strategically placed near the entrance of the famous Khân al-Khalîlî, the bazaar in Cairo that draws tourists and Egyptians alike. The area remains awake practically night and day, with restaurants and cafés frequented at all hours of the night. During the month of fasting, Ramadân, in particular, people gather in al-Husayn after the evening meal following the fast, walking the historic streets and participating in cultural activities. It is not unusual for people to be seen, in the nonholiday season, enjoying a snack in the area long after midnight.

For an inhabitant of the greater Cairo area to plead ignorance of al-Husayn is interesting, indeed. But when this ignorance of the particular site is compounded by another ignorance, that of the Azhar administration, it begins to dictate a different language, the language of a deep secularism.

This secular language was there earlier in Karîmân's journey, beginning with her entrance into the religious institute. With al-Husayn, the secular language takes a different twist, one that relates directly to geography. This neighborhood functions as a microcosm of the religious/ secular discourses in Karîmân's text.

There is another geographical locus that partakes of the secular, in which Karîmân's more religious life is put under review, and this is the social club, "al-nâdî." Neither the location nor the name of this club is specified. One day, Karîmân goes to pay her yearly membership and meets a group from Heliopolis, comprised of family and neighbors. One woman, particularly well placed both socially ("the wife of so-and-so. . . . and the daughter of so-and-so") and intellectually (she is also "a poet and littérateur" who attends various poetic and intellectual gatherings), is in the position of secular authority. The women, noting Karîmân's absence and her loss of touch with the newest fashions, advise her against her newly acquired religious leanings. Instead of reading the likes of Shaykh Mahmûd, she is told, she should read western writers and secularized Arabic writers: Jean-Paul Sartre, Simone de Beauvoir, Jean-Jacques Rousseau, Guy de Maupassant, and others, on the one hand, and Ihsân ᶜAbd al-Quddûs, Yûsuf al-Sibâᶜî, and the like, on the other. In the course of this well-intentioned advice, the women make pronouncements on Shaykh ᶜAbd al-Halîm Mahmûd.[31] Striking about the entirety of this discourse are the levels of language: some of the women hold forth in dialect. The presence of the Egyptian dialect contrasts sharply with the standard literary Arabic, not only of Karîmân's responses in this heated interchange but of the remainder of the work.[32] Fushâ, or the literary language, becomes associated in this work with the religious tradition (though most of the secular authors discussed above write in fushâ).

Karîmân is, of course, not the only individual who has to resist different forces on the path to salvation. Margaret Miles, in her *Desire and Delight,* notes Augustine's "penchant for contrasting people who helped him toward his conversion to Catholic Christianity with those who encouraged him to resist conversion."[33] A similar contrast is there in Karîmân's saga. That Karîmân feels this pull between the two life choices is evident in the structure of the chapter itself. The incident in the club is embedded in a chapter whose title bears the name of her new spiritual brother. The incident with the women in the club closes with Karîmân's excusing herself and returning home to meet her new friends in the evening, the members of her new spiritual family.

This incident in the club does not represent a chronological intrusion in the journey. It seems to surface at the right chronological moment in the life of the female hero. But what the women in the club do not know is that Karîmân had already had intimate experiences with the secularized Arabic writers. In a powerful analepsis, the narration of an event that took place earlier in time than its actual narrative location, Karîmân reveals a telling incident.[34] At age thirteen, the reader learns, Karîmân had read the novel *Anâ Hurra* (I Am Free) and was greatly influenced by its liberated female hero. When her father did not wish her to go out because it was late in the evening, she theatrically declared: "I am going out now. I am free." Her father slapped her and she ran to her room and cried all night. In the morning, she apologized to him and explained that she was imitating the hero of the story *Anâ Hurra*. Karîmân's father called out to her mother and asked her to choose something else for the young girl to read. The mother then explained that such books were written for fame and economic gain.[35]

Anâ Hurra is a famous work by the prolific Egyptian writer Ihsân ᶜAbd al-Quddûs, whom Roger Allen qualifies as "the Arab world's most popular writer of fiction, in that more copies of his works have been sold than of any other Arab novelist."[36] As Roger Allen further puts it, this particular novel "proclaims a defiant message that is typical of a number of works which have appealed to successive generations of adolescents and young adults faced with the task of reconciling traditional mores with the forces of change in the postrevolutionary Arab societies." For Karîmân, the novel becomes a symbol of a literature whose only virtues are economic.

The female friends in the club who recommend reading the likes of ᶜAbd al-Quddûs are not privy to the information about Karîmân the teenager, who is slapped by her father for disobeying his orders. His chronologically earlier direction to the mother that she find something else for Karîmân to read runs counter to their advice. Even more interesting is the fact that the western writers mentioned as worthy of reading by the female club members are all French. Is it a coincidence that in the beginning of her spiritual journey, Karîmân had mentioned that her mother was French-educated?[37]

It is precisely this background of cultural secularism, the nonreligious lifestyle with its westernized clothing and its ignorance of Islamic space, that brings about that initial experience of alterity, of alienness, in the religious location and during which Karîmân becomes the object of the male gaze. That experience is so powerful that it creates its own intertext. The ultimate transgression: thus did the narrator express her physical penetration into the enclosure of the lecture hall and the hostile glances directed at her. "The Ultimate Transgression with the Doctor" is a chapter title that, by virtue of its words, ties the adventure in the lecture hall with another, and equally important, transgression. These transgressions share more than mere words: their hero is identical, Shaykh ᶜAbd al-Halîm Mahmûd. This latest transgression bears examination not only in the context of Karîmân's spiritual trajectory but also in the larger context of Arabo-Islamic letters and culture.

Karîmân decides to visit ᶜAbd al-Halîm Mahmûd and get his advice on her thesis. A male family friend, Muhammad Shalabî, will accompany her. Two days prior to the visit, she begins to think about her impending visit and her short clothing. Where will she get modest clothing? She poses the problem to Shalabî, who suggests her mother's overcoat. She tries on the overcoat and discovers that it covers about ten centimeters below the knee. Her hair is still hanging down. So she puts it under the coat. But the female hero is still displeased with her looks. It is her hair. Her mother provides her with a scarf, which she places on her head. Now she is happy to go and see the shaykh. Karîmân and her male companion get in the car, and near the institute, she closes the coat, ties up the scarf, and places her cigarettes in her bag.

They enter the institute and head for the shaykh's office. The shaykh is late. Karîmân takes off her overcoat, which is quite warm, and places it on her knees, just in case the shaykh should enter. Soon she is uncomfortable with the scarf and removes it, letting her hair hang down. A knock on the door makes her jump to put on her coat and gather her hair. But it is only the office boy bringing two glasses of tea. She takes one and begins to drink. She feels the need for a cigarette, having given up hope of the shaykh's arrival, and having decided to leave after finishing the tea. "So I lit a cigarette and put one leg over another, and I started watching the smoke, trying to see the future in it." She thinks about her thesis and becomes quite distracted.

> Suddenly, I saw Dr. ᶜAbd al-Halîm Mahmûd in the middle of this smoke, with his tall stature and his pious face. . . . Oh, how terrible!! I was nailed to my place. . . . I cannot throw the cigarette on the ground, the ground is furnished with rugs . . . nor can I put out the cigarette since there is no ashtray close to me. . . . The shaykh sat at his desk, looking at us. . . . I cannot grab

the coat to hide the extreme shortness of the skirt. . . . since the glass is in one hand and the other hand is busy with the lit cigarette. . . .

What do I do?? Excuse myself?? Do I put out the cigarette or do I quickly gather my hair in the scarf, or what do I do?

The shaykh asks how he can help them, but Karîmân is unable to speak. Muhammad Shalabî saves the day, and the shaykh provides them with the necessary references. Questions plague her after this visit: Why is she so ashamed? Why did she lose her ability to speak in front of him? Why did he come late after she had already taken off her coat, let loose her hair, lit her cigarette, and put one leg over another? Is the miniskirt illicit? Did God not create her legs and her hair? [38]

In fact, even before she goes to meet the learned man, Karîmân worries about her external appearance. Her two body parts that will be the foci of her obsession throughout the chapter are her hair and legs, both of which she covers.

Karîmân's smoking incident is embedded in the larger passage detailing the visit to the older spiritual leader. This visit, the reader understands, is momentous, entailing for the young woman a change in her daily appearance: she must cover her hitherto uncovered female body. The corporal concealment is an elaborate process performed in stages, involving first the body and then the hair. The cigarettes make their appearance even before she enters the religious setting. As she and her male companion near this setting, she begins at the beginning as it were, by closing the coat, the first element in her new covered-up persona. Then comes the scarf, the second element. Her body contained, she places her cigarettes in her handbag. Like her body which must be covered, the cigarettes are placed in a closed environment where they will not be seen.

Once inside the sacred enclosure, the religious environment, Karîmân, impatient with waiting for the shaykh, begins the unveiling process. She proceeds to actively shed one covering after another, effectively performing a striptease of sorts. First she removes the coat, the first item used in the cover-up. Then follows the scarf, the second item, whose removal will liberate her hair. It should not come as a surprise, perhaps, then, that the cigarette should be next. Just as her body left its hiding place, so will the cigarette be made to emerge from the handbag. That this sequence is important is evident by its repetition during the narrator's musings after she arrives at her home after the interview. "Why did he enter late, after I had removed my overcoat, given free rein to my hair, lit my cigarette, and crossed my legs?" [39]

The appearance of ᶜAbd al-Halîm Mahmûd in the smoke transforms the episode. It is not simply that Karîmân is at a total loss over what to do with the burning cigarette. When Mahmûd asks how he can be of service, she is unable to answer. It is her male companion's voice that responds to the request. Is this inability to speak related to the fact that the hero's mouth (and mind) is otherwise occupied with the cigarette? The narrator is quick to assert: "I did not answer because words did not help me." [40] Her original intentions had been to speak. Had she not, after all, declared to the reader after locking up the cigarettes in the bag, while on her way to her appointment, that she had begun to think about what she would tell "the man?" [41] The lit cigarette will make her telling that or anything else impossible.

The cigarette, in fact, does more than silence the young woman during the interview with the learned older man. Most recently, Richard Klein has examined the cultural and literary constructions of cigarettes and smoking. Although his work is based on a western corpus, it nevertheless exposes some potentially universal concerns about women and smoking. [42] Speaking of war fiction, he notes that "lighting the cigarette is a measure of the time of decision." [43] Though Karîmân's textual world is autobiographical, nevertheless the act of lighting a cigarette is critical. Klein also notes the offense engendered by a woman's smoking in public, a fact that will be central as one encounters the text by Hamza's countryman, Yûsuf Idrîs. [44] More importantly, confronting the transgressive nature of smoking female bodies calls up Richard Klein's words: "even today, when a woman smokes she is seen as performing a brazen, transgressive act." [45]

In Karîmân's case, the cigarette is a sign of her complete perdition. The reader is aware that the very word she uses in the chapter title indicates the act of transgression itself. Up to the moment she lights the cigarette, she might have been able to keep her honor intact. She could still have rushed to put on her coat and gather her hair, as the unexpected arrival of the office boy almost makes her do. But the cigarette turns all that into an impossibility. It is the last element in a sequence of disrobing that will lead to the crossing of the legs. Only later as Karîmân is pondering the incident and asking herself questions about her corporal comportment does the reader learn that she had actually been wearing a miniskirt. (All she had previously indicated was that her clothing was short.)

After Mahmûd provides his guests with the necessary references, the hero thanks him and puts on the overcoat. This confirms her earlier confession that because she held the tea in one hand and the lit cigarette in the other she was unable to grab the coat to hide the "extreme shortness" of her skirt. The entirety of the interview, then, occurred with Karîmân's body uncovered. The cigarette, meanwhile, evaporates from the narration after its task is accomplished: the reader never learns its ultimate fate.

The gaze, however, far from disappears. When ᶜAbd al-Halîm Mahmûd first appears, Karîmân sees him in the middle of the smoke. Thus does the scopic game in this incident begin. Then the shaykh "sat at his desk looking at us." It would seem initially that both older male and younger female are participating in the scopic game. After Karîmân quickly leaves the learned man's presence, she decides that she will not come back "to him," since he has seen her in the state which she had gone to so much trouble to hide. The narrator's obsession is with the fact that Mahmûd "has seen" her.

But, in fact, the scopic game is not so simple in this cigarette incident. The concern with the gaze here speaks to the earlier encounter in the Institute of Islamic Studies in which Karîmân was subjected to the probing stare of the male students. There, also, it was her short clothing and her wild hair that turned her into a "strange creature." That earlier incident, in a sense, sensitizes Karîmân to her corporal deficiencies.

It should then perhaps not come as a surprise that the female hero should be so preoccupied with the visual activity in the interview with the shaykh. The male religious figure is very carefully kept out of the play with the gaze. He is not once shown to be looking at the young woman. When he looks, it is at both of his guests. After all, does not the narrator use the first-person plural to describe the shaykh's action ("looking at us")? The use of the plural turns this activity into a glance that is not specific to the feminine gender. Only after the episode with the cigarette as Karîmân is reliving the incident does she transform the shaykh's gaze into the singular "as long as he saw me." [46] The male religious figure progresses from looking at both his male and female guests to only seeing the female guest's body. It is Karîmân who recognizes the power of the gaze and its influence on her corporality. The scene she paints is a sign of her initial downfall: after all, the shaykh caught her not with her pants down but with her skirt up.

More than that, the incident is also quite provocative for an Arab audience: a young woman in a miniskirt, legs crossed, smoking a cigarette. Enter the male physician-writer, the Egyptian Yûsuf Idrîs. Many of his texts single themselves out by their frank exploitation of sexuality and their exploration of male-female relations.[47] More important, one of his short stories can shed light on Karîmân's transgression.

In Idrîs's fascinating narrative, "In Flagrante Delicto," a third-person narrator weaves the tale of a male dean watching a female student smoke a cigarette.[48] His initial reaction is anger. But this anger is not that of a dean but rather that of a child born in the Egyptian Delta. It is this upbringing that allows him to understand that such an act, while permitted to men and considered shameful for male youth, was completely forbidden to children and was a crime and a disgrace for women. This student was a young woman not more that seventeen years old. The dean compares her initially to his daughter. He watches the female student first light up the cigarette and then smoke it. In the process, he reassesses her age: she is surely older than his daughter. The dean's gaze continues, leading eventually to orgasm. The end of the cigarette brings an interesting end to the game with the gaze. The student looks up and spots the dean. Their eyes meet: "The two gazes were electrified with shame." She proceeds to take out a book and become the serious student, while he returns to being a dean.

The superficially "simple" nature of the narrative does not mean we should dismiss it so easily.[49] The story functions almost as a contemporary ode to the gaze and the complicated sexual games it can generate. At the same time, investigating the Idrîsian game with the gaze will shed light on the way Hamza plays that same gaze game. Yûsuf Idrîs's narrator will be the guide in this scopic maze. The short story begins with the act of looking, and this act takes on dramatic proportions as the dean finds himself in the position of voyeur. Being alone facilitates this unnatural act. The narrator is sure to tell the reader that the dean intended to call for someone when he first saw the girl smoking. "Had someone been in the room—a professor or a committee or even if he were waiting to meet someone or other—the movement would have been completed and his hand would have reached the button."[50] But the university official was isolated in a big room with a narrow window, a fact that seems to invite a greater desire for looking. The female student, like Karîmân, liberates the cigarettes from her carrying bag and proceeds to light one. The older man is drawn to the scene at the same time that he feels "a strong fear of continuing to look."[51]

The power of the gaze is such that it keeps the dean from taking action against this smoking female body. He decides, for example, that he will have the student called in when the cigarette and the crime reach exactly the midpoint. Note that the smoking of the cigarette has once again been classed as a crime, as it was in the opening passage of the short story. That midpoint comes and goes with the university official still the victim of the visual. Even more dramatic, this middle point in the cigarette if anything intensifies the man's gaze. He continues to observe the young woman. His body parts, from his eyes through his tongue to his legs, become active participants in this pastime: "all of them watch." [52] As the dean's entire corporal entity seems to partake of the visual operation, so the narrator seems to exploit the entirety of Arabic lexicography to describe this activity from its beginning to its end. The male body looks (*yanzur*), sees (*yarâ*), contemplates (*yata'ammal*), watches (*yushâhid*), observes (*yurâqib*), and so forth. [53]

But it is not merely verbal prestidigitation that is at play here. The visual act with the young, puffing, female body becomes the occasion for the older male voyeur to muse about society. He who had begun the narrative thinking that smoking was a "crime" for women begins to question these societal values. What is the difference between the girl's smoking as a student or her smoking after she graduates? This and other questions occupy him. After all, he muses, his country will not achieve any scientific, industrial, or civilizational progress unless complete freedom exists, "even the freedom to make a mistake." [54]

These lofty musings and ideals will not, however, keep the older male from continuing his voyeuristic activities. As his body increases its perspiration, he quickly wipes his glasses so as not to cut off his vision. A strange silence pervades the scene, "the silence of a world completely devoid of life, with no living being in it except him and her . . . she is in the ultimate stages of pleasure and he is in the ultimate stages of excitation . . . and between them, separating them completely and tying them together completely, was that cigarette." [55] The lit cigarette unites the female object of the gaze with its male perpetrator, isolating them from the world. Her pleasure is countered by his arousal. Is it a surprise that their eyes should meet at the end of this performance, before each returns to his or her previous existence?

Yûsuf Idrîs's third-person narrator, like Karîmân Hamza's first-person narrator, paints an interesting textual world in which woman's body, equipped with a cigarette, can become a pawn in intricate sexual games. Karîmân is involved in a vestimentary cover-up: the superficial donning of conservative clothing that is quickly abandoned as the female hero falls into the debauchery of smoking a cigarette in a religious establishment. But perhaps the locus is not so important: after all, the unnamed character in Yûsuf Idrîs's short story is not puffing on her cigarette in a sacred space.

It would seem that the two texts united by a smoking female body are worlds apart. Yûsuf Idrîs provides his reader with a fictional short story, presented by a third-person narrator. Karîmân Hamza's cigarette episode is part of a larger autobiographical spiritual journey narrated in the first person. More importantly, in the short story, the narrator concentrates on the male gaze and its ramifications. The smoking female body in the Idrîsian universe remains at a distance as the provocative object of the gaze. The Idrîsian narrator leaves no room for his reader's imagination, providing the sexual impact of the young, puffing, female body on the voyeuristic older male.

Not so for the smoking literary cousin in Hamza's world. Here, the female body is conscious of its power as the object of the male scopic act. The male religious authority may well first emerge in the smoke, but he does not appear disturbed by either the smoke or the puffing body. Rather, he remains above it all, providing an impressive array of religious sources the female student should investigate in her academic work, ranging from Qur'ânic commentaries through Islamic history to contemporary legal works. The learned religious figure apparently feels no temptation, being outside and beyond the gaze. The concern with her smoking body would seem to be Karîmân's alone. The cigarette here is not a mediating instrument, as it was in Idrîs's narrative, but the opposite, separating the secular younger woman from the religious older male. This will not always be the case for Karîmân.

Differences between Idrîs and Hamza aside (neither would probably enjoy the comparison), the two narratives from opposite sides of the cultural and religious divide highlight common concerns, chief among which is power. To say "power," however, is to say many things. Both texts star a younger woman and an older man. And both texts direct this age difference through the educational medium: the two women are students with the men hierarchically superior to them. In one, the short story, the older male is a dean; in the other, he is a highly placed religious functionary. The power relationship is stronger in Karîmân's case, since she instigates the encounter to get guidance in her academic work.

The older male-younger female association also partakes of the parental. There is an underlying father-daughter relationship in both encounters. With Karîmân, this relationship has already been exposed. The spiritual path will seal the issue of paternity by taking the young woman out of her secular existence and permitting her to join the spiritual family of ᶜAbd al-Halîm Mahmûd. With Idrîs, however, the father-daughter link is clearly enunciated in the beginning, when the dean realizes that the smoking student is almost his own daughter's age. As the visual experience intensifies, the narrator declares that the student is undoubtedly older than the dean's female offspring.[56] This change in the student's age is important: it distances the otherwise naturally incestuous undertone of the entire voyeuristic episode.

This potentially incestuous situation is a reminder that sexuality is part and parcel of the smoking female body. Even Karîmân does not escape this. And this despite the fact that she ventures on her visit to the older man with a male guardian, the socially determined proper course of action. The position of the Idrîsian dean is more ambiguous. After all, his social and hierarchical position in the university would have permitted him to call someone in at any time, hence putting an end to the voyeuristic encounter. But, of course, he does no such thing.

Is it surprising, then, that when the eyes of the male dean meet those of the female student at the end of the explosive situation, the narrator adds, "The two gazes were electrified with shame [khajal]"? Shame is the sign that a transgression has taken place. Both parties feel this shame, confirming the illicit nature of the long-distance encounter mediated by the cigarette. Shame is also what Karîmân feels: shame (khajal) over her hair and legs, the identical word found in Idrîs's narrative. But in her journey, the religious male, unlike his secular cousin in the Idrîsian textual universe, is free of this shame. Clearly, the transgression in My Journey from Unveiling to Veiling is the domain of the woman alone. And perhaps the reader should not be overly surprised: the obsession with the gaze in the smoking incident was solely hers.

Be it in the secular textual universe of Yûsuf Idrîs or in the religious one of Karîmân Hamza, the disgrace is common to both smoking bodies. This shame is an indication that the gaze and the scopic regime in which it exists transcend social and religious allegiances to speak to a larger cultural discourse. In fact, both narratives are operating in a scopic system in which the female body as object of the gaze can be nothing short of dangerous.[57] This would not be a surprising fact on the religio-cultural map in the Middle East today. One of the most popular religious figures in the Arab world is the television preacher and personality Shaykh Muhammad Mutawallî al-Shaᶜrâwî, already familiar as the author of a spiritual autobiography.[58] In one of his discussions on the status of women, al-Shaᶜrâwî argues that "the glance is the beginning of desire with relation to men and women. Once the glance has begun, you will not be able to control yourself relative to what can happen after that."[59] Shaykh al-Shaᶜrâwî's warning, grammatically constructed in the masculine gender, seems to be directed to a male audience. Certainly, the Idrîsian university official would not need a commentary to comprehend its import.

Nevertheless, and oddly enough, both Yûsuf Idrîs's narrative and that of Karîmân Hamza, despite their differing allegiances, are questioning that scopic regime in which the glance plays such a potentially dangerous part and yet ultimately resigning themselves to it. The dean's idealistic musings about society do not keep him from being trapped in the sexual game in which the gaze suffices to generate a host of illicit sentiments on his part. As for Karîmân, she questions her feelings of shame, especially about the two body parts she holds so dear. Yet, like Idrîs's dean, she is involved in a game in which society sets the rules. This transgression will be significant for her eventual covering.

Just as the cigarette united the male dean and the female student in Yûsuf Idrîs's short story, so a cigarette will link that same short story to a spiritual journey emanating from a revivalist woman writer. The two narrators put up a united front on smoking: this is an illicit activity whose sexual ramifications are powerful, especially when tied to the gaze. In Idrîs's case, smoking and the gaze have the potential of transforming every puffing female body into a sex machine. In Karîmân's case, woman's smoking body mixes with the gaze in a formula guaranteed to produce dissolution.

How interesting it then becomes to see the place that smoking holds in contemporary revivalist discourses in the Middle East. In these religious discourses, smoking is considered anathema.[60] Karîmân Hamza, the religious authority, writes about this noxious habit. In a provocative work in which she answers questions about women's problems, Hamza addresses smoking. She receives a letter from a recently veiled woman who confesses that despite this new religious existence she cannot keep herself from smoking. After welcoming her new "sister" into the fold, Hamza proceeds to give her counsel on smoking. Her attacks on this noxious habit are largely health-related. But cigarettes will also change woman's voice and make it manly in the same way that they distort her fingers and teeth. And this is not to speak of breast cancer. Hamza does add that cigarettes are forbidden according to Islam.[61]

In a pamphlet entitled *al-Islâm wal-Tifl* (Islam and the Child), Hamza addresses smoking by parents and the harm that this can cause. In addition to its direct health hazards, smoking becomes the first step to various types of addiction, ranging from alcohol to drugs.[62] The personal experience so eloquently presented to the reader of *My Journey from Unveiling to Veiling* is occulted. In fact, once that cigarette serves its purpose in Mahmûd's office, it seems never to reappear.

After Karîmân has lit her cigarette and crossed her legs before the shaykh's entrance, she begins to look at the smoke, trying to see "the future." On this word, the text appends a footnote in which Karîmân is quick to inform her reader that she stopped smoking "after that."[63] Is the time reference an allusion to the upcoming ill-fated event with Mahmûd or is it a general comment meant to indicate a more generalized future? The reader is not told. The presence of the announcement about her having given up cigarettes helps to soften the blow of the upcoming interview with her spiritual guide. When I discussed this episode with Karîmân Hamza in Cairo in January 1996, she made certain that I understood that she had indeed given up the nicotine habit.[64]

For Karîmân, in the narrative of the spiritual journey, the smoking body has engendered a host of other issues. She is unable to cover the two body parts she had gone to so much trouble to conceal with her mother's clothing. She is angry at the shaykh and at his delay. Her anger combines with the deep shame already signaled in the analysis. "Is the miniskirt illicit?" This seemingly naive question transports Karîmân into a quasi-obsessive monologue on the by-now-familiar body parts: hair and legs. Did God not create them? Why is she ashamed of them? These are two body parts she has always held dear.

The discourse of corporality is part and parcel of Karîmân's conversion experience. This will not be the last time she feels shame, nor will it be the last time she has a dialogue with herself over her various body parts. As she is leaving the television building one day, the protagonist spots Shaykh ʿAbd al-Halîm Mahmûd approaching it. His eyes fall on her uncovered arms. He looks at her with displeasure and averts his eyes. She, however, feels that when his eyes fall on her arms, it is as if "a whip had strongly stung my uncovered arms."[65] The male gaze has once again had its effect. True, it is averted, but its metaphorical violence remains.

Karîmân is becoming slowly persuaded. Her corporality is problematic and earns her the displeasure of the male religious establishment. She visits Shaykh Muhammad al-Ghazâlî at the Ministry of Pious Endowments daily. He welcomes her, but she always sees displeasure in his eyes. She wonders if the Deity might be angry because her appearance is that of a person not committed to the cause. "I notice this in his eyes every day. . . . And I swallow it. . . . I lower the skirt a centimeter or more each day. . . . And I break the rules of fashion. . . . Out of desire to see some approval in the eyes of my teachers . . ." [66] The teachers here are of the male gender. The protagonist plays the scopic game by looking for approval in their eyes, something she does not see. She lowers her skirt, that piece of clothing that caused her such shame in the office of ᶜAbd al-Halîm Mahmûd. Thus far, these vestimentary games are of no avail.

But it is the look that is always primary: how Karîmân looks at the religious males who are in turn looking at her. She continues to see displeasure in their eyes. A friend and brother in spirit to whom she has grown close assures her that her appearance "does not befit a believing individual!!" [67]

What is left for Karîmân to do? Her corporality continues to be a problem. Fortunately, her full religious awakening will take place and she will emerge from it not naked like a baby but fully covered as befits a Muslim woman. She has by now covered her arms, hidden her legs entirely, and broken all the rules of fashion. Still, the male eyes do not show approval. "I think there is nothing remaining visible of me that points to my femininity but my hair." [68]

One day, a young man delivers an invitation to Karîmân from the Faculty of Medicine of al-Mansûra to come and speak on "The Position of Women in Islam." The official paper arrives two days later, and in it she is asked to cover her hair in a scarf. "Oh, how terrible." Her hair is the most beautiful thing she has, and she remembers an incident on a ship during which a man even wrote her a poem praising it. The woman's magazine, *Hawwâ'* (Eve), also gives her advice about what to do with it: "Your crown, Madam."

Nevertheless, she takes a black embroidered scarf along with her on the trip. In front of a mirror, she tries to put it on in a reasonably fashionable way. On the train, she runs into Shaykh Salâh Abû Ismâᶜîl and talks to him about her speech. As the train approaches al-Mansûra, he tells her to go to the rest room and straighten her head covering because a piece of hair is showing. "And it was as if a scorpion had stung me!!" She jumps up and screams at the man, citing a Qur'ânic verse, "and as for thy Lord's blessing, declare it," as part of her right to show all her hair should she so wish. [69] The shaykh grows angry in turn, but she nevertheless goes to the rest room and hides all her hair.

The festivities proceed and Karîmân is seated next to her train companion. Her own presentation includes the Qur'ânic verse (al-âya al-karîma), "And let them cast their veils over their bosoms,"[70] which she is incapable of understanding. Fortunately, Shaykh Salâh Abû Ismâ^cîl explicates the verse, ending with the injunction that women should cover their hair, for "hair is ^cawra." (We shall return to ^cawra below.) The shaykh's words have quite an effect on the protagonist. She checks her head to make sure that all her hair is hidden. Her heartbeat rises and she breathes quickly. Her Lord does wish this. She does not hear the rest of the shaykh's words, swimming as she is in the "seas of the verse." "Suddenly, I opened my eyes and saw the veiled young women, as though they were angels in the clothing of obedience, the clothing of the Merciful." She decides to return to Cairo with Shaykh Salâh Abû Ismâ^cîl. "And on the way, I began to think about how I would hide my beautiful hair. . . . My treasure and my ornament and on which I rely in beautifying myself . . . And in the scarf, I will look unsophisticated and will no longer be fashionable or beautiful or radiant." But God answers her immediately. She sees the beauty of the nature surrounding her and remembers her mother's words: "God is beautiful and loves beauty." She realizes that God who loves beauty would not want the Muslim woman to be less beautiful than others. Surely, God would want woman with this clothing to be more beautiful and more perfect. She asks the shaykh about his explication of the verse. Yes, he assures her of his interpretation and adds that "the entire body of woman is ^cawra, except for the face and the two hands." This discussion decides it for Karîmân: she will cover her body.[71]

Shaykh Salâh Abû Ismâ^cîl is the male religious figure whose authority is invoked in this particular incident. Karîmân may well have recited a Qur'ânic verse in the train, which turns out to be the last verse from the Sûrat al-Duhâ. But it is ultimately the shaykh who is the holder of religious knowledge. Karîmân is unable to understand a verse about women covering themselves, which the shaykh must repeatedly explicate. But in fact, what she does not indicate to the reader is that this injunction is part of a much longer verse, the famous verse 31 from the Sûrat al-Nûr, a verse that also addresses the averting of the gaze. The male religious expert is the conduit to the holy book, and his knowledge will permit the young woman to continue on the proper religious path.

Yet, oddly enough, there is another authority, a woman, whose presence is noted at these festivities but who does not participate directly in the dialogue with Karîmân. This is the prominent Islamic spokes-woman, Ni^cmat Sidqî. Sidqî's presence is signaled initially when the in-vitation comes to Karîmân to participate in the public event. Sidqî re-appears on the stage, as the participants are seated, and once again when she delivers her message. The content of that message, however, remains occulted.

But to say "Ni^cmat Sidqî" in this context is to say a great deal. The reader conscious of the intricacies of the Islamic revival knows that Ni^cmat Sidqî is not simply another female voice advocating the Muslim way of life for women. Sidqî is the author of one of the most popular booklets on female adornment, *al-Tabarruj*.[72] This booklet has gone into multiple editions in multiple countries and has traveled the world. Part of the power of Sidqî's prose is that, like that of Hamza, it partakes of the personal. In her case, the story of her veiling is tied to a personal illness, presented to the reader in the introduction of the book. I have discussed elsewhere the importance of Sidqî's personal experience, which resur-faces without attribution in other contemporary revivalist materials.[73]

This incident in al-Mansûra will bring about a full realization of the need for modest dress on Karîmân's part. It is not an accident by any means, therefore, that the message in favor of this Islamic dress is deliv-ered repeatedly and by males of all ages. First, the young male student transmits the invitation orally. His visit entails his looking at Karîmân once in a while but being ashamed to say anything. When the invitation arrives, there is a clear message that she "hide" her hair "in a scarf." On the train, she receives an oral request from Shaykh Salâh Abû Ismâ^cîl to fix up her head covering because a bit of hair is showing on the side. Her sensation that "it was as if a scorpion had stung" her testifies, once again, to the violence of the male glance. Then this same religious authority delivers the message first in a public setting and then over and over again in answer to Karîmân's repeated questions in the car to Cairo. Shadowing the male authorities in their verbal delivery of this all-important message, Ni^cmat Sidqî remains in the background as the fe-male but silent exemplar.

In explaining the full import of the Qur'ânic verse about female cov-ering, Shaykh Salâh Abû Ismâ^cîl instills in Karîmân the notion of woman's body as *^cawra*. This is powerful stuff. *^cAwra* is a concept em-bodying a complex range of significations including that of shame, the pudenda, that which must be covered, and so forth. The term also links directly to classical Islamic discussions of woman's body, since the de-limitation of the domain of *^cawra* determined not only what parts of a woman's (and also of a man's) body were to be covered but also effectively the degree to which a woman could be involved in social life outside the house.[74]

In this context, Shaykh Salâh Abû Ismâᶜîl's position is by no means the most conservative possible. Karîmân Hamza authored a guide for the Muslim woman, *Rifqan bil-Qawârîr*. This work received a conservative rejoinder from Yusriyya Muhammad Anwar on the Islamic right, a reply that clearly demonstrates that Hamza's positions (like those of this shaykh) on woman's body and its covering are not as strict as some would like.[75] Karîmân Hamza was quite surprised when I raised this work with her in Cairo. "You are well read," she said to me with a tone that implied that she would rather I were not so well read.

Hamza's assessment of Yusriyya Muhammad Anwar's work was extremely telling. First, she revealed to me that Yusriyya Muhammad Anwar was a *munaqqaba*—that is, one who wears the *niqâb*, the extremely conservative dress for women that dictates the covering of the hands and the face but for the eyes. Hamza also dismissed the work by Yusriyya Muhammad Anwar by claiming that she had not written it, but rather that her husband composed it and published it under her name. Further, according to Karîmân Hamza, the husband had not only written the book in fifteen days, but it was extremely sloppy as well. Hamza informed me that she, on the other hand, had taken years to write her work, long years in which she had thoroughly researched the traditions of the Prophet, the *hadîth*s.[76] Karîmân Hamza's attribution of Yusriyya Muhammad Anwar's work to the latter's husband is used to dismiss its more conservative position. But what I did not raise with Karîmân on that occasion was the fact that, as Joanna Russ has so eloquently demonstrated, attributing women's works to men is a common technique for occulting women's authorial voices.[77]

Nevertheless, by inserting the word ᶜ*awra*, a term redolent with taboo, into the dialogue, Shaykh Salâh Abû Ismâᶜîl has effectively convinced Karîmân of the error of her ways. From one lock of hair, the corporal geography of ᶜ*awra* has been extended to the entirety of woman's body. Like the male gaze, the male discourse of the body is powerful. It will determine the future behavior of the narrator. Other discourses, especially more feminine ones (like those of the women's magazines) are nullified. Her hair may well be her "crown," or it may be her "treasure." It will be covered.

The resistance to the cultural discourse in the women's magazine that woman's hair is her crown can take other forms, as it does in El

Saadawi's feminist novel, *Mudhakkirât Tabîba*. There, the female hero runs to have her hair cut. Her "crown" falls at her feet rather than disappearing under a head covering, as with Karîmân.[78] Strikingly, for both the feminist and the revivalist woman, the crown of the women's magazine must be negated.

With this, Karîmân has completed the transition. She has recuperated from the initial striptease performed in Shaykh ʿAbd al-Halîm Mahmûd's office. Just as her uncovering in his office was accomplished in steps, so has been her recovering. The males may be pleased, but they do not seem to understand the extent of her sacrifice. The conversion experience has confirmed the gender hierarchies with which the text started. True, Karîmân is no longer an alien creature. She has accomplished the rite of passage successfully. But she could not have done this without the help of the males, from their disapproving glances to their unsolicited advice to their explanation of the religious tradition.

And one male stands out above all others, ʿAbd al-Halîm Mahmûd. From the beginning of the book to its end, he is a presence. He dies at the end of the narrative, but that oddly enough does not diminish his power. That he is a father figure is by now obvious. But he is more than that. The attraction the narrator feels for him is almost sexual. His voice is compared to the finger of the physician: phallic imagery indeed.[79] When she speaks to a young man about him, she says that she is "enamored of" him.[80] His words run through her body, shaking her limbs.[81] "I am strange, myself, in my love for this Imam," she muses.[82]

This infatuation, this love, penetrates into the verbal texture of Karîmân's spiritual journey. In her first encounter with the shaykh (as a lecturer at the Institute of Islamic Studies), she removed herself from the narration and surrendered the first-person voice to him. At this point, his identity had not yet been revealed. Once his name is uncovered, however, once that voice is attached to a corporal entity, he not only shares the narration but also appropriates large segments of the text. Karîmân summarizes his books. She quotes from them. Entire chapters are devoted to his works. These are not mere intertextual references. These are entire passages and sections transposed from the shaykh's books into Karîmân's book. His textual identity becomes enmeshed with hers. That seemingly false modesty in her own preface was but a literary ruse to allow the male voice to insert itself into that of the female. And this despite the already-discussed change in title and direction of the work.

The gender politics are clear. A woman's spiritual journey remains tied to the male. Her saga is always seen through his eyes. She looks for his approval. She worries, as most women do, about whether or not she will still be pretty. More than that, female discourse may become subordinated to that of the male. Karîmân discovers on the pilgrimage to Mecca that she has been sharing space with "the shaykh's sister." This sister remains unnamed, unlike the shaykh's brother, who is identified.[83] The female is defined by her relationship to the male.

The two mystics whose conversions as related by the shaykh had acted as catalysts for Karîmân were, of course, both males. The underlying message is that this is a male activity. Should it be a surprise that toward the end of her saga, Karîmân should be called by the *Majallat al-Idhâ^ca wal-Tilifizyûn*, the "mystic announcer?"[84] The last work by ^cAbd al-Halîm Mahmûd she quotes is on a famous medieval male mystic, al-Hârith ibn Asad al-Muhâsibî (d. 243/837).[85] The reader has come full circle. Karîmân has learned her lesson well.

Gender politics also appear in the physical product that is the book itself. The first edition is visually relatively spare. A cover painting features a woman, seen from the back so that no face is visible, against the background of an Islamic cityscape (Figure 1). No other illustrations are provided, and even the back cover is merely text. The second edition of *Rihlatî min al-Sufûr ilâ al-Hijâb* is a far more iconographically oriented object. The cover features a line drawing of Karîmân Hamza holding an open Qur'ân. She is wearing the *hijâb,* the veil, and is in outline against a skyline of mosques. The entirety is colored in shades of green, black, and white. The holy book is open in the direction in which the reader will open Karîmân Hamza's account of her journey (Figure 2). The last page of the book is a black-and-white photograph of Karîmân Hamza in the same pose, this time without the skyline, but facing in the opposite direction—in cinematic terms, a countershot (Figure 3). This photograph is preceded by another photograph on the penultimate page, of a dreamy or spiritual Karîmân Hamza in quarter profile with a fashionable *hijâb* with floral print (Figure 4). Karîmân-with-Qurân is preceded by Karîmân-Islamic-fashion model.

The Qur'ân in the photograph on the last page is pointing to the book the reader has just completed. Karîmân Hamza has effectively beckoned the reader to her life story, and the open book is but a sign of that. Intertextually, there is also similarity between the book that is Karîmân Hamza's saga and the book she holds. Is it an accident that the first work by

Figure 1.   Cover of the first edition of *Rihlatî min al-Sufûr ilâ al-Hijâb.*

Figure 2. Cover of the second edition of *Rihlatî min al-Sufûr ilâ al-Hijâb*.

Figure 3. Photograph of Karîmân Hamza on the last page of *Rihlatî min al-Sufûr ilâ al-Hijâb*.

ᶜAbd al-Halîm Mahmûd that she exposes is a biography of the Prophet? Did Karîmân not, after all, early on in the book, present the reader with a discussion in which it becomes clear that the Prophet Muhammad not only represents the Qur'ân but that he is indeed the Qur'ân?[86] She asks God's forgiveness for having always compared herself with the Prophet. Now she realizes that her own behavior must be a Qur'ân.[87] The symbolism of the holy book in the picture is then all important. It is not simply that Karîmân Hamza's life is an open book. Her path is one to be followed, like the Qur'ân. As Khamîs put it in the introduction, her book is "a book of propaganda for Islam."[88]

Equally important, this visual reinforces a verbal description by Khamîs in his eloquent introduction. As he singles out Karîmân Hamza in the domain of the media, he repeats that she is the only television announcer who possesses certain unique qualities. He, interestingly enough, chooses to begin with the body: "She is the only television announcer who adheres to Islamic dress, so nothing shows of her body but the face and the hands."[89] The insistence on the corporality of the television personality

كريمان حمزة

بقلم : الداعية الإسلامي الكبيــر
الشيــخ محمد الغـزالي

Figure 4. Photograph of Karîmân Hamza on the penultimate page of *Rihlatî min al-Sufûr ilâ al-Hijâb.*

is reinforced in the visual materials, where only Karîmân Hamza's face and hands are bared.

Just as the first words in the work are not those of Karîmân Hamza, so it is with the last words. The final speaker is the religious leader Shaykh Muhammad al-Ghazâlî. His two-page contribution is entitled "Karîmân Hamza." Each of the pages is itself made up of a picture of the female personality and below it the words of the shaykh. Al-Ghazâlî is providing a minibiography, one that must be read alongside the first-person saga of Karîmân herself. As a male speaker, he also provides the official closure to the text.

What about the pictures? One, on the penultimate page, is a close-up of a fashionably veiled Karîmân Hamza. The other, on the final page, shows her with an open Qur'ân, but one whose marginal decorations seem to match those on the sleeve of her dress. How interesting that the name of the studio should have been left visible on the pictures: Mûnâ-lîzâ, Mona Lisa. How even more interesting that the shaykh's opening words should explain that he met Karîmân Hamza as she was abandoning western customs and following Islamic teachings. But how many traditional Muslim women would flaunt their pictures in such a way in the back of a book? Not many. The end of the book is a reminder of the importance of the external. Words can adequately convey a spiritual odyssey. The photographs give a centrality to the physical image well known from the less modest culture of the contemporary West.

Many elements of Karîmân Hamza's saga are familiar from the more or less autobiographical works of other Arab women. The female narrator of the first-person novel of the Egyptian feminist Nawal El Saadawi, *Mudhakkirât Tabîba* (Memoirs of a Female Physician) felt the shock of the notion that her body was *ᶜawra*, when her mother censured her for exposing her legs.[90] In the autobiography of the Palestinian poet Fadwâ Tûqân, *Rihla Jabaliyya, Rihla Saᶜba* (Mountainous Journey, Difficult Journey), it is an older woman, Shaykha, who delivers the admonition.[91] But in these cases, social authority comes from the female. With the contemporary Egyptian Muslim writer, however, the disapproving glances, the instructions, all came from males, usually authority figures as well. Karîmân's mother in this whole debate remains on the margins. Muslim sisterhood is barely visible. Few are the women who help Karîmân on her journey.[92]

But why this gender difference? El Saadawi's heroes were young women escaping from the constraints of a traditional culture to the greater freedom made available by secular lifestyles.[93] Older women are frequent (and negative) symbols of traditional culture in modern Arabic literature (as they are in other non-Middle Eastern traditional cultures).[94] What is interesting here is the precise opposite. Karîmân's mother is French-educated, with all that implies of modernity. The daughter, on the other hand, is moving toward a less secular and, hence it could be argued, more traditional culture. No older women are present here to urge Karîmân along on her new path. If women can signify tradition negatively, men signify it positively.

Karîmân Hamza is coming from this relatively secularized society and reveiling. The Muslim revival movement of which she is an exemplar is, her narrative would suggest, a movement whose motive forces are male. That is why she is textually handed over from one father to another. This neopatriarchy (to use Hisham Sharabi's apt term)[95] is necessary because Karîmân's original social authority, her parents, did not bring her up in an appropriately Islamic manner. Hence the need for a new father.

And if for just one moment the father, patriarchy, is envisaged as the basis of social authority and, in effect, as the state, then Karîmân's saga can be read as an allegory of the political ambitions of the Islamist movement. The new (Islamic) state must reimpose values the former (secularizing or westernizing) state has allowed to fall away. But the woman is more than allegory. For it is her body that must be veiled.

Gender and Spiritual Vision

The reader of Karîmân Hamza's powerful spiritual autobiography watches as the young woman moves from a secular lifestyle to a fully religious one, along the way covering her female body. But Hamza's *My Journey from Unveiling to Veiling* is more than a story about a female body that must be covered. It is also an eloquent demonstration of the power of the Arabo-Islamic tradition in the contemporary Arab world. Karîmân's spiritual journey is defined with reference to Islamic mysticism or Sufism, and specifically to medieval male mystics. Gender and mysticism might seem an odd couple indeed in the context of the contemporary revival movement. But Karîmân demonstrates that this odd couple is alive and well. (This is not just the case for her but for other women in the revival.)[1] Not only that, but mysticism is a prime mover behind the young woman's complete integration into her new spiritual family and away from her biological one. Along the spiritual path, the reader of the journey also participates in other experiences that partake of the spiritual and religious, including dreams and the pilgrimage to Mecca. The physical pilgrimage adds a transnational level to the geographical discourse, as Karîmân joins a community in one of its most important religious rituals.

Karîmân the university student, married, and seemingly happy ends her journey as a highly visible public persona involved in the media.[2] Her transformation from a more secular lifestyle to a more religious one is dramatic indeed. The distances she has to traverse are not only vestimentary but geographical, as her newly acquired knowledge of Islamic religious sites demonstrates. Thus she can go from someone who does not know the location of al-Husayn in Cairo to someone who navigates the holy sites of Mecca with her religious sisters, all under the guidance of Shaykh ᶜAbd al-Halîm Mahmûd.

This transformation has its roots in Karîmân's fateful entrance into the Institute of Islamic Studies. The importance of this initial encounter for the discourse of corporality has been amply demonstrated. But no less significant is the impact of this first meeting for the discourse of spirituality.

Karîmân's entry into the religious institute, which defined her as a being apart, also propels her into the spiritual universe that she will end up inhabiting. The momentous event is that lecture to which Karîmân listens in fascination. The male religious figure delivering these words, the as yet unnamed shaykh, begins with Islamic religious formulae, something alien to the university student. Then he continues: today he will speak about two important mystics: al-Fudayl ibn ᶜIyâd (d. 187/803) and Ibrâhîm ibn Adham (d. 161/777–78). The stories follow. Al-Fudayl was born to a pious father in Khurâsân and, against his father's wishes, became a successful highway robber. He was in love with a slave girl and one night, after attacking a caravan, was on his way to her house. While scaling the wall, he overheard a voice from the sky addressing him: "Is it not time that the hearts of those who believe should be humbled to the Remembrance of God and the Truth which He has sent down?"[3] Every time he tried to cross the wall, the voice would repeat its message. So al-Fudayl responded: "Yes, it is time, my Lord." He descended from the wall, with his heart beating in fear and shame, and his body shaking with sorrow and pain. He has heard the divine call. He also overhears some people speaking about their travel plans and deciding to delay their trip until morning, because al-Fudayl will hold them up. The highway robber repents and proceeds to immerse himself in learning in order that his repentance be based on true knowledge.[4]

The second Sufi the shaykh speaks about is Ibrâhîm ibn Adham. Ibrâhîm hailed from a well-off family in Khurâsân. He was out on a hunt one day, and just as he was approaching the prey, he heard a voice saying: "Were you created for this? Or were you ordered to do this?" He stopped, looked right and left, and saw no one. The voice continued to repeat this to him. Ibrâhîm came to his senses and changed his life.[5]

The lecture ends and the students go to the shaykh. Karîmân "awakens" (though when she actually went into a sleeping state is not indicated!) and realizes that she has heard the entire lecture. She suddenly remembers her father. She runs out to the car and apologizes to him. But he quickly informs her that he learned that his friend to whom she was to deliver the books died two days ago. She herself begins to tell him about the shaykh's lecture. She repeats the story over and over, and when her father asks her who the shaykh is, she answers that she does not know.

From the visual world in which she is the undesirable object, Karîmân has been transported into the intellectual oral world of the shaykh's lecture. The significance of this oral communication is such that the first-person female narrator exits the text, allowing the religious figure of the shaykh to speak for himself. He introduces the two conversions in the first person: "I will speak to you today about two great Sufis." [6] From the moment the lecture begins until the moment it ends and the narrator awakens, the voice heard is that of the shaykh. Karîmân's exit has been more than narratological. The voice of the lecturer has transported her into a world different from that of her everyday reality. She must awaken from this experience.

This oral aspect is crucial. Karîmân hears the shaykh tell the two conversion narratives. The two stories, in turn, revolve around orality/aurality. Both males hear the divine voice calling them to change their ways. And this is an insistent voice. It does not cease repeating the message. Al-Fudayl's oral experience is twice enriched. Does he not also overhear voices speaking about his activities as a highway robber? This contrast between oral and visual (with preference for the former) is familiar in Arabo-Islamic culture. [7] Distinctively, it resolves itself here into a contrast between immodest body and healing word, the visual/external being the sign of the heroine's spiritual deficiency.

This will turn out to be a momentous event in Karîmân's life. Not only does she spend a sleepless night, but she hears the voice of the shaykh repeating over and over the Deity's call to the two medieval mystics. Her life is laid bare before the reader, as is her personal distress (which translated itself into a desire to die). [8] In the morning, Karîmân hears that same voice while listening to a radio program on the Qur'ân. This time, the male voice is recounting the saga of another male mystic, Sahl ibn ᶜAbd Allâh al-Tustarî (d. 283/896). The announcer thanks the speaker, thus identifying him as no less a figure than the prominent religious leader Dr. ᶜAbd al-Halîm Mahmûd. Karîmân calls her father to share this information, "and I told him, while in a quasi-dream state, what he said on the radio. . . .

"What is this that the shaykh is saying . . . How his talk runs through my being, shaking my limbs and yielding them to the Lord, may He be exalted."[9] What an effect the voice has on the narrator! Its balm is mental and physical.

Karîmân has crossed an important threshold. She has listened to three narratives, all dealing with male mystics. Each narrative, in its own way, has great relevance to her own experience. The first two males, Ibrâhîm ibn Adham and al-Fudayl ibn ʿIyâd, came from opposite social classes, and knew one another in Mecca.[10] Both are examples of the early Muslim ascetic movement (zuhd), one that involved an individual spiritual experience, as distinct from the later phase of mysticism, in which mystics or Sufis attached themselves to a particular teacher and a brotherhood.

Karîmân's presentation of Ibrâhîm (it is she, after all, who has recounted the lecture) is not devoid of significance. In the contemporary setting, Ibrâhîm is a lone figure, traveling from place to place, "a tourist in the tourism of God." He contemplates creation, he battles Satan, he flees from that which is forbidden.[11] His is a lonely path: his interactions with either his contemporaries or with those who may have asked him for spiritual advice are occulted.

This twentieth-century Ibrâhîm, hence, differs from his medieval persona. Ibrâhîm ibn Adham's pre-Hamzian saga is perhaps one of the most enticing of those of all the mystics, reaching at times the legendary. From the earliest to the later sources on asceticism and mysticism, Ibrâhîm is there. His story shifted from Arabic to Persian and then to Turkish and even to Urdu and to Malay, along the way becoming more and more fanciful. Russell Jones argues that the Arabic sources are really the most trustworthy.[12] And of these, al-Qushayrî (d. 465/1074) is, in the words of A. J. Arberry, the "author of the most famous and authoritative treatise on Sufism in Arabic."[13]

Al-Qushayrî's vision of Ibrâhîm is, in a sense, more social. Certainly, the asceticism is there, as is the piety. But the Qushayrian Ibrâhîm is a generous soul who cares both financially and emotionally for the plight of his fellow humans. To take but one example: Sahl ibn Ibrâhîm relates that he was Ibrâhîm ibn Adham's companion. Sahl became sick and Ibrâhîm ibn Adham paid the cost, and when he had a craving for something, Ibrâhîm sold his donkey and spent the money on his friend. When the friend asked where the donkey was, Ibrâhîm replied: "We sold it." So his friend asked: "And on what will I ride?" Ibrâhîm ibn Adham replied: "O my brother, on my neck." And he proceeded to carry his friend.[14]

The transformation of the medieval Ibrâhîm into the contemporary one who inhabits a modern woman's religious narrative is significant. The medieval accounts show a multifaceted character, whose ascetic life is as important as—if not more important than—the actual call he receives.[15] Not so in Karîmân Hamza's book. In the contemporary setting, the call is primary and is in a certain sense the culmination of a previous life away from God. How interesting it then becomes to realize that ᶜAbd al-Halîm Mahmûd, Karîmân Hamza's spiritual guide, was co-editor of al-Qushayrî's work.

As for al-Fudayl ibn ᶜIyâd, Hamza's book elaborates that he kept reciting the Qur'ân and the Prophetic traditions (the *hadîth*) until he devoted himself to the study of religion. He then adhered to the Sharîᶜa (the revealed or canonical law of Islam) and emulated the Prophet as much as he could.[16] The Arabic word for al-Fudayl's study activities is *tafaqqaha,* which also means to study the *fiqh,* the science of Islamic jurisprudence. This might seem incongruous in an Islamic mystical account. But the immediate reference to the Sharîᶜa and to the emulation of the Prophet makes it clear that more is at stake here.

What Karîmân Hamza's narrative has done is to redirect ever so subtly al-Fudayl's asceticism. According to Annemarie Schimmel, al-Fudayl is "a typical representative of early orthodox asceticism." And though he was married, he considered family life "one of the greatest obstacles on his way to God." Schimmel notes that, for the early ascetics, "a preference for celibacy was common in spite of the Prophet's example of married life and his advice to raise a family." [17] Clearly, the contemporary al-Fudayl has acquired a slightly different identity from his medieval persona.[18]

In the modern text, al-Fudayl's call has primacy. His earlier life, painted by the male lecturer in the female's text, was that of debauchery. His family is presented as pious, with a father attempting in vain to guide his son on the right path. But the divine call is more powerful. Whereas Ibrâhîm is summoned to the ascetic life while hunting animals, al-Fudayl hears the divine voice while pursuing a slave girl.

The medieval intertext is, therefore, not innocent. The message inculcated by the twentieth-century teacher is quite powerful and serves as a reminder that spiritual sagas do more than portray a religious transformation. This process of redefinition of the medieval male mystics will facilitate the spiritual experience of the contemporary female.

The two mystics, Ibrâhîm ibn Adham and al-Fudayl ibn ᶜIyâd, play similar roles in Karîmân Hamza's *My Journey from Unveiling to Veiling.* The call was foregrounded in their contemporary presentation, and just as the call becomes of primary importance in their lives, so it is also for Karîmân. But whereas the call for the two medieval figures instigated an almost instantaneous change in lifestyle, for Karîmân the call will be but the first step on the path to salvation. Clearly, the attention to the two calls in the female contemporary account makes it clear that their purpose is to sanction her own call by ᶜAbd al-Halîm Mahmûd.

True, like her medieval male predecessors, she has heard the voice. But her oral experience differs. The two men had a direct link to the Deity: when called on the religious path, they could answer without intermediary. Not so in the case of the contemporary female protagonist. She is not addressed directly; her call is mediated through different male voices. The contemporary shaykh is but a transmitter of the original story in which the voice calls on the two males to change their ways. One of them, al-Fudayl, answers: "Yes. It is time, my Lord," a phrase that is taken out of his mouth, placed in the mouth of the venerable lecturer at the institute, and from there transported into the mouth of the female narrator, who repeats it to herself. This double mediation also occurs with the questions posed to Ibrâhîm—"Were you created for this? Or were you ordered to do this?"—questions filtered through the voice of ᶜAbd al-Halîm Mahmûd, only to be repeated by Karîmân.

Another important difference surfaces between the contemporary female and the medieval males. The call for Ibrâhîm and al-Fudayl represented salvation from a life away from the Deity. The ascetic path will save them from eternal perdition. For Karîmân, the call is much more substantial. For her it represents rescue from physical destruction. She must be saved not only from a spiritual death but from a physical one as well. Her call has permitted her rebirth of sorts in new clothing.[19] It will also fully provide her with a spiritual family.

Ibrâhîm adds an additional role to the one he shared with al-Fudayl. His presence is not simply to endorse the call, but more importantly, it is also a sign of vestimentary transformation. He, after all, shed the clothing of "arrogance and pride and wore the clothing of sincere obedience to God."[20] And this is precisely what Karîmân herself does throughout her narrative.[21] But unlike Ibrâhîm, who dons his new clothing immediately, her response is much more gradual and entails much more resistance: the shedding of the westernized clothing in favor of the Islamic dress occupies much of the narrative and involves a great deal more soul-searching. Since her salvation culminates in the proper Islamic dress (if nothing else the title of the work tells that!), the sartorial switch will not come about easily, as it did for Ibrâhîm. In fact, much of the contemporary female journey is devoted to a step-by-step covering.[22]

The call is, however, but one component of the religious experience, the teacher being the other. Here, again, a medieval male mystic provides the clue: Sahl ibn ᶜAbd Allâh al-Tustarî. Sahl is the mystic about whom ᶜAbd al-Halîm Mahmûd is speaking as Karîmân tunes in to her favorite radio program on the Qur'ân. Sahl in the radio account was in need of a teacher, a shaykh, to help him understand his exact position vis-à-vis the right path. Sahl, therefore, differs from the two previous mystics. He does not receive a call. And, that is what the medieval accounts substantiate. Abû Muhammad Sahl al-Tustarî was pious from early childhood. His devout uncle taught him early on to say "God is my witness" over and over again, increasing the number of times the boy was to say this. This the young Sahl did, deriving pleasure from the experience. He was eventually sent to the *kuttâb* (Qur'ânic school), but even here he made a condition: that he would attend for an hour, only to leave after that for contemplation. He memorized the Qur'ân while still a child of six or seven. His asceticism started early in his life, when he began fasting at noon. It was at the age of thirteen that he had a "problem," and that is the point at which he went out in search of someone to help him cure this dilemma. He found his mentor and returned to his home town, where he maintained his ascetic lifestyle.[23]

Once more, a medieval mystic and his twentieth-century counterpart are not identical. In the medieval biography, Sahl's visit to the spiritual healer is embedded in an otherwise contemplative life. (In one medieval account, it is simply his contemplative life that is presented.)[24] In Karîmân Hamza's rendition, this visit to the shaykh is the central issue of the radio message.

Like Sahl, Karîmân is afflicted with a spiritual malaise. Sahl did not need a call from the Deity to pursue the religious life, and at this point, neither does Karîmân. Her call has been already twice delivered. Like Sahl, she will seek out her own shaykh, ᶜAbd al-Halîm Mahmûd.

The arrival of the teacher in the young woman's life leads to a transformation whose culmination is the all-important pilgrimage to Mecca. This ultimate geographical displacement that Karîmân undertakes is heralded by several major incidents, all of which tie the young woman to the centuries-old Islamic tradition. These events can be divided into those that take place before the pilgrimage and those that occur during the holy month.

Before the pilgrimage, the narrator will have to veil herself. She herself puts it eloquently in the title of the section: "The Veil before the Pilgrimage" (al-Hijâb qabl al-Hajj).[25] And veil herself she does. Observe the female hero's description of herself in this new religious garb. She dons a light green head covering with a dark green velvet suit. The entirety was "of extraordinary elegance and modesty" (anâqa wa-hishma). These two terms, elegance and modesty, become very significant. Karîmân Hamza will use them as the title of an annual fashion catalog in the form of a magazine designed for the veiled woman and entitled Anâqa wa-Hishma.[26]

As the young woman is heading toward the Ministry of Pious Endowments in this new clothing, she hears people calling out to her with the honorific title of al-Hâjja, she who has performed the pilgrimage. This word seems strange to her. She had not hoped to perform this ritual, which for her should fall later in life, both her mother and father having been much older when they accomplished it.[27]

Dressed in this new clothing, she enters the office of ᶜAbd al-Halîm Mahmûd. She is anxious to hear his opinion about her new appearance. She gives the Muslim greeting, which he proceeds to answer. He then tells her calmly that her clothing is "not bad." She almost begins to cry and wonders whether the shaykh is aware that she has broken all the rules of fashion and gone against the currents of the age. She goes home immediately and addresses the Deity, asking him if He is pleased with her. "Are you pleased? Nothing pleases your servant Dr. ᶜAbd al-Halîm Mahmûd. . . . He did not encourage me. . . . Nor did he praise my position. . . ." Then Karîmân begins to cry. This will incite her to ask herself if she has done all this in order to please Shaykh al-Ghazâlî and Shaykh ᶜAbd al-Halîm Mahmûd or to obey God and his Prophet.

In the evening, she is reading a book by another religious personality, and she spots the hadîth: "Man will be resurrected with whom he wishes/loves." She jumps up, runs to her husband, hugs him, and informs him that she will be resurrected with Shaykh Mahmûd. The husband is confused but she provides him with the Prophetic saying. Despite the fact that her accomplishments are not identical to her mentor's, she will nevertheless be resurrected with him.

Karîmân falls asleep and dreams that Mahmûd and a group of learned men (ᶜulamâ') are sitting in a room overlooking a big sea in Paradise. Among them is her spiritual brother, ᶜAbd al-Khâliq ᶜAbd al-Wahhâb. The room resembles a coffee shop. The young woman is with them. Suddenly, the shaykh gets up, stretches his hand, "and brings my head to his chest," saying, "Yes. Man will be resurrected with whom he wishes/loves." Karîmân awakens, very happy, and heads for the Ministry of Pious Endowments. She is surprised by the fact that ᶜAbd al-Halîm Mahmûd has included her in that year's pilgrimage deputation, of which he is the leader.[28]

These prepilgrimage events are extremely important, spanning as they do the corporal and the spiritual. This is the time during which Karîmân becomes increasingly conscious of male dissatisfaction with her appearance and finally takes the full vestimentary plunge. The opening section of "The Veil before the Pilgrimage" is imbued with the disapproving male gaze and a preponderance of the masculine plural. This grammatical usage has the added benefit of encompassing the entire range of males who have been influential in the young woman's transformation, including the two preeminent shaykhs, al-Ghazâlî and Mahmûd.

Once the corporal change is effected, the fashion-conscious narrator does not shy away from describing her appearance, taking special pains to inform her reader that the new clothing is not only color coordinated but also extremely elegant and modest. Her own assessment of this vestimentary cover-up is confirmed by the external world around her, as evidenced by the title of al-Hâjja with which people address her on her way to see Shaykh ᶜAbd al-Halîm Mahmûd. This honorific means that she has successfully traversed the clothing barrier.

Karîmân is, however, much more concerned with the opinion of the male religious leadership than with the opinion of the people in the street. Her prominent mentor notices her new appearance, but is not terribly effusive in his compliments. Karîmân appeals to the Deity. This appeal attests to a critical change. On the one hand, it signals that she is now, because of her clothing and her training thus far, without need of an intermediary, as she was early on in the spiritual journey. She can address the Deity directly, in the same way that she knows male mystics centuries before her have done. On the other hand, this appeal sets up the male religious establishment on one side, and the Deity on the other. Shaykh Mahmûd's earthly opinion is less important than the divine one. This incident serves to set the young woman on the right track and make her redirect her efforts away from pleasing the venerable earthly masters and toward obeying the directives of God and His Prophet.

And how quickly the benefits from this new trajectory will flow! First, Karîmân runs across a tradition of the Prophet about resurrection, which, as far as she herself is concerned, inextricably links her fate to that of ᶜAbd al-Halîm Mahmûd. But that is not enough. An oneiric experience will put the final Islamic touch on this union between male spiritual mentor and female disciple.

"*Ra'aytu fîmâ yarâ al-nâ'im*" (I saw as the sleeper sees): thus begins the dream sequence. This phrase is a relatively unusual way in modern Arabic for expressing the idea of dreaming. The word normally used to express the dream state is *halama* (*yahlumu*), to dream. This phrase emanates from the classical Arabo-Islamic tradition, in which dreams played an extremely important role. *Ra'aytu fî al-manâm* (I saw in a dream) or *ra'aytu fî al-nawm* (I saw in sleep) were the favored classical ways of signaling to a reader that an oneiric narrative was in the process of unfolding, with a clear stress on the idea of seeing, from the verb *ra'aytu*.[29] Of the various forms of divination of non-Islamic origin, oneiromancy was the only one fully accepted by the Orthodoxy. A cursory glance at the *hadîth* material is sufficient to demonstrate the level of integration.[30] There was also in the Islamic Middle Ages an important Greco-Islamic oneirocritical tradition that blended the Greek science with its Islamic counterpart, much as was done with Greco-Islamic medicine.[31] This oneirocritical tradition has continued with some significant adaptations down to the present day as a vigorous form of popular culture.[32]

It is perhaps not an accident that another contemporary writer, the 1988 Nobel laureate Naguib Mahfouz also exploits this phrase in a short-story cycle composed of dreams and in which the rich Arabo-Islamic tradition, the *turâth*, plays a critical role.[33] Once again, and in an odd textual twist, the female revivalist writer, as she did with Yûsuf Idrîs, comes close to another male secular literary cousin, this time the Nobel Prize winner.

In the complex medieval Greco-Islamic world of dreams, there were oneiric experiences that needed no interpretation. Most often, these should predict a future event and not be allegorical.[34] And this is precisely where Karîmân's dream fits in: it needs no interpretation. Instead, the female dreamer, in the morning, rushes to the ministry without so much as a question about the meaning of this oneiric experience.

Karîmân's dream takes place in Paradise and is entirely populated by men, with the exception of the female hero. All the learned men present are unnamed, but for Shaykh ᶜAbd al-Halîm Mahmûd and Karîmân's spiritual brother, ᶜAbd al-Khâliq ᶜAbd al-Wahhâb. But Karîmân is far from an outsider in this distinguished company. The action of Mahmûd will testify to this, as he gets up, stretches his hand, and brings her head to his chest. This intimate gesture seals the emotional bond between teacher and pupil. To add to the power of the corporal gesture, the shaykh repeats the words that Karîmân herself uttered during her waking state prior to the dream. Corporality and orality come together to assure the fate of Karîmân's resurrection experience.

Not only that, but the dream expresses a reciprocity of desire: both Karîmân, in the nondream world, and her shaykh, in the dream world, have the same wish, to be resurrected with one another. Significant here is the fact that the young woman did nothing during the course of the oneiric events themselves to instigate the older male to express this desire. His action would appear to be self-motivated, demonstrating an affection for his young pupil that will go beyond this world.

The corporal action undertaken by Shaykh ᶜAbd al-Halîm Mahmûd is significant in yet another way. The hug desexualizes the relationship between the older male and the younger female, since the action clearly hierarchizes the two as father and daughter: no male would touch a strange female in this way in the contemporary Middle East.[35]

On a certain level, Karîmân has been fully adopted by the religious leader. The substitution of spiritual father for biological father seems now complete. Those two crucial meetings in the beginning of the journey have borne their fruit: "The First Meeting" (al-Liqâ' al-Awwal) signaling that fateful entrance of Shaykh Mahmûd into Karîmân's life, on the one hand, followed almost immediately by "The Last Meeting" (al-Liqâ' al-Akhîr) signaling the death of the biological father, on the other.

This dream clearly constitutes a sign to the female dreamer. Her ensuing visit to the Ministry of Pious Endowments reveals to her that her shaykh has included her in the pilgrimage deputation—and this without her request. She has been metaphorically resurrected with those whom she wished, as has the shaykh.

The veracity of this oneiric experience is established by various means that tie it directly to the entire centuries-old Arabo-Islamic dream tradition. One of the indications of the veracity of a dream is the presence of one of a number of figures, chief among them the Prophet. These figures include one's teacher. In addition, true dreams tended to be those whose interpretation was obvious, clearly the case for Karîmân. The time of the day at which a dream took place also bore upon its veracity. The Prophet was quoted as saying that the dream that is most true is the one that is seen at dawn. While Karîmân does not specify dawn, she indicates that she awoke extremely happy and, when morning appeared, headed directly for the ministry.[36] The locus of Karîmân's dream could not be better than it was: Paradise.

Perhaps the reader should not be overly surprised that such an action involving the shaykh's new relationship to his pupil should be heralded by means of a dream. The entire states of sleep and wakefulness have been crucial ones for Karîmân from very early on in her spiritual journey. After all, had she not awakened after the learned shaykh's initial lecture, though the text never revealed when she actually fell asleep?[37] Then she tells her father about hearing the shaykh's words while she was in a state of semi-dream. (Here, she uses the word *hâlima* [dreamer].) Only after the shaykh has been fully identified is she able to enjoy a deep sleep after her previous period of insomnia.[38]

The female narrator is well aware of the importance of the oneiric in Islam. She herself cites another dream, preceding the one that takes place in Paradise, in which her shaykh is also present.[39] More importantly, Karîmân flaunts her knowledge of the rich Arabo-Islamic dream tradition. During the October War, Shaykh Mahmûd, in a sermon he delivers in al-Azhar, cites a contemporary dream in which the Prophet appeared and performed the crossing of the canal with the dreamer. In a discussion Karîmân has with television announcers over this sermon, one of the high officials in the television industry makes fun of the sermon, claiming that the world will laugh at the Egyptians, since wars are not fought with dreams. Karîmân rushes in, in response to everyone's laughter, and quotes the famous *hadîth* of the Prophet: "He who sees me in a dream truly sees me. For the devil does not impersonate me."[40] This, of course, argues for the veracity of the oneiric experience and for the validity of the historical crossing. This testimony, however, testifies to something else: the young woman's knowledge of the rich Islamic tradition, given not only the popularity of this tradition but its discussion and elaboration in medieval works.[41] And this tradition will reappear in the spiritual narratives by both the Moroccan Leïla Lahlou and the Belgian Sultana Kouhmane.[42]

In Karîmân's trajectory, the dream is a prelude to the pilgrimage to Mecca. This pillar of Islam, which the young woman performs, will permit her to reaffirm her allegiance to the shaykh's family. It is during this religious ritual that she meets her teacher's biological sister, a woman whom she does not initially recognize. It is only when someone comes asking for her that her identity is revealed. The sister's name remains occulted during the entire pilgrimage. Karîmân Hamza mentioned to me how impressed she was by the modesty of the shaykh's sister. The dynamics of female solidarity, as well as the general attitude of the women during this holy season, will be discussed in comparison with Leïla Lahlou, for whom the trip to Mecca is central. Suffice it to say here that there is a drastic difference in the portrayal of this sacred ritual between the two spiritual journeys.[43]

For Karîmân, the journey to Mecca seals her fate as a member of Shaykh ᶜAbd al-Halîm Mahmûd's spiritual family. Yet her full integration into the revival movement will not be accomplished until yet another medieval male mystic enters the text. This time, the male medieval figure is the well-known Sufi al-Hârith ibn Asad al-Muhâsibî (d. 243/837). He will make his guest appearance in the twentieth-century narrative toward the end of the work. Unlike Ibrâhîm, al-Fudayl, and Sahl, al-Hârith is not the subject of oral discourse. His intertextual presentation is through written discourse: a book on him authored by ᶜAbd al-Halîm Mahmûd, which the learned man presents to his female pupil.[44]

Al-Muhâsibî breaks into the Hamzian text after an introduction about the social and political conditions that permit such a character to flourish. The Islamic world, the reader discovers, was undergoing a battle between two forces: on the one hand, the Orthodox at whose head was Ahmad ibn Hanbal, and on the other, the Muᶜtazilites, with representatives in Basra, Kufa, and Baghdad. Shaykh ᶜAbd al-Halîm Mahmûd explains that such a conflict is a natural one, from which no religion has ever escaped: "It is the eternal conflict between the textualists and the intellectualists. It is the everlasting struggle between those who say that religion is a text which can be explained by the revelation, and language, and transmission, and those who say that religion is a text which can be explained and clarified by the intellect."[45] Ahmad ibn Hanbal (d. 241/855) is the famous legist and founder of the Hanbalî school, the most conservative of the four canonical schools of Islam. The Muᶜtazila were "important in the history of Islamic theology . . . for initiating the discussion of Islamic dogmas in terms of Greek philosophical conceptions." The battles between the two groups were ardent ones dealing with, among other things, the createdness of the Qur'ân, with the Muᶜtazilites opting for the created nature of the sacred text.[46]

Enter al-Muhâsibî, the third fighter in this battle in the eyes of ᶜAbd al-Halîm Mahmûd. He took on the Muᶜtazila and was himself attacked by the Orthodox. His weapons? Awe of God and knowledge. His message in Karîmân's text is one of asceticism (*zuhd*), piety, fearfulness of God, and so forth.[47]

Al-Hârith al-Muhâsibî was, according to Arberry, "the first Sufi author of the foremost rank whose preserved writings may truly be said to have formed to a large extent the pattern of all subsequent thought."[48] He did, in fact, have run-ins with Ahmad ibn Hanbal.

But unlike the other three medieval mystics, al-Muhâsibî and his intellectual milieu receive from Shaykh ᶜAbd al-Halîm Mahmûd an interpretation that makes them relevant for contemporary Islamic thought. "These three powers are still in conflict down to our present day, and we believe that they will continue to be." This is due to people's nature: some people are realistic and prefer a text, some are more intellectual, and some are more sensitive and lean to Sufism.[49] Karîmân's response? Long live the three orientations. "May they live in the service of God's religion, in the service of Islam." Yes, she continues, she was truthful when she declared her love for all who serve Islam, even if their paths differ, be they using intellect, or ecstasy, or text. "The difference of their ways is mercy."[50]

How interesting it then becomes to have Karîmân herself labeled "the Mystical [Television] Announcer" (*al-Mudhîᶜa al-Mutasawwifa*)[51] by the *Majallat al-Idhâᶜa wal-Tilifizyûn,* a popular illustrated Egyptian weekly that caters to a mass audience and presents various cultural and media news, extending from the secular to the religious. On the same day, Karîmân goes to the High Council for Islamic Affairs and reports the following conversation:

> "Welcome to the Mystical Announcer . . . We thought you were one of the Muslim Brothers. . . ."
> I said to them:
> "The truth is that I do not say that I am a Sufi nor one of the Muslim Brothers. . . . I am a Muslim. . . . A Muslim and someone who professes the unity of God only."[52]

The dialogue continues with Karîmân arguing that she cannot possibly attribute to herself the honor of being a member of the Muslim Brotherhood, since she has not suffered all they have suffered of torture, imprisonment, and so forth. When her interlocutor then replies, "Then

you are a Sufi like your shaykh," Karîmân's reply is adamant: she is only
a Muslim. She continues, "Sufism is a special grade of worship, piety,
abstention, asceticism, and sincere fearfulness of God. . . . And commitment. . . . And contentment. . . . And I am not like that. . . . I am a be-
ginner, I love Islam. . . . And I love the Muslims only. . . . Do you not understand?"[53] This futile dialogue between the two is not so quickly
resolved. First, the male speaker warns Karîmân to stay away from the
Muslim Brothers, but she defends them. Then he warns her not to become a Sufi like her shaykh and be one of "those of al-Ahwâl wal-
Maqâmât." She replies: "Who are those of al-Ahwâl wal-Maqâmât? I
do not understand what you mean."[54]

The *ahwâl* and *maqâmât* are, of course, code words for the discern-
ing reader that the subject has moved seriously into the area of mysticism. The *ahwâl* (sing. *hâl*) are the mystical states, or more properly, "the
hâl is a spiritual mood depending not upon the mystic but upon God."
The *maqâmât* (sing. *maqâm*) are the stations on the mystical path. "The
maqâm is a stage of spiritual attainment on the pilgrim's progress to God
which is the result of the mystic's personal effort and endeavors. . . . 'The
states,' says al-Qushairî, 'are gifts; the stations are earnings.' "[55]

These are such basic concepts in Sufism that it is difficult to believe
that Karîmân does not comprehend what her interlocutor is saying. The
well-versed reader will have already become aware of Karîmân's knowledge of mysticism in the earlier quote. The language she used to explain
her refusal of the label of the Mystical Announcer is imbued with mystical terminology: for example, *wara^c* (abstention), *zuhd* (asceticism),
khushû^c (fearfulness), *ridâ* (contentment).[56]

Hence, Karîmân's supposed ignorance of the *ahwâl* and *maqâmât* is
but a ruse. The reader knows that she had already had exposure to
Sufism and to various political and cultural dialogues revolving around
it.[57] Not only that, but her interview with this aggressive male is preceded by her immersion in Mahmûd's book on al-Hârith al-Muhâsibî.
More telling is that the section detailing this run-in is entitled "al-
Mudhî^ca al-Mutasawwifa" and is part of the larger chapter on al-
Muhâsibî, or more correctly on Shaykh ^cAbd al-Halîm Mahmûd's book
on al-Muhâsibî. And this book by Mahmûd is a wealth of information
on Sufism, including the famous *ahwâl* and *maqâmât*.[58]

This ruse is, then, extremely significant. It permits Karîmân to draw
out the enemy. And this she does. First, her adversary asks if she has noticed individuals in rags, dirty and smelly, in the mosques. Yes, she admits she has. These she learns are those of *al-ahwâl*, who believe that

they have a great rank with God. They speak to the angels and to the Prophets. Karîmân objects to this qualification. The dialogue becomes more and more violent as she persists in asking questions that relate to Sufism and her interlocutor persists in qualifying mystics as social marginals. When Karîmân points out that her own shaykh does not fit this description, the man is not appeased. His closing argument on the Sufis leaves her without a counterargument: the Islamic world is drowning and both the East and the West are hurrying to swallow it up. This is happening at the same time that the mystics are not thinking about ways to save Islam. Karîmân changes tactics and moves to the Muslim Brothers: why should her interlocutor be so negative on them since their way is one hundred percent positive? The man is nonplused: she is clearly one of them. He continues to rant and rave. And whereas before he had laughed "like a wolf," now he speaks like "a raging bull." [59] These images are significant. The man has been turned into an animal, no longer in control of his emotions. Karîmân will leave the premises, but not before she has called for the vengeance of God on this man, whom she perceives to be "an enemy to himself . . . to others and to Islam." [60]

It is not accidental that as the argument progresses, the male speaker delves into dialect rather than maintaining his speech in the more literary language, the fushâ. This distinction between the dialect and the literary is not insignificant in Karîmân's narrative. The secularized women in the club, it will be remembered, addressed her in dialect.[61] And the role they were playing in attempting to keep the young woman away from her chosen religious path is by now well known. Dialect becomes a level of the language associated with antagonism to Karîmân's spiritual mission and an interrogation of her by forces hostile to her sacred travails.

What a timely debate! Its locus is perhaps as significant as its subjects. The High Council for Islamic Affairs is an organ of the Egyptian government. Of course, nowhere does the text state that "the man" is expressing the government's views, but his enemies are, oddly enough, the Muslim Brothers, on the one hand, and the Sufis, on the other. The bloody history of the Muslim Brothers with the Egyptian government goes back many years and needs no commentary. The relationship of the government with the Sufis has been less conflictual, but it is certainly not one of love and admiration.[62]

Karîmân tries to keep herself above the fray; however, she cannot combat the man's argument about the political ineffectiveness of the Sufis in defending Islam. What the dialogue makes clear is that Karîmân's perspective on Sufism is not identical to that of her coconversationist. His view, ironically enough, comes closer to the lives of the ascetics whom Karîmân called up in her text. When the man informs her that these people in rags stink, certain stories come to mind, stories that have attached themselves to some of the medieval mystics, who "cared neither for their outward appearance nor their attire, and although they strictly observed the ritual purity required for prayer, Ibn Adham was proud of the huge number of lice living in his coat, and as late as 900, a maidservant of a Sufi from Baghdad exclaimed: 'O God, how dirty are Thy friends—not a single one among them is clean!'"[63] Ibrâhîm ibn Adham was once asked if he had ever been happy in this world, to which he answered, "Yes, twice," one of those times being when he was sitting one day and someone came along and urinated on him.[64] This anecdote is meant to explain the mystic's high character, but it can be read corporally as well, testifying in that case to a total insouciance toward the physical entity that is the body.

This dialogue also points to another difference between the contemporary Mystical Announcer and her medieval male predecessors. The male ascetics were moving away from the ease of the world, something Karîmân has not done. Her trajectory has been, in a sense, the opposite. She has moved into the world rather than away from it, having picked up a public and visible persona. The Karîmân on the first pages of *My Journey from Unveiling to Veiling* was a university student like many others. The Karîmân who ends the narrative has been singularized and thrust into the public domain.

The debate between the female hero and her male opponent became itself an extended subject of discussion between Karîmân and me. Karîmân Hamza, the historical individual, it turns out, paid a price for her eloquence in this lively interchange in the High Council for Islamic Affairs. She was anxious to tell me that the official with whom she was at odds was quite highly placed and created problems for her later in her career. Despite my insistence, she refused to go into detail and would not name the person.[65]

For me, this incident was extremely crucial, since it raised questions that went beyond the spiritual saga. I was interested in knowing precisely where Karîmân Hamza stood in relation to Sufism. She explained to me that though she is not a Sufi, she loves Sufi gatherings, which she attends continually, no matter what the *tarîqa* (order). On that particular day when she and I discussed the question, Hamza was wearing a dress trimmed in fur. She asked me how she could possibly be a Sufi, since Sufism is asceticism (*zuhd*) and there she was wearing fur?[66]

Since the male interlocutor also raised the question of her allegiance to the Muslim Brothers, I asked Karîmân Hamza about this as well. Hamza did not shy away from her affection for the Muslim Brothers. But she insisted, as she does in her autobiographical journey, that she had not suffered as they had and expressed to me her opinion that the group had been badly mistreated by the Egyptian government.[67]

If Karîmân is the Mystical Announcer, she has accomplished this through the guidance of medieval male mystics. An announcer, by definition, is someone operating in the public sphere. And interestingly enough, this translates into the fact that Karîmân is still the object of the gaze. In the preconversion incident, Karîmân was the object of the male gaze and tried to hide from it. Now the Mystical Announcer is an even greater object of the gaze, this time that of television viewers. Yet being in this position is what permits Karîmân Hamza to earn another appellation, that of missionary—female—(dâ‘iya) for Islam. This honorific was bestowed upon her by Khamîs in his introduction to *My Journey*.[68] This label is powerful, indeed. It confers a responsibility on Karîmân and allows her to share in a different way in the larger mission of the Islamic community. Such an appellation is normally reserved for someone of the stature of the older prominent woman activist Zaynab al-Ghazâlî.[69]

The dialogue with the aggressive male speaker must be juxtaposed with the initial scene in which Karîmân received the call. Both incidents are set in an official Islamic environment: the first in the Institute of Islamic Studies and the second in the High Council for Islamic Affairs. In the first, Karîmân enters in a state of deficiency, even her dog playing a role. This animal companion will return momentarily.

The juxtaposition of the two scenes also highlights Shaykh ‘Abd al-Halîm Mahmûd's role. In the first, he enters the narrative as the voice that beckons the young woman to the religious path. In the second, he is there as a textual authority validating his female disciple's religious transformation. It is she who must now carry forth the message. The heated dialogue she has with the interlocutor in the offices of the high council is embedded within selections from Shaykh Mahmûd's work on al-Hârith al-Muhâsibî. This will be, in fact, Mahmûd's last appearance in Karîmân Hamza's book. His disappearance will signal first a textual death, as Karîmân calls forth various other religious authorities to testify to her shaykh's good actions. And this textual death will be followed by his physical death. He has, in a sense, performed his function in Karîmân's saga. He has helped to rectify the deficiency with which she began her trajectory. She is now a full member of the religious community.

Is the reader to conclude from all this that the mystic intertext played no role in Karîmân's saga? On the contrary. It is perfectly possible to read *Rihlatî* as a modern Sufi parable. The *zâhirî*, or external, message is that of a young woman adapting herself to an Islamic community. The internal, essential *bâtinî* reading would be that of a soul finding the path. Similarly, one could see the vestimentary transformations as *maqâmât* and the spiritual fruits of these changes as *ahwâl*.

But, to return to the clear signs in Hamza's *Rihlatî*, the intertext of the medieval male mystics not only redefines the young woman's religious experience but places it squarely in a male religious tradition. And in this mystical tradition, the dog plays an important role. The dog is not only a sign of the westernization of the young woman.[70] In the mystical discourse that imbues Hamza's narrative, the dog is not merely a random animal but is associated with the baseness of the world from which a mystic must flee, and symbolizes at times man's lower nature.[71] That this dog should be present for the initial call and disappear without a trace by the end of the narrative is not accidental.

Karîmân Hamza the historical individual recognizes the significance of the dog in Islam in general. In her guide, *Rifqan bil-Qawârîr*, she devotes a chapter to this animal, citing Prophetic *hadîth*s on dogs (for example, that angels do not enter a house in which is a dog) as well as some contemporary anecdotes and general advice for the potential contemporary dog owner.[72] Her objections to having canines inside a home are primarily cleanliness- and health-related: dogs urinate all over the house and carry germs. In a very telling conversation that she presents in the guide and that she has with the prominent journalist and author Ahmad Bahjat, he angrily chastises "their" attitude to dogs, and this despite the animals' faithfulness. "Do you not know that a man entered Paradise because of a dog?" he asks her, summarizing the popular *hadîth* about a man in the desert who gave a thirsty dog water from a well. This action, which involved the man's descending into a well and carrying the water in his shoe, assured him an entry into Paradise.[73] Karîmân Hamza's response to Ahmad Bahjat is addressed to "them." She acknowledges the existence of this popular *hadîth*, but for her, the Prophet's attitude to dogs was that they should be kept out of the house. This *hadîth*, in fact, transcends both speakers here and is quite popular in contemporary Islamic materials, including children's literature.[74]

The dynamics of this conversation between Ahmad Bahjat and Karî-mân Hamza are fascinating, indeed. Both parties use the plural in their respective words, and this despite the fact that Hamza began the interchange by stating that "the great journalist Ahmad Bahjat said [masculine singular] to me . . ."[75] The subsequent grammatical usage of the plural is clearly an indication that the dialogue is addressed to a much broader audience, one beyond the confines of an interchange between two people, a prominent male journalist and writer and an equally prominent female television personality and writer. In her footnote introducing Bahjat to her readers, Hamza is careful to add that he loves cats and dogs and "raises them in his apartment and takes care of them himself."[76]

This is all obviously a far cry from that primal scene in *My Journey from Unveiling to Veiling* in which Karîmân ventured forth into Shaykh ᶜAbd al-Halîm Mahmûd's lecture with her canine companion in her arms. In one of my numerous conversations with Karîmân Hamza, I asked her about the dog. She laughed and said, "The dog? I gave him away as a gift." She then added that the dog loved her so much that every time he saw her he would run to her and "do his toilet" around the house. So she gave him away.[77] Hamza's personal experience with the pet concords with her warnings about canine behavior and soiling in *Rifqân bil-Qawârîr*.

Karîmân Hamza's explanations to Ahmad Bahjat notwithstanding, the journalist's anger may not be so misplaced. One need not look very far to find hostility to animal companions in the Islamic revivalist vision of the world. In Turkey, for example, in 1995, I had the occasion to spend some time with a Turkish friend who owns a little dog. This friend happens to live in an apartment building in one of the bourgeois suburbs of Istanbul (which had an Islamist municipal governor). She was constantly attempting to keep her dog from barking—his barking would signal his presence to more conservative neighbors. The consequences of this would be drastic: the neighbors would alert the appropriate religious authorities and the dog would be taken away and most likely killed.

Hamza's argument that the Prophet Muhammad did not order the destruction of dogs is countered by her own citation of another *hadîth*, in which the Prophet states that if dogs were a community/nation, he would order its killing.[78] In her intertextual exploitation of this *hadîth*, however, Karîmân Hamza omits a part of this *hadîth*, in which the Prophet enjoins the killing of the jet black ones ("kill among them every jet black one"). Al-Tirmidhî, who relates this saying in his collection, adds material that makes it clear that the dog indicated here is the one with no white coloring whatsoever and that "the jet black dog is a devil."[79] Investigating canine politics in Arabo-Islamic culture, while an extremely interesting topic (no book like Marjorie Garber's *Dog Love* exists), would unfortunately pull the critic away from Karîmân's spiritual journey.[80] Suffice it to say that the giving away of the pet is certainly a more compassionate action on Hamza's part.

The verbal war between Hamza and Bahjat in the guide is but a manifestation of the tendency already observed in the spiritual journey: a tendency for Karîmân to engage her adversaries in various dialogues in which she demonstrates her intellectual and textual prowess. Nevertheless, the verbal and textual eloquence of the males in this female's text cannot eliminate one of the most important silences and absences in Karîmân Hamza's *My Journey from Unveiling to Veiling*: the medieval female mystical and ascetic experience. One of the most famous early ascetics, and one of the most famous of all Sufis, was a woman: Râbi͑a al-͑Adawiyya (d. 185/801).[81] Yet, she has no role to play in this contemporary account. In his introduction to *Rihlatî min al-Sufûr ilâ al-Hijâb*, Muhammad ͑Atiyya Khamîs singles out the importance of the gender issue in Karîmân Hamza's journey. He correctly notes the presence of notable women in the medieval period, beginning with the Prophet's wives.[82] Missing from his enumeration is the great mystic, Râbi͑a. This is all the more striking since Khamîs authored a popular biography of Râbi͑a, which much like Karîmân Hamza's book is available on streets and in bazaars in the Middle East and North Africa.[83] There have, of course, been many other Sufi women of note, but none is alluded to.[84]

Clearly, more is at stake here than mere literary categorization. What emerges is the complexity of *Rihlatî min al-Sufûr ilâ al-Hijâb,* a text whose internal dynamics bring together gender and religious and political issues. The textual validation by the male mystics is but an internal reflection of the external sandwiching of Karîmân Hamza's text between the introduction by Muhammad ͑Atiyya Khamîs and the epilogue by Shaykh Muhammad al-Ghazâlî. Much as her book is embedded between two male textual voices, so her spiritual trajectory is validated by men.

CHAPTER FOUR

Breast Cancer, Medicine, and the Transnational Body

If Karîmân Hamza's spiritual journey saved her from a potential physical death, how much more dramatic a story is that of the Moroccan Leïla Lahlou, afflicted with a very serious disease, breast cancer. Lahlou's saga is quite memorable, detailing the case of a body ravaged by cancer and submitted to medical treatment. Ultimately, however, it is religion that will bring the cure. The intersection of this afflicted body with religion and the divine will be explored in chapter 5. The nexus of the female body and medicine is equally crucial, as the corporal intertwines in fascinating ways with the medical and the geographical. Various geographies manifest themselves as the mutating cancerous body traverses the globe.

Like her sisters in the Islamic revival movement who undergo dramatic spiritual experiences, Leïla Lahlou relates her journey in the first person.[1] *Do Not Forget God* (Falâ Tansa Allâh) is the title of her book.[2] More correctly, the title should be translated as *So Do Not Forget God,* but it will be rendered here as *Do Not Forget God.* Originally written in Arabic, the work has appeared in multiple editions and was translated into French as *N'oublie pas Dieu.*[3] This French translation is unfortunately littered with errors (mistranslations, omissions of important materials like the religious intertext, etc.). Nevertheless, it will be used below at a specific stage in the analysis.

The injunction not to forget the Deity is in the masculine singular. True, strictly speaking, grammatically the use of the male gender could include the female. But why stretch the linguistic limits when one is speaking, of all things, about breast cancer, an essentially female affliction?[4] The significance of this grammatical choice will become evident as the analytical journey continues.

This title also stands out not so much because of what it includes (i.e., the male gender) as because of what it excludes. In the context of other works written by women and emanating from the Islamic revival movement, *Do Not Forget God* also singles itself out because of its absence of the personal. There is no reference here to "my journey," as in the work of Karîmân Hamza or in the work briefly discussed, *Rihlatî min al-Zalamât ilâ al-Nûr* (My Journey from Darkness to Light) by Shams al-Bârûdî.[5] *Do Not Forget God* is also far from *L'Islam, la femme, et l'intégrisme: Journal d'une jeune femme européenne* (Islam, Woman, and Integrism: Journal of a Young European Woman), the spiritual saga of Sultana Kouhmane, the Moroccan-Belgian Islamic activist who will figure prominently below.[6] It is precisely its nature as an injunction that permits Lahlou's title to transcend the personal and address itself to both the male and female genders.

But the story Leïla tells about her breast cancer is quite gender specific.[7] Leïla's narrative eschews absolute chronology: the sequence of events is there but not their dates.

Leïla discovers her breast cancer herself as she is taking a bath. A visit to her Moroccan physician is followed by more medical tests in Belgium: she is diagnosed with cancer. The chemotherapy treatment is administered in Morocco, but due to illness Leïla is obliged to return to Belgium for more medical attention. Belgium is then followed by a diagnostic trip to France. All the physical examinations confirm the identical result: a serious cancer which has already metastasized. In Paris, before undertaking further treatment, Leïla and her husband decide to perform the *ᶜumra*, the little pilgrimage to Mecca.

On the *ᶜumra*, Leïla maintains an ascetic regimen consisting of an egg, bread, and water from the sacred well of Zamzam, a regimen that leads to the disappearance of the lumps in her body.[8] Medical tests in France after the *ᶜumra* confirm this finding. Nevertheless, the French physician recommends treatment to eliminate any vestige of the cancer in her lungs. Leïla returns home, where she becomes ill. Then follows a series of treatments in both Europe and Morocco. Her return to Morocco only means time spent between the hospital and her home. The month of Ramadân finds her in a worsened state in which she is losing consciousness, and the physician decides to send her home to her family. Her family members are worried that Leïla's end is near and have very little hope of her coming out of her coma. She, however, felt that she was not in a coma, but rather in an extended sleep. It is during this state that the Prophet Muhammad appears to Leïla in a dream and wipes his hand on her head, effecting a cure. Leïla awakens, walks energetically, and recounts the incident to her family, whose members are very pleased. She spends much of the night in prayer, and this happy event signals at once the end of Leïla's first-person narrative as well as her cure "from this dangerous illness." [9]

In her introduction, Leïla Lahlou alerts her reader to the fact that hers is a factual story. But this is not only a true story—it is a highly dramatic one as well. It is not just the corporal cure from a dreaded breast cancer that the reader witnesses. Throughout the drama, the female body plays a most important role. This should not perhaps come as a surprise, since, after all, breast cancer is first and foremost a condition of the female body.

This cancerous female body which is Leïla's plays, however, on more than just the narrative stage that is the spiritual journey detailed in *Do Not Forget God.* What can be called breast-cancer narratives—that is, texts recounting a woman's experience with breast cancer— are proliferating, much as the illness seems to be. Be it in English or other western languages, women rush to narrate their experience with the disease. The task here is not bibliographical. As Barbara Seaman puts it: "Breast-cancer books written by patients are not entirely new." [10] Simply, by calling attention to the generic types of works that discuss breast cancer, it becomes easier to see the contribution of the Moroccan Leïla Lahlou.

Discussions by women of breast cancer can be on the level of cultural discourse analysis or on the level of personal testimony. Susan Sontag's groundbreaking work, *Illness as Metaphor,* is one of the best-known studies of the cultural languages of cancer. Emanating from a personal experience (the author was diagnosed with breast cancer), Sontag's work goes beyond the personal to comment on societal attitudes to disease.[11] The personal narratives of women suffering from this killer condition abound, and they can range from autobiography, such as Joyce Wadler's *My Breast,* to play, such as Elisabeth Gille's *Le crabe sur la banquette arrière.*[12] These examples, which can be multiplied, demonstrate clearly that a woman's detailing her experience with breast cancer is not a peculiar phenomenon. On this world literary stage, Leïla Lahlou becomes one of many female players.

If one moves, however, from the world stage to the Islamic stage, be it in North Africa or the Middle East, then the story is different, Leïla's role becomes more unusual. Other women have written of cancer. ᶜAbla al-Ruwaynî's eloquent work on her late husband, the poet Amal Dunqul, who was afflicted with this disease, would be one such example.[13] Then there is a short story by the Egyptian feminist physician-writer, Nawal El Saadawi, in which the central character is diagnosed with breast cancer.[14] Other narrative differences aside, this fictional creation, by its nature as a short story, cannot be seen in the same way as Lahlou's extended narrative.

One Arab woman has written of her breast-cancer experience: Evelyne Accad. A Lebanese-American, Accad was diagnosed with breast cancer in 1994. She published excerpts from her cancer diary in *Al-Raida,* the Lebanese journal of the Institute for Women's Studies in the Arab World. Professor Accad's cancer entries, detailing as they do her diagnosis and her treatment, are quite revealing. Following a surgical procedure, she writes: "From now on, I belonged to all my sisters who have been mutilated, subjected to a mastectomy, hysterectomy, clitoridectomy, i.e., all the ectomies." [15] Despite the explicit link to clitoridectomy, Accad writes from an extra–Middle Eastern locus: her diagnosis is in the West, as is her treatment.

This western perspective means that Lahlou's text is still part of a minority opinion. Something else sets Leïla Lahlou apart in the Middle Eastern and North African context, however: her frank discussions of the female body. To bare this body before the reader is, to say the least, striking.[16] The female body is an obsession in certain contemporary revivalist discourses, but it is the female body as an object that must be occulted rather than the female body as an object to be examined and analyzed, as it is in Lahlou's autobiographical narrative.[17] When one adds to this the fact that Islam is part and parcel of Leïla's text, the fact that she exposes her female body when this body should literally be covered is significant.

Even more extraordinary is the trajectory that this body takes on its journey from a medical diagnosis of breast cancer to a spiritual "cure" from this dreaded disease. The female body crosses geographical borders as it crosses medical frontiers, becoming along the way a participant in a transnational discourse of the female body. From Casablanca to Brussels, from Paris to Mecca, the reader follows the female hero on her various trajectories.

The centrality of the geographical component appears in the opening sentences of this spiritual journey. The first words Leïla utters as a narrator are: "From the plane . . ." She is on the plane, returning from her journey to Mecca.[18] This beginning underlines the significance of geography and displacement. In addition, this is an event that takes place later than its actual narrative location, given that the reader does not yet know from the journey itself (though that is clear from the introduction) that the narrator: (*a*) has breast cancer; (*b*) will pursue medical treatment; and (*c*) will have a corporal intervention in Mecca. To use Gérard Genette's terminology, this constitutes a prolepsis, a chronological intrusion in the narrative in which an event occurs chronologically after its actual placement in the narrative. While the present task is not the examination of these intrusions in the narrative, one needs nevertheless to keep in mind the nature of this event and its importance as a marker. It sets the entire breast-cancer journey under the sign of religion and the holy. And since the narrator makes a point of bragging about her health on this return journey from Mecca, it means that the reader is alerted from the beginning of the work that the narrator will win her corporal battle with cancer.

If, however, the journey from Mecca is viewed not so much as a prolepsis in the cancer narrative but as the true beginning of the narrative of spiritual salvation, then the entire following story becomes an analepsis, an event that takes place before its actual location in the narrative. In fact, any autobiographical project constitutes an anachrony of sorts, since the events narrated have all taken place before the process of narration has even occurred. In Leïla's case, this process is heightened by the opening setting of the narrative, in which the chronology of salvation is the opening marker.

Leïla's body is, hence, from the beginning, a body in movement. Perhaps one of the most important loci for an analysis of this body in movement is the medical environment, an environment that shifts continuously between two continents, Europe and Africa. It has been decades since Michel Foucault made it clear that the clinic and medicine are their own purveyors of discourse.[19] Of course, Foucault is far from alone now. Western cultural critics have delved into the fruitful areas of medicine and literature and, recently, Kathryn Montgomery Hunter has eloquently demonstrated the textual strategies inherent in medical texts, from the fictional to the case history.[20] And this is not to speak of Elaine Scarry's groundbreaking work.[21]

The nexus of medicine and the body, as cultural constructs, has, unfortunately, only barely begun to attract the attention of critics in the area of Middle Eastern studies. And this despite the fact that the physician-writer looms quite large on the literary scene. Names likes those of the male Yûsuf Idrîs and the female Nawal El Saadawi should already be familiar.[22] Both are exceptionally conscious of the body and capitalize on their medical knowledge in much of their fiction.[23]

Of course, fictional creations exploiting medicine and corporality are one thing, autobiographical journeys involving a diseased body, another. Medicine in Leïla's journey is a powerful tool that vies with religion in its efficacy. In her narrative, however, it is not simply medicine that plays an important role. The appended medical documents themselves create their own alternate narrative, providing a parallel reading of the spiritual saga. Perhaps, for a western audience, it needs to be said that these Moroccan physicians in Lahlou's text are working in the identical western-origin scientific medical tradition as their western counterparts. There is no discordance or break between the two groups.

To start at the beginning may seem like an obvious step. In this case, however, it is more than that. Leïla's initial visit to her physician in Casablanca immediately after her own discovery of the abnormality in her breast proves to be a crucial event. With one voice, the members of Leïla's family urge her to go to Dr. Yacoubi's clinic.

> "The doctor . . . Your doctor . . . The specialist in women . . . Are you going to go to him?" I did not answer . . . And it was as though the questions had been posed to an individual other than me . . . I threw myself on them and hugged them warmly as though I were asking for help even from the doctor . . . Yes . . . The doctor . . . The examination! The questions! Pressing on my breast . . .[24]

Leïla imagines a conversation with the physician in which she beseeches him not to inform her family of her condition and asks him if her breasts will be cut off, "like the breasts of so-and-so were cut off?" She continues: "No. By God I will not go and will never go. Leave me alone. I want to sleep." Despite her hesitation, Leïla goes to the physician. Dr. Yacoubi, the gynecologist, appears in the text as jovial and friendly. Nevertheless, Leïla is speechless once she enters his office and wishes that her husband would broach another topic with the medical specialist. This inability to speak stands in opposition to the imaginary conversation between Leïla and her physician. There, the female patient could give voice to her fear about her potential physical mutilation. Of course, this imaginary dialogue remains precisely that: imaginary, with the voice of the physician occulted.

This does not mean that Yacoubi is absent in the text. Far from it. The gynecologist is the one who examines Leïla's body. He presses on her breasts and she, sweating and quite uncomfortable, merely moves her body in various ways to facilitate the physician's task. Hers is the diseased passive body, subjected to the physician's procedure and gaze. Is it a wonder that she was "no longer anything but a doll in the hands of the physician"?[25]

When Leïla actually speaks in the physician's office it is after the examination. It is then to confront the medical specialist and ask about the size of the lump and insist that the object in her breast is small. "Then what I have is not cancer," she ascertains. Yacoubi's response argues for logic: after all, he cannot declare anything before verifying the diagnosis, something that necessitates examinations. He does, however, confirm the presence of calcification in the breast.

Leïla's corporal entity has begun to transform itself. Her body may be that of a doll, only insofar as it seems to have lost any will of its own; however, if a doll is understood as the representation of an idealized body, and more importantly of a static and unchanging body, then Leïla's corporal entity is far from that. The visit to Dr. Yacoubi and the following medical examinations reveal that she is indeed afflicted with a serious condition. This new corporal reality will begin to dictate a geography of its own, as the Moroccan physician explains the European options open to Leïla on her search for medical treatment. The choices are two: Villejuif in France or Brussels. Because of her fearful negative associations with Villejuif and cancer, Leïla chooses Brussels. It would be a mistake to read in this choice a negative reaction to the name of the town, Villejuif. Among the physicians consulted by the patient was a Dr. Israël, about whom Leïla has only positive things to say, not to mention Dr. Lévy-Lebar of Casablanca.[26] Not only is her text free of any sectarianism, but all the physicians, whether of Jewish, Christian, or Muslim background, are treated in totally nonreligious terms. They are pure representatives of science.

The visit to Dr. Yacoubi's clinic in Casablanca is the focal point of Leïla's pre-European medical experience in the text. But this visit that ultimately determines the ill state of Leïla's body will also signal the physical migration of this body, as the female patient pursues treatment in

Europe. Her trajectory begins in Casablanca. She is sent by her physician to Brugmann Hospital in Brussels.[27] Unlike Yacoubi's clinic in Casablanca, this locus in Europe receives a detailed description. It was "all roses/flowers, and water, and trees. As though with the beauty of nature those in charge wanted to lighten the pain of the patient or make him forget that he [masculine singular in the Arabic] was in a clinic. . . . Especially if he is told that he has a dangerous illness . . . cancer?!"[28] Brugmann Hospital is a large hospital with signs directing individuals to where they should go. And should someone lose the way, there are women who will guide him [masculine singular]: "if you find yourself in a wing other than the one to which you should be going, there are women who point out the right way to you." The narrator notes that the radiology specialists try as hard as possible to make the patient [male singular] feel better and more confident so that "those large instruments and frozen rooms do not frighten him."[29]

Leïla continues. "What I also liked were the women who are entrusted to help the female patient take off her clothes . . . and uncover the afflicted side of her body so that the female patient feels a bit better about that. . . ."

> In the waiting room I found women speaking or, more correctly, telling stories and debating their problems . . . and they would speak about cancer as something normal, which surprised me. . . . Among them would be one who complained about a pain she had once in a while in her lower abdomen, and another who wondered why her chest swelled . . . and I almost screamed in her face that I also complain of a swelling in my breast . . . and all wait patiently to be called on. . . . And while I was in my frightening dreams a woman asked me which country I was from. . . . no doubt it is my accent that caught her attention, making her ask about my country. She smiled upon hearing "Morocco" because she had visited Marrakech and Fez and, oh, how much she liked them . . . and how much she wished to return to Morocco to stay a longer time there . . . and after a long and extensive discussion of my illness, she made me frightened and calm at the same time . . . and I knew that she had had an operation six months ago. . . . her physicians in America had agreed to take out her breasts . . . so she left them and came to Belgium where her family was, to perhaps find a second solution, i.e., cobalt treatment or chemotheraphy. . . . Two nouns that will undoubtedly enter the dictionary of my new life. . . . then she moved to France and she did not finish her conversation when I was called. I rushed, following the nurse, fulfilling all the requests like a polite child undergoing a difficult examination. I took off my clothes in a cold room. . . . I stayed in this state for five minutes and my body was shaking from the cold. But it was a necessary and natural matter, which had to be gone through before beginning the medical examinations. During the entire examination time, the nurse was asking me about the weather, and

my occupation, and my country. She also was impressed by my home country of Morocco [literally: my Morocco] and loved it a lot . . .[30]

This is a highly complex incident with multiple discursive layers, in which the geographical mixes with the corporal. The female body stands at the center of much of the discourse, and specifically the baring of this female body, its uncovering.

Take the geographical layer first. Geography here is, on the most obvious level, that of the world. But this incident makes it clear that even this world geography is not so simple. There are a geography of tourism and a geography of medicine. Tourism involves Morocco. In the medical setting, Leïla hears admiring comments from both a female patient and a nurse about "my Morocco." The patient had visited Marrakech and Fez, liked them a great deal, and wished to return there to spend a longer time. As for the nurse, she also engages Leïla in a conversation about her home country.

The geography of medicine is the all-encompassing geography that subsumes the geography of tourism within it. After all, it is in the medical establishment that Leïla hears tourist praise of her country. The discourse of the clinic is not identical in Europe and Morocco. In Europe, Leïla becomes the exotic other. And this even in the medical environment in which she is surrounded by women who, like herself, are afflicted with cancer.

This complicated geography of medicine involves an elaborate set of physical displacements in which the diseased female body is shuttled from one continent to another in search of medical treatment. The narrator hails from North Africa and finds herself at the time of this incident in Europe. Her corporal trajectory takes place between Africa, Asia, and Europe. The difference is that the tourist geography is one generated from Europe, whereas the other geographies (both medical and sacred) come from within the Moroccan cultural sphere.

Leïla is not, however, the only character involved in this medical geography. One of the female patients in the Brussels clinic explains that she hails from America and has been crossing geographical borders in search of a solution to her physical dilemma: breast cancer. She had had an operation six months earlier and had left the physicians in America who wished to remove her breasts in order to come to Belgium for a second opinion. Then this patient moved to France. This breast-cancer victim textually disappears as Leïla is called, and the reader never discovers what France will hold for her. As Leïla's own narrative develops across geographical and national borders, she finds herself eventually in France, much as her copatient did in this incident.

This larger medical geography of countries and national borders in which the female body travels and that subsumed within it a geography of tourism is offset in this incident by another sort of geography, that of the European clinic. When Brugmann Hospital makes an entrance in Leïla's life, it is immediately introduced as "a hospital which is all roses/flowers, and water, and trees." This is an interesting description indeed. It draws away from the institutional aspect of the building as an architectural entity designed for medical purposes and turns it almost into a natural park. Notice the inclusive quality of the "all," which initially leaves no space for other physical characteristics. The "nature" aspect of this is not foreign to Leïla. It is she, after all, who declares that through this environment of "nature," those in charge in the medical institution wished to lighten the burden of pain from those afflicted with serious illnesses, like cancer.

This idealized description of the nature-filled hospital is soon abandoned in favor of an intricate physical geography of the hospital. Like the female body that must be uncovered, so the reality that is the physical hospital is also uncovered, one level at a time. The reader discovers that the entity that begins as "all roses/flowers, and water, and trees," Brugmann Hospital is, in fact, a large complex with elaborate signs directing people to where they should go. Someone lost is given guidance by women who are there for that purpose.

These women guides help individuals navigate the labyrinth of the medical institution. But the textual appearance of these female guides is not without importance. They do more in Leïla's journey than just point out the right hospital hallways. They signal a female presence that will be significant for Leïla as she enters the world of the European hospital. And this female presence is intimately tied to the corporal component in the text. The women guides function as the links between geography and corporality.

In much the same way that women help lost individuals find their way, so it is that women help other women bare their bodies and locate the afflicted area. This baring of the female entity is not simply one involving the divesting of clothing. When Leïla enters the world of the European hospital in Brussels, she becomes part of a corporal female community defined by physical illness.

In fact, the uncovering of the female body takes place on two levels. On the one hand, there is the verbal undressing, what one could call the telling event, and on the other hand, there is the physical undressing, what one could call the examination event. Both events, the telling and the examination, occur in a medical setting, the clinic, and are heralded by the women guides. The telling event is embedded in the examination event, in that it is while awaiting the examination that the women tell their stories and debate their problems.

What these women create in the European clinic is a female group linked by a common corporal problem. This bonding represents a homosociality that permits the women to discuss the body and its afflictions.[31] The clinic, a closed space in which individuals come together out of a unifying principle, here cancer and female maladies, is an ideal environment for the creation of homosociality. In this homosocial environment, the female diseased body becomes an object that can be discussed and in the process transformed into a public entity. Another form of female homosociality, one based on religion, will be significant below.[32]

The women form a community sharing their illnesses. Leïla "almost" participates in this event of women speaking their bodies when she nearly screams out about the swelling in her chest. But she does not. She remains textually, for the purposes of this event, an observer and not an active participant. She confesses that it is her accent that alerts one of the female patients to ask her about her country. The reader remains in the dark about what she might have said. Her precise role in any dialogue is a mystery and her actual words are hidden in the narrative.

There is an inherent tension between the homosociality of this incident in which the women share both their stories and their bodies and the fact that Leïla appears to stand alone. She does not relate her own experience to the other women and, even more important, she appears to undress alone. And all this despite the presence of women whose aid in this area is praised. The situation in this instance is not entirely dissimilar to that in Dr. Yacoubi's clinic in Casablanca. There, Leïla was unable to utter a word. She was like a doll. The experience in the hospital in Brussels turns her into a "polite child undergoing a difficult examination." The Arabic word here refers to an educational examination, not a medical one.

In the company of women, though, there is progress. From a doll, Leïla becomes a young child. She moves from inanimate object to human being, albeit a still immature one. Is it a wonder then that she speaks of a new life and of learning a new vocabulary, much as a child might? In her case, however, it is the language of medical treatment: cobalt and chemotherapy, "two nouns that will undoubtedly enter the dictionary of my new life."[33] This is a language taught her by other women in the homosocial environment of the diseased female body.

The female homosociality inherent in this incident stands in contrast to the experience in Casablanca. There, the initial consultation with Dr. Yacoubi is followed by a visit to a laboratory. The narrator undergoes a mammography, coldly described as "a big instrument with which they press on the breast from every side." Leïla initially stands alone, without the companionship of other women suffering the same fate. This homosociality in the European hospital will become important later, when viewed against the female homosociality in Mecca. There, religion will bring Leïla close to her Muslim sisters who are party to her cure as they examine her body for any signs of abnormalities.[34]

Notwithstanding her eloquent aside about having to learn a new language, the narrator had already demonstrated to the astute reader a conceptual sophistication when discussing her physical condition. As she ponders, in the beginning of the journey, whether or not to tell her daughter that she is afflicted with cancer, she notes the difficulty of expressing the existence of this disease, which is referred to by all sorts of names except that of "cancer, its true name." These linguistic subterfuges and euphemisms include "a deadly illness, a dangerous epidemic," and similar terms. Leïla's own metaphors are imbued with the language of incarceration and punishment. The elegant clinic of the physician becomes a dark prison, and the narrator feels that her fate is capital punishment: "my name was registered in another world. . . . the world of cancer is the world of the death sentence."[35] As Leïla moves geographically from North Africa, she describes this as moving "the battle abroad."[36] Of course, this terminology and the concomitant images would certainly not be alien to someone like Susan Sontag.[37] They simply confirm that the discourse of cancer has a quasi-universal substratum that permits its migration and its existence in a transnational language of the diseased body.

As Leïla moves from medical environment to medical environment, in the process crossing continents and national borders, her medical dossier moves with her. This file makes its first entrance in the text in Leïla's initial visit to a medical setting, that of Dr. Yacoubi's clinic in Casablanca. The narrator notes that it is the custom of the Moroccan gynecologist to "ask about the state of his female patient while he reads her dossier and writes in it the date of her last visit."[38] On his request, following her mammography, the folder is quickly returned to him on the same day.

This first appearance of Leïla's medical dossier is far from being devoid of interest. The record surfaces in the text at the same time as Leïla's predicament and will maintain its existence alongside her cancer. The creation of the medical record is a process in which the patient and the physician partake. The gynecologist inquires about his patient's condition as he reads and writes in the dossier. The words of the patient are transmuted into a written record that will form part of a dossier, intimately linked to the medical professional who manipulates it and controls it. After all, the gynecologist dictates to the laboratory the speed with which the results of the patient's examination are to be returned, and the medical laboratory complies with the physician's wishes.

This medical dossier will continue to resurface and will transform itself as the female body changes. Leïla's initial visit to "Fu" in Belgium will signal the dossier once again.[39] Like his Moroccan colleague, Fu also examines the female patient and reads her dossier. "And how small and thin it was at the beginning. . . . And he opened a new folder with my address in my home country and my life from my earliest youth to this very day, with all its happenings."[40] With this official birth of a new medical file in Europe, Leïla's medical record takes on a life of its own. This dossier is now able to grow and get bigger.[41] Not only that, but it seems to have an uncanny ability to cross national boundaries, much as its subject does. Leïla returns to North Africa after her medical bout in Belgium: "I returned anew to my energy and vitality . . . and my life became the life of any normal woman. . . .

"My dossier arrived at Mr. Yacoubi's and in it was the treatment plan! . . . And the treatment began in 'Anfa' Hospital."[42] Just as she arrives (*wasalnâ*) in Casablanca airport with her husband, her dossier arrives (*wasala*) at Yacoubi's, one assumes from Europe as well.

Perhaps the most dramatic moment for this medical record occurs after the first religious intervention in Mecca. As is to be expected, the medical record makes no appearance during Leïla's journey and subsequent visit to the holy places of Islam. The reader knows that it is in Mecca that the physical symptoms of her illness disappear. She is very anxious to visit the various medical specialists who had predicted no cure whatsoever for her. She leaves them complete freedom to repeat their examinations anew, including a biopsy. "They were detailed, difficult, long, and repeated examinations." The physicians are nervous. They begin to ask her, "Are you really so and so? The daughter of so and so? The wife of so and so? Do you have two children, Nadia and Karim?" She answers them sarcastically and without fear, "Yes! Yes!"[43]

The examinations were all negative, a fact that leaves the physicians confused and surprised. "They compared the first dossier and the last dossier."[44] The evaluation of the two files is much the same as the evaluation of the female patient's body, which is first afflicted with the breast cancer and then seemingly not.

And when Leïla travels to Paris to consult with a French oncologist after the first religious intervention in Mecca, her medical record goes with her. This time the file is even bigger, thanks to the fact that all her examinations have been repeated, as have the x-rays of her entire body. Professor "I" examines this "strange dossier" very carefully and prescribes more treatment.[45]

Patient and medical dossier are leading a quasi-parallel life. This "strange" medical record is nothing but a kind of external manifestation of the narrator's illness and corporal reality. Much like her own physical body, it moves across various sorts of boundaries, from physician to physician. By not venturing forth to Mecca along with the narrator, the medical file remains, as it were, in the "scientific" realm and not in the spiritual one. After all, there was nothing to keep Leïla from consulting with physicians in Saudi Arabia, but she does not. Her consultations there are restricted to the domain of the religious. The medical practitioner, be he in the hospital or the clinic, is replaced with the religious figure of the Imam of the mosque.[46]

Just as the narrator's body undergoes a radical change in Mecca with the disappearance of the lumps, so her medical and social identity must be reestablished after this corporal and spiritual intervention. That is in essence why the questioning about her family identity becomes so crucial. Her sarcastic and proud response helps seal the social identity in the face of the changing body.

This medical folder that registers the life of the protagonist from her earliest days and exists alongside her through her medical journey is reminiscent of the Book of Judgment. In Leïla's case, however, this Book of Judgment records the medical and corporal, the religious being left aside. The essential irony of this, of course, is that the salvation from the dreaded cancer comes through the spiritual interventions, both that in Mecca and that in Morocco through the oneiric experience.[47]

The parallel life of the patient, on the one hand, and the medical dossier, on the other, is confirmed in the physical entity that is the book, Do Not Forget God. In fact, the book as physical object pulls together the two narratives, of which one (that of Leïla) claims to be the interpreter between the other (that of the physicians) and the resulting book.

As the reader follows the trajectory of the medical record and the discussion of the various examinations to which the narrator submits, the reader may well become aware that behind this inspiring journey to a religious cure from breast cancer lies a variety of medical documents. The reader is not to be disappointed. Leïla, as if she were herself conscious of her own reader's mind, obliges. At the end of her corporal and spiritual journey, Leïla is cured by the Prophet Muhammad by means of a dream, an incident to be investigated in detail below.[48] The dream and its cure signal the end of the narrative text. This is confirmed by the table of contents at the end of the physical entity that is the Arabic book. In the original Arabic text, the medical documents are not evident from the table of contents, in which they are not listed. In the French text, however, their existence is signaled in a section entitled "Documents annexes."

Before presenting these medical documents, the narrator advises her reader that some may find her account fanciful. The medical documents are there to avert this possibility. She invites the doubting reader to "examine them carefully." She is permitting the documents "to speak for themselves" so that readers can see through them the power and wisdom of God, as evidenced by part of a Qur'ânic verse, "When He desires something, He says to it: 'be' and it is."[49]

By arguing that the medical materials should "speak for themselves," the first-person female narrator is alerting the reader that another voice has entered the work, the voice of medicine. This is a "cancer in two voices," but not like that of Sandra Butler and Barbara Rosenblum. Their two voices are a patient and her partner;[50] Leïla Lahlou's are a patient, on the one hand, and the medical establishment, on the other. The medical voice in Lahlou's text is not introduced, however, for its own sake but rather as proof of the divine word. Yet, an examination of the entirety of her medical documents demonstrates that not a single one, be it from North Africa or Europe, broaches the issue of religion.

So what kind of documents are these whose power goes beyond their mere medical validity to support the power of the Deity? The medical documents, unlike the first-person narration by Leïla, are dated. They provide a real chronological frame for the events in the work. Further, the medical documents in the Arabic original and in the French translation are not identical. The French work includes more documents than its Arabic counterpart. Nevertheless, the nature of the documentation does not differ substantially from one text to the other. The diagnostic reports range from laboratories in France commissioned to perform blood tests to radiologists in Morocco providing the results of various x-rays. The reader will also find statements and certifications from physicians attesting that they have indeed been following the female patient, and providing their medical judgment of her state.

Leïla's invitation to her reader that he or she examine the documents carefully is a bit disingenuous. Most readers will find themselves at a loss when facing these scientific papers. Or, at the very least, they will be intimidated. The average reader will be looking at a medical certificate drafted on letterhead bearing a physician's name, the name of a laboratory, or the name of a hospital. Some of the documents are handwritten, rendering them more difficult to decipher. The Arabophone reader, with the Arabic text in hand, will be facing an even greater dilemma: all the medical documentation is in French. The only Arabic he or she will encounter in that section of the work will be the names and addresses of the Moroccan medical practitioners. These essential facts about the practitioners, along with their medical degrees, are displayed both in Arabic and in French (one facing the other on the same letterhead). For the reader of the French translation, the alterity between Leïla's first-person narration and the medical testimonies will not be as radical.

Nevertheless, there is an inherent discordance between the personal breast-cancer narrative as told by the female patient and that other narrative of her condition, the narrative of the medical establishment. The scrutiny of one medical document will demonstrate the complexities of this alternate medical discourse in the work.

This document is a letter addressed to Dr. Yacoubi in Casablanca from a Belgian oncologist, Dr. H. M. Tagnon. The document appears in both the French and the Arabic editions of Lahlou's work. Dr. Tagnon types his missive on the letterhead of the European Organization for Research on Treatment [sic] of Cancer in Brussels, of which he is the past president. "Cher Confrère," begins Tagnon. This letter is in the first-person singular: Tagnon has seen Madame Lahlou, whose cancer has metastasized. The metastases are "unfortunately" partly due to the chemotherapy and to the fact that this treatment did not include endoxan, "following the flat refusal of the patient to take this medication, which causes hair to fall out" (à la suite du refus absolu de la malade de prendre ce médicament qui fait tomber les cheveux). Tagnon continues by informing his Moroccan colleague that he has convinced the patient to follow the enclosed treatment, with which he has provided her and which includes endoxan. "She has promised me to submit herself" to the new plan. Tagnon thanks Yacoubi and adds that this patient is extremely sensitive and needs con-

siderable moral support, which the two of them should be able to provide. He has promised her that he will see her as often as she would like.
Noting when he would like her next visit to be, the Belgian oncologist
signs off with the usual French formalities.[51]

This French missive from Tagnon to Yacoubi is telling. It is a document that indeed speaks for itself, to quote the narrator of *Do Not Forget God:* it is narrated in the first person. And this first-person male narrator, a medical specialist, is a favored speaker, addressing himself to
another male specialist. True, the sender is in Europe and the recipient
in North Africa, but no matter. This is the privilege of the transnational
body. It can become the subject of the identical medical discourse, be it
in Morocco or in Belgium.

In Tagnon's narration, the female patient surfaces only as an object of
the discourse. She is now "Madame Lahlou," whose concern over her
physical appearance and fear of hair loss prevented her from following
the prescribed medical treatment, thus helping the cancer to spread
throughout her body. This is also a fairly weak individual, in need of a
great deal of support. But the missive is reassuring on that front. The
voice of the physician is at once superior, strong, and protective. Tagnon's
englobing *nous* (we) speaks to himself and his Moroccan colleague: they
should be able to provide the breast-cancer victim with the moral support
she requires.

The female patient may be painted here as a weak individual in need
of help. But there is an essential irony to Tagnon's words that only appears when his letter to Yacoubi is placed in the context of Leïla's first-
person female narrative. Tagnon had confidently assured his Moroccan
colleague that "Madame Lahlou" promised him that she would "submit herself" to the new treatment.

Submission is an interesting term indeed. Tagnon's letter is dated
April 4, 1979. It will be remembered that Leïla's Arabic text contains no
dates. Nevertheless, an archaeology of the appended medical documents
reveals that Tagnon's letter immediately precedes the visit to Paris, during which Leïla consulted the French oncologist, "I," who confirmed the
diagnosis of his Belgian colleague. This is Dr. Israël of the Hôpital Avi-
cenne, whose handwritten testimony is included in the appendix to the
Arabic text, but not in that to the French text. It is after the visit to "I"
that Leïla and her husband perform the *ʿumra* to Mecca. And, of course,
this pilgrimage will bring about the first religious intervention, in which
the physical symptoms of the cancer disappear. Islam is the triumphant

hero here: *Islam,* a word that means "submission." Lahlou has submitted herself, as Tagnon so eloquently put it. Her submission, however, was not to medicine but to religion—not to the physicians but to God.

Leïla invites the medical records to "speak for themselves." But she attempts to orient the reader's perspective with the intertextual game of inserting a Qur'ânic verse in the course of this invitation. The astute reader who listens to these documents speak will hear a narrative, predominantly male (the laboratory results are not gender coded), that redefines and recontextualizes the first-person narrative of the female patient. The French medical documentation serves as testimony to the Arabic verbal journey narrated in the first person, in which Leïla takes the reader from the discovery of the cancer to its cure. These materials do not form a closure as such to the case, but they do provide the work with a medical, scientific cover.[52]

In the medical documentation, Leïla is the third-person object. The story of the ravaged female body told by the first-person narrator is transmuted into the words of the physicians, who turn the female narrator into the object of a medical discourse generated by scientific personnel and laboratories, stretching from Casablanca through Bordeaux to Brussels.

The transformation of the female narrator into the object of the discourse is, in its own way, not dissimilar from the phenomenon of Karîmân Hamza, whose spiritual journey was sandwiched between the introduction and the epilogue by men.[53] In Karîmân's universe, however, all the parties involved in the creation of the various discourses of which Karîmân is either the subject (as narrator) or the object (as "narratee") belonged to the identical universe, the spiritual one. Leïla's mutation is different because she herself acts as the mediator between her own narration and the testimony of the medical establishment, introducing the documents and encouraging her reader to immerse himself or herself in them. Leïla's situation of go-between means that she is endorsing her own change in status from first-person narrator who controls the personal journey to object of the medical discourse.

This entire game with narration and the medical documents calls into question Leïla's agency in the text. The analysis of the Belgian physician's letter made it clear that he and the narrator understood the issue of submission quite differently. While he wished her to submit herself to medicine, she instead submitted herself to religion. This personal act on the part of the female narrator demonstrates what appears at the outset as full control over her destiny.

But the issue is much more complicated. Control over her destiny and her body is not so simple for the breast-cancer victim. There are two issues central to this question of control, and both relate to Leïla's agency in the text. On the one hand, there is the issue of knowledge, and on the other hand, there is the issue of the body. Of course, knowledge constitutes, among other things, awareness of the narrator's physical condition, a condition ultimately linked to her body. For the moment, however, one needs to separate the body as an abstract entity from the body as a corporal phenomenon undergoing transformation as the disease progresses. This latter involves knowledge of what is transpiring in that changing body.

Take the body as abstract entity first. From the initial discovery of the abnormality in her breast until the final cure from this dreaded cancer, Leïla's body seems to be under the control of other characters in the text. This external control effectively begins early in the journey. After all, the initial push to visit the Moroccan physician in his clinic comes from various family members and not directly from the narrator herself. And as her body travels from North Africa to Europe and Asia, that body undergoes various examinations and treatments partially administered by other characters in the story. Be it in Yacoubi's clinic or in the Belgian hospital, Leïla's body is turned into a public object.

This public aspect of her body is not alien to Leïla. Perhaps the most significant element of the body as public object is the gaze. The gaze surfaces in the opening pages of the text. As the central character of the spiritual journey begins her saga with the cancer, the visual component reigns supreme. The reader watches as first the narrator and then the various members of her family gaze at her body, specifically at her abnormal breast. Verbs expressing the action of looking and observing abound, as this activity is pursued. And, of course, there is the all-important medical gaze that haunts the breast-cancer victim. The gaze even reappears in the religious setting of the pilgrimage to Mecca.[54]

Leïla herself, however, is not immune to the exploitation of this all-powerful gaze. In a manner that is quite out of character in the Middle East and North Africa, she declares her wish to show off her body. On her return to Casablanca after the initial operation in Belgium that left her diseased breast intact, she triumphantly boasts: "I arrived at the Casablanca airport. . . . and I almost opened my shirt out of joy . . . and if I had been able to, I would have said to the passers-by: I was cured . . . my cancer has left me."[55]

This desire to exhibit the body is, on one level, understandable, and demonstrates the excitement of the female narrator over the fact that physicians in Europe had not performed a mastectomy and that her body remained whole. She had already discovered this herself, but her inclination to share this information with mere strangers by taking off her shirt in a public place like the Casablanca airport is, to say the least, unusual. In the Islamic cultural context in which Leïla is operating, displaying the female body is taboo.[56] Displaying this body naked would be an even greater cultural challenge.

But beyond simply a mere allusion to a passing desire for body display, this incident in the Casablanca airport signals much more for the body. It is now that Leïla feels she can speak about her breast as though it were like any other piece of her body, without shame.

> And how proud I was . . . and who is the woman who would not take pride in this? A cancer in her breast? And this diseased part was not taken out . . . was not cut . . . and her chest was not disfigured. . . . who is the woman who will not look in the mirror after this illness and not have a smile mixed with tears to praise God over what the mirror reflects to her. . . . everything as God wanted it is in its place . . . as though nothing had happened.[57]

This aside on the body is embedded in Leïla's narration of her arrival in Casablanca, an event to which she returns immediately after these happy observations.

This return to the homeland, this geographical displacement from Europe to North Africa, necessitates these comments on corporal stability and the unchanging body. Interestingly enough, all the observations about the body are based on external and superficial criteria dealing with appearance. Leïla's pride in her body is based on the fact that that body is complete and undamaged: no mutilation has taken place, no "ectomy," to use Evelyne Accad's terminology.[58] The narrator is not happy leaving the issue here. She feels the need to bring in the Deity, who must be praised for the fact that the body parts are where they should be.

The concern with the outward appearance of the body as a whole entity, as something that has not been mutilated, is not too dissimilar from "the same as before" phenomenon that Audre Lorde discusses. In *The Cancer Journals,* Lorde speaks about the breast-cancer victim who chooses prosthesis following a mastectomy as someone who "wishes to be 'the same as before.'"[59] Of course, Leïla's concern here is precisely because she has not lost a breast but instead can have the same body she has always had. Nevertheless, there is a nostalgia here for the body as undamaged goods.

This assessment of the body as a sum of its parts that are not disturbed, as the gaze and its reflection in the mirror verify, leaves aside the entire question of the internal cancer plaguing the female narrator. In fact, knowledge about the inner workings of the body and not its exterior appearance is a question that occurs over and over again in the narrative and leads to the area of the agency of the narrator and control over her body.

From the first medical encounter between Leïla and a physician, which takes place in Yacoubi's clinic, Leïla seems to be arguing for the integrity of her body. It is here that she declares that the size of the lump in her breast is proof that she does not have cancer. This negation of the corporal reality is immediately questioned by the attending physician. Dr. Yacoubi informs her that they have found calcification.

It is really at this point that medical certainty establishes that Leïla's body, as a corporal entity, has begun to be transformed. And these corporal transformations will continue throughout the narrative as the cancer first metastasizes, then goes into remission, then is seemingly cured. At the same time the physical reality that is Leïla's body undergoes radical modifications as it encounters the various medical treatments and the ascetic regimen in Mecca. The body becomes an evolving, mutating unit and a complex of parts: as the cancer changes and moves, as the various medical treatments enter the body, so the body is altered.[60]

Throughout many of these variations, Leïla remains, as it were, outside her own body, calling her own agency into question. She is certain, for example, that her husband asked the Belgian specialist "to hide the truth from me." Nor did this physician "answer my questions."[61] After certain treatment decisions are made, including the use of chemotherapy, Leïla notes that she was not asked what she herself would prefer.[62] She does, of course, as she herself admits, overhear her husband speaking to the oncologist about her cancer, leaving no doubt that she was quite aware of her own physical condition. In fact, she overhears her husband crying out to the physician, "No. . . . She will never die in three months." Leïla moves away after she hears the physician prescribing a mastectomy and chemotherapy—all to the husband.[63]

Leïla's protestations are a clear sign that she felt no control over her own fate, no sense of agency when dealing with her malignancy. In this, she differs drastically from many western breast-cancer victims. In a

series of commentaries from women with breast cancer, a recurring topos is that of "taking control." Listen to Kathleen M. Hoffman, a breast-
cancer patient, explaining her position on the question of control: "I
agreed to a lumpectomy, but I refused to sign consent to 'perform whatever procedures' the surgeon deemed necessary during the surgery. Ultimately it meant two surgeries, not one, but I needed to feel in control." [64]
In Audre Lorde's journals, the decision to follow certain treatment is
made after long and due consideration of all the possible alternatives.
And she, like Hoffman, had wanted "a two-stage operation anyway, separating the biopsy from the mastectomy. I wanted time to re-examine
my decision." [65]

Part of Leïla's dilemma with agency is, without doubt, cultural. It is
not considered appropriate in the Middle East to inform ill patients of
their medical plight. Instead, a consistently optimistic attitude is taken
with the patient, assuring him or her that the illness is but a passing
thing, even when it is as serious a condition as a terminal cancer. Family members and friends, however, are normally advised of a patient's
predicament and counseled to keep the secret from the diseased individual. This is a situation that I myself have encountered with terminally
ill friends in the Middle East, like the famous film director Shâdî ʿAbd
al-Salâm. As he suffered and screamed in agony from bone cancer, everyone assured him he would be fine. Part of Leïla's problems arises
from these cultural practices.

As Leïla is outside this diagnostic universe, she has recourse to an interesting metaphor, that of acting. After Yacoubi's announcement about
calcification, the narrator states that she is no longer a normal individual; rather, her name has been registered in another world. She delves
into "the scenario":

> I became the star of the most wicked and worst film in my life. . . . True, since
> my childhood, I used to dream of acting. . . . I would stand in front of a mir-
> ror for hours and hours imitating the actress whom I admired. . . . But I did
> not expect that I would undertake the most dangerous role . . . and that I
> would live the worst days. . . . Would that I had not gotten up on that stage
> full of thorns. . . . Would that I had died before reading the chapters of this
> sad and painful show. [66]

The entire idea that Leïla is but an actor on a stage is, of course, related
to her passivity and to her absence of agency. This is rendered all the
more pathetic in that a childhood fantasy of acting as agency becomes
an adult experience of acting as loss of control.

The opening of the journey stands as an interesting moment in this question of agency. As the narrator is addressing the importance of health (presumably on the plane from Mecca), she notes that she did not concern herself with her health until she had almost lost it, "and until the conflict began, a conflict between me and an illness that was almost dangerous and deadly were it not for the mercy of my Lord."[67]

Beginning a journey with a conflict is far from unusual: one has but to think of the popular novel by Nawal El Saadawi, *Mudhakkirât Tabîba* (Memoirs of a Woman Doctor), which begins with the notion of conflict between the first-person female narrator and her femininity.[68] The difference here is that in Leïla's struggle, it is the Deity, through his mercy, who brings about a resolution. The religious intervention will be addressed below.[69] Here, it is the agency of the Deity that is important. Religious agency means that the narrator need not take any action vis-à-vis the dilemma between her and her own corporality. The Deity will battle the cancer alongside the male representatives of the medical establishment. And, it is no surprise that the Deity should be the winner.[70]

Female patient, male physicians; a first-person narration in Arabic in which the female patient is the subject of the narrative, controlling and manipulating it; appended medical texts in the French language, in which this female patient becomes the object of the discourse—an inherent multilingual quality permeates Leïla Lahlou's book, in which various languages, ranging from the corporal to the geographical, sit side by side.

And this is not to speak of the Arabic and French languages that coexist for this North African writer. Beginning with the first pages of *Do Not Forget God,* there is an essential bilingualism that exists for the narrator and for the general medical universe that she will soon be inhabiting. She appears to be equally comfortable in both Arabic and French. Those initial moments of discovery of the abnormal body part also recall to Leïla's mind the French-language magazine *Constellation* and what she read in one of its articles about cancer in general and breast cancer in particular.[71] This reference to the magazine does not end there, however. Leïla notes that she kept this magazine and would come back to it from time to time "as if I wanted to read about the new discoveries and what medicine had accomplished in terms of great advance or fast steps in this area . . . or as though I wanted to memorize the names of the medicines and the medical instruments specialized in cancer."[72]

Here the narrator is attempting, first and foremost, to demonstrate the importance of cancer as a presence in her life. But what also comes through is the association of this dreaded illness with the West and with the French language, the language of Morocco's principal colonizers. Although politics and history play no overt role in this breast-cancer narrative, one cannot ignore the importance of medicine and its association as a western transplant. Once this geographical component becomes clear, the absence of the medical file in Mecca takes on even more importance. Science becomes associated with the West and spiritual salvation with the East. This is not to imply that one should not have recourse to medicine. Far from it.[73] Medical geography and spiritual geography can coexist, but theirs is not a comfortable alliance.[74] The geography of tourism, with its constant praise of Morocco, was embedded within the geography of medicine.

Leïla's intense cancer journey appears to be quite uplifting, as it chronicles a religious cure from a dreaded medical condition. The only discordant element in this story is the fate of Leïla Lahlou herself. She died of an intestinal cancer not too many years after her miraculous cure.[75]

CHAPTER FIVE

Corporal Geographies
of Salvation

Leïla Lahlou's breast cancer narrative is inherently dramatic. The reader follows the narrator as she is first diagnosed with the cancer and then cured of it. The movement of Leïla's body, as she traverses national and linguistic borders in search of a solution to her corporal dilemma, heightens the drama. Even more sensational will be the movement from a secular to a religious lifestyle. Leïla's is not just a traveling body that moves across national geographies. It is also a traveled body, itself the subject of discovery not only by the narrator but by other individuals as well.

The examination of several incidents will elucidate this corporal geographical component, central to the narrator's spiritual journey, incidents that will help bring religion into focus. The first incident involves Leïla's discovery of the abnormality in her breast. Although religion is not overtly present in this particular event, nevertheless it sets the background against which the diseased body and the spiritual redemption will interact in provocative and important ways.

It is August and Leïla is returning from the swimming pool with her husband and children. She plans on taking a bath at home. She notices redness in her left breast, but is not surprised, attributing it to the sun. So she begins to compare the two breasts, both their color and their size. She notices that the left breast is swollen and that the swelling is increasing minute by minute. Not only that, but there is a hot liquid emanating from the breast: "it was almost black and not red in color like the red of blood . . . nor yellow like the yellow of pus."[1] This is followed by pain. Leïla then remembers a problem she had with the same breast fourteen years previously when her son was nursing and she had undergone a biopsy. But, as she adds, she is not nursing now.

Leïla screams and the first person to respond is her daughter, Nadia. The daughter looks at her mother, asking herself how it is possible for her to scream "after a warm bath, full of soap and perfume."[2] "How can this be since five minutes ago you were in your bath[room] singing and playing with the water like a child . . . and now you are screaming?"[3] Nadia asks her mother what happened, and since the mother's finger has not left her breast, the daughter notices what is going on. She attempts to smile and then throws herself at her mother, hugging her while taking off the soap and covering her mother's chest to keep her from seeing anything. Leaning on her daughter, Leïla leaves the bathroom as though she were paralyzed. Leïla then remembers the article she had read in the French-language magazine *Constellation* on cancer in general and breast cancer in particular. Questions begin to plague her: should she tell her children? Should she ask her daughter to read her the section on breast cancer? No, she decides, she does not have cancer. In fact, she enumerates all the other names one calls this illness. She is crying so hard that her hot tears "almost burned my cheeks."[4] Nadia leaves her mother and returns with her father. Questions are also running through their minds. When Leïla opens her shirt and the two of them look at her red swollen breast, they are dumbfounded and motionless. They both hug her and kiss her so much that she does not need to wipe away her tears. Leïla's son, Karim, returns from visiting some family members and finds them in this state. He does not understand what is happening but nevertheless hugs his mother. The family sleeps together in one room.

Thus does Leïla's adventure with cancer begin. The reader meets her in August as she is returning home from a day spent in the sun with her family. In fact, she initially attributes the noticeable redness in her left breast to the experience outdoors. But the physical abnormalities she discovers in one breast (e.g., swelling, liquid) are enough to cause her a great deal of worry, especially given her earlier history with that breast. Leïla's problem with her left breast is attributed immediately to the fact that her body had been exposed to the sun. In other words, her body was uncovered, and that in a public place.

The narrator's scream brings forth her daughter, Nadia. The self-questioning on Nadia's part to which Leïla calls attention opposes the contrast between the mother's present scream and her previous singing in the warm perfumed bath. The two oral activities are juxtaposed as the physical well-being of a close-knit family returning from a day in the sun is shattered.

The discovery of the abnormal breast creates a disruption in the nuclear unit. The mother becomes the child and the weak female who first is playing in the bath and then is being protected by the daughter. This protection is corporal: the daughter puts her arms around the mother and attempts to wipe off the soap from her body, with Leïla leaving the bathroom and leaning on her daughter as though she were paralyzed. The daughter will bring the father into the picture, and the two of them will look at the swollen body part. Finally, the son arrives, completing the family unit. The ordeal of discovery will have the family members sleeping together, united as they had been earlier during their excursion in the sun.

This reunion of the nuclear family is mediated through Leïla's body, which progressively disappears as a corporal entity with the appearance of each family member. Leïla first discovers the physical abnormality, touching her breast in the process. Her daughter will spot the problem when she sees her mother's finger still lying on that breast. The young woman will then proceed to clean the soap from what one assumes to be her mother's naked body. The corporality of the incident is heightened by the mother's hot burning tears. The father and daughter also look at the abnormal breast, but this time it is Leïla herself who invites them to perform this act by opening her shirt. When did she put on clothing? The reader is not told this information. The tears that had earlier almost burnt Leïla's cheeks now disappear through the hugging and kissing emanating from the father and daughter. By the time the son, Karim, arrives, the corporality of the female body is no longer in question: in fact, the son does not understand what is happening but nevertheless hugs his mother.

The female body that the son does not see is the object of scrutiny by the other family members. More importantly, the discovery of the abnormality in Leïla's left breast has started a delicate game involving the female body. The body moves from partial uncovering, at the swimming pool, to complete uncovering, in the bath, to covering, with the arrival of the son. In the process, the female body part is explored and described for the reader, down to the black liquid oozing out of this abnormal breast.

But this discovery incident does more than introduce a geography of Leïla's body. It also introduces, though covertly, a cultural divide. Leïla's discovery of breast cancer is associated with swimming in a public pool, and in a context in which sunburn on the breasts is normal. This reveals that this Moroccan woman has been wearing a western-style bathing suit. Readers from Muslim countries do not need to be reminded that public swimming of this sort (and in mixed company) is considered immodest and un-Islamic behavior (as will be made clear by the Belgian Sultana, below).[5] The emphasis on the heartwarming solidarity of the nuclear family in crisis may distract from this religious subtext, but it cannot eliminate it.

Alongside the corporal geography of Leïla's body and the medical geography of treatment is a sacred geography, combining with and redefining the other two. After all, the sacred geography was presented in the beginning of the book with the reference to travel to Mecca. Nevertheless, it is a European capital that sees the junction of the geography of medicine with that of salvation. In Paris, after making the decision to perform the *ʿumra*, Leïla and her husband leave the hospital, while doing a *takbîr* (reciting the formula, *Allâhu Akbar*, God Is Most Great) "that could be heard in the streets of Paris" and praying loudly. All this the couple does while heading for an Arabic bookstore to buy a copy of the Qur'ân. The sense of belief was so strong in Leïla's heart that she kept imagining the Kaʿba in front of her eyes. The narrator confesses that it was in Paris, "the city of skyscrapers," that God guided her on the right path. "Yes, we came out of the physician's clinic doing a *takbîr* whose echo was heard from afar." The biggest and most crowded Parisian streets become the site for the couple's prayers.[6]

On the one hand, this description plays up the contrast in religious geography: Muslim thoughts in a western city, and the Kaʿba, an Islamic sacred place, transported to the boulevards of Paris. On the other hand, the Arabic bookstore in the French capital is a testimony to the presence of Islam within this western city. This is also clearly either a new or a renewed spirituality on Leïla's part, because even though she was gravely ill, she had not brought a copy of the Qur'ân with her.

Paris functions as the transition between the medical and the spiritual. It is in the French physician's office that Leïla's husband first proposes the idea of going to Mecca, an idea that meets with no resistance on the part of the French specialist. It is also in the French capital that the cancer victim is addressed by a *hâtif* (literally: an invisible caller or a voice—a well-known term from Islamic mysticism), enjoining her to perform the pilgrimage to the holy city of Islam. And the couple's search for an Arabic Qur'ân in Paris proves to be critical. Not only is this the book that will accompany the narrator on the trip to Mecca, but it is also "the great book of God and the cure and medicine of the hearts." This terminology is crucial, bringing together the corporal and the spiritual, as geographical boundaries are crossed. At the same time, this description of the religious book effects a redefinition of cure and medicine. These are no longer referents simply to a physical illness but can now include a spiritual condition as well. Medical terminology then becomes an integral part of the religious world Leïla will inhabit. She can, henceforth, speak of "a pharmacy left to us by the Seal of the Prophets, a pharmacy that can only increase you in strength and hope." [7]

On the way to Mecca, Leïla forgets the "physicians of Belgium and France . . . and the analyses . . . and the treatments and the hospitals." The movement from Europe eastward to Mecca permits the full blossoming of that sacred geography that will help bring about the spiritual corporal interventions. The couple lands in Jedda and proceeds by car to Mecca. The road is extremely crowded "as though it were the *hajj* season." Both men and women are dressed in the appropriate clothing, and Leïla feels that she is "in another world, or, more correctly, in a new world." [8] The allusion to the pilgrimage or the "new world" is a sign of the importance of this geographical movement to the holy sites of Islam. It may be officially just the *ᶜumra* that the Moroccan couple is performing, but that is unimportant, since for the narrator, the event is compared to the *hajj*.

On the small pilgrimage, Leïla follows for four days an ascetic regimen in which her daily intake consists of nothing but some bread, an egg, and holy water from Zamzam. On the fifth day, she feels a great power pushing her to feel the lumps on her body; however, she ignores this impulse and returns to drinking the water of Zamzam. But she is once again urged on by a *hâtif*, and she begins to look for the lumps.

Here is Leïla as she explores her body: "I found myself looking for those lumps and did not find even a small one. . . . I was surprised at first, then I slipped my hand inside onto my body. . . . I took off my heavy *jellaba* . . . and put my hand inside my shirt to make sure. . . . I pressed on my skin . . . and uncovered my arms." She asks her female companions—Egyptians, Syrians, Iraqis, and Turks—if they can see anything on her arms, under her armpits, or on her neck. They look at her and then at each other, but say nothing. Instead, they scream at once: "God is most great, God is most great, everything is gone." [9]

Leïla repeatedly puts her hands under her shirt while shaking and sweating. She finally calms down, and it is as though she hears a voice addressing her and reassuring her, at the same time reminding her of what she should have heard already about the positive effects of Zamzam water, especially when compared to medicine. Leïla continues to praise the Lord and cry and laugh, as everyone around Zamzam wonders what is going on. She dons her *jellaba* and finds her husband, to whom she gives the good news. She almost stops people in the street to tell them that God is present and that He is all-powerful. She calls Him "the Greatest Physician." She had been told that her cancer was dangerous and that no one could cure it, but she asked God to cure her, and He led her on the right path.

In the hotel, her husband "searches" and she searches as well. "He examined my entire body and did not find anything." [10] She continues, "My Lord afflicted me and my Lord cured me." Her husband throws himself on the bed crying, declaring that this is "impossible." He then reveals to her that the physicians had said that she had only three weeks to live. The Belgian physician had refused to treat her, claiming that no cure existed for her dangerous disease. "I hid this from you," he continues, "and said to myself: 'let us do the ʿ*umra*.'" She replies that she had heard the dialogue that took place between him and the physicians and that his recourse to the Deity was, indeed, the only solution. "Now you see with your own eyes what you see," she tells her husband. [11] She then gives him some Zamzam water to drink and drinks some of the holy water herself. Both perform the ablutions anew to return to the House of God. There she thinks about her salvation from a death sentence as well as her repentance. This leads to an attack on the base world and on the nominally Muslim but actually secular lifestyle she had previously lived. She may have known the Muslim creed, having learned it as a child, but did she really know its true meaning? At the mosque in Mecca, she searches for the Imam and tells him the news. He congratulates her and teaches her more prayers, at the same time enjoining her to recite the Qur'ân. With this Leïla returns to the Kaʿba and to her normal religious routines. [12]

This is clearly a momentous event in the narrator's life. She discovers that the physical symptoms of her malignancy seem to have disappeared. But once again, like the incident of the discovery of abnormality in the breast, the discovery of the disappearing symptoms involves an intricate corporal game. This corporal game also involves a display of the body, not too dissimilar from the narrator's exhibitionist desire at the Casablanca airport. [13]

The incident in Mecca is couched in an intertextually complex religious discourse that Leïla enriches with verses from the Qur'ân, citations from the *hadîth,* and so forth. The theological component exists alongside the corporal, at once defining it and enlarging it. Even the discourse on the Deity involves this. As Leïla enters the new religious universe of Mecca, she addresses God: "I have come to you, O Greatest and Most Powerful Physician." She continues by detailing that she is afflicted by a dangerous illness, a cancer, against which physicians have been powerless, and she beseeches the Almighty to cure her.[14] This direct appeal to the ultimate religious authority links the Deity directly to the world of medicine.

The corporality in Mecca initially appears in tandem with the spirituality. And this crucial duo of corporality and spirituality is constantly reinforced. Leïla follows a diet of nothing but some bread, an egg, and water from Zamzam. This ascetic regimen calls attention at once to the body and to the spirit. Leïla is not alone in her attempt to restrict her alimentary desires as she performs the religious ritual. Karîmân the narrator noted in her journey that her spiritual guide, Shaykh ʿAbd al-Halîm Mahmûd, while on the pilgrimage, also pursued a modest regimen: some bread and a banana, followed by black coffee (prepared and served by the narrator—an act whose gender implications are transparent). As Karîmân relates the shaykh's daily habits on the pilgrimage, she asks her reader to imagine this example of self-control.[15] Her tone is one of wonder and awe. True, she notes earlier in her account of these habits that she used to observe her spiritual leader closely and aspired to imitate him in everything. Does this mean that she emulated him when it came to her own alimentary conduct? The narrator does not say.

That it is not a coincidence that the spiritual and the corporal are both parts of Leïla's discourse in Mecca becomes clear on the fifth day of the regimen. On this day, Leïla senses a great power pushing her to feel the lumps on her body; however, she ignores this impulse and returns to drinking the water of Zamzam. Drinking is, of course, a corporal activity, but drinking the holy water of Zamzam is a corporal activity that partakes of the spiritual as well. Feeling the lumps, however, is a purely corporal activity that is painted as almost self-indulgent.

The spiritual here will not let go. Like many of those medieval Muslim mystics who are called on the path by a *hâtif,* Leïla hears a *hâtif* urging her to look for the lumps.[16] This is not the first time that a voice moves Leïla to a specific action with ultimately grave consequences. Remember that it was in Paris that a *hâtif* enjoined her to perform the pilgrimage. Since it was not the month of the pilgrimage, she and her husband decided to perform the *ʿumra.*

What is interesting about this particular call in Mecca is its evocation of the corporal. Leïla gives in to the urges and begins her actual search for the lumps. This personal exploration is followed by that of the narrator's female companions. Her question to them—whether they can see anything on her arms, her armpits, and her neck—remains technically unanswered. They simply look at her and at one another and then scream: "God is most great, God is most great, everything is gone." [17] Now she receives the answer to her corporal question, but couched in a religious formula, uttered by a multiplicity of women speaking as one voice. The incident accentuates the scopic and the gaze. Leïla does not simply inform her female copilgrims that the lumps have disappeared from her body. Rather, there is a collective effort at the examination of the ill body.

Leïla repeats her own exploration of her body, putting her hands under her shirt to check for lumps. The voice that is there soothing her also reminds her of what she should have known about the positive effects of Zamzam water. The corporal is the site of this triumph of religion over medicine. It should not come as a surprise, then, that as Leïla is winding her way through the streets of Mecca, she should call the Deity "the Greatest Physician." [18]

But, as with the incident detailing the initial discovery of the breast abnormality, the husband must partake of the corporal exercise. His emotional response to the absence of symptoms on Leïla's body leads him to reveal the conversation between himself and the Belgian physicians, a conversation Leïla had overheard, but without disclosing this fact to her husband. The husband repeats the medical claim that no cure existed for her disease and reminds her that his reply to this medical prognosis had been to suggest the *ʿumra.* The husband's reaction clarifies the miraculous nature of the cure.

What Leïla discovers on her own in the sacred spot of Zamzam, the husband discovers in the hotel room: recourse to the Deity was, indeed, the only solution to her dreaded illness. This knowledge unites them in religion: she gives him some Zamzam water to drink and imbibes some of the holy water herself. Does this knowledge also unite sexually? Possibly. The narrator is careful to add that they both perform the ablutions anew to return to the House of God. Sexual relations are one of a number of actions that would have required renewed ablutions.

Leïla has come full circle. She starts in the mosque examining her body and ends in the mosque informing the Imam of her "cure." In between, her body has been explored by her female religious colleagues as well as by her husband. Four groups are party to the miraculous cure: Leïla, the women, the husband, and the Imam. Two female constituencies followed by two males. The first three (Leïla, the women, and the husband) physically ascertain this cure in the body; the fourth (the Imam) is, from the corporal perspective, almost irrelevant. He derives his importance from being able to narratively bring closure to the incident by giving Leïla specific religious advice.

This circular structure echoes that in the first incident, involving the discovery of the abnormality in the breast. There were also four parties involved: Leïla, her daughter, the husband, and the son. Two females followed by two males. The first three see the body, the fourth one, the son, does not. Like the Imam, the son is, corporally speaking, also almost extraneous. The narrator even mentions that he did not know what was transpiring. If the Imam's function is to bring religious closure to the miraculous cure, the son's function is no less important. Without him, the nuclear family would not have been complete. Males confirm, and provide closure to, female corporal discoveries.

The protracted event in Mecca spells more than a religious intervention in Leïla's corporal odyssey. The incident transcends the issue of the disappearance of the symptoms to touch on the question of identity. For the narrator, Mecca is not just a new geographical environment. It is a new world that signals a chronological movement backward, a regression. But this is a positive regression in which the narrator seems to be getting younger and younger. As she explains her diet, she notes that her physical strength had increased to the point that she felt she was "a young woman, sixteen years old." [19] But this is not enough. Leïla informs her reader that she performed two prayers at the Maqâm Ibrâhîm, near the Kaᶜba. To this she then appends a *hadîth* in which the Prophet said that he who performs two prayers at this locus leaves his sins "as on the day his mother gave him [masculine singular] birth." [20] Gender aside, Leïla is, indeed, reborn, as the questions regarding her identity by the medical establishment subsequent to the ᶜ*umra* testify.[21]

But the change in age is not the only transformation that the narrator undergoes. The metamorphosis will also involve a quasi sanctification of the female hero. First the decision to go to Mecca and then the actual trip facilitate the narrator's ability to address the Deity directly, and this on several occasions.[22] She even becomes a spiritual teacher to the other women in Mecca.[23] More dramatic still, the women, upon their departure from the sacred space, seek her blessing, touch her clothing, and wipe themselves, saying to her, "Blessed, blessed, blessed." [24] Leïla derives her own knowledge from the male Imam and transmits this knowledge to the women, forming part of the homosocial unit.

The relationship, both corporal and spiritual, between Leïla and her female coreligionists in the sacred sites of Islam testifies to a strong homosocial bonding. In fact, the husband virtually disappears during the Meccan episode, only to reappear when it is time to confirm the disappearance of the lumps. Leïla notes initially that "I lived with a group of women believers, who knew about my illness. They used to follow all my steps and would go with me to anything I undertook. . . . They used to surround me with care and solicitude." These female companions even incited her to patience, telling her that God had chosen her for this. She was advised to practice this quality and take it as a sign of strength.[25] Here, as later, the women speak with one voice, the voice of a deep and abiding homosociality defined by a common religious experience. As Leïla puts it so eloquently herself when the women are bidding one another farewell at the end of the visit to the holy sites of Islam, "the bond of religion is stronger than any other bond." [26]

The reader should not be misled into assuming that this female homosociality is automatic among copilgrims of the same gender. Karîmân paints a different picture in her journey, where there is a visible absence of spiritual bonding among the women on the pilgrimage. Aside from Karîmân, the only other woman to display any sort of religious fervor is a "pious country woman," who turns out in the end to be Shaykh ʿAbd al-Halîm Mahmûd's sister.[27] More significant are the derision, frustration, and disdain Karîmân's coreligionists display toward the pilgrimage activities. Karîmân notes that she would sleep immediately after the evening prayer to escape the "chatter of the women." [28] Not only that, but these women complain about their physical surroundings and the crowds. They would mention their well-furnished homes and the absence of comfort in their Meccan accommodations. One of them even referred to their well-appointed (according to Karîmân) space as a "prisoners' ward." [29] These women, however, reach the height of their arrogance when they proceed to mock the country woman and her pious behavior. When, one day, a man comes asking about the minister's sister, one of these women replies, "No. Naturally, she is not here. Is it believable that the sister of the minister would be in this stable?" Karîmân realizes immediately who the sister is, and she stops the man before he leaves and informs him that Shaykh ᶜAbd al-Halîm Mahmûd's sister is, indeed, among them. The other women are, of course, surprised, and their reaction testifies to their superficiality: "Why had she not announced herself so they could get close to her?" [30]

All this is a far cry from Leïla's Meccan universe, in which all the women share in the religious experience. Even the linguistic aberrations that Leïla mentions and that she finds entertaining (such as the Turkish pronunciation of Arabic consonants) do not detract from the affection the narrator displays for her female companions.[31] This homosociality is what will ultimately permit the Moroccan hero to reach the rank of the blessed.

The geographical displacement to Mecca permitted the narrator to feel that she was in "another world or, more correctly, a new world." [32] This is not the only new world in Leïla's spiritual journey. When Dr. Yacoubi first informed Leïla that she had calcification in her breast, her reaction was that her name has been registered in another world, that of cancer and that of a death sentence.[33]

These entries into and exits from different universes reflect the tensions in Leïla's first-person account. The world of illness and medicine, in which her name has been metaphorically registered in Yacoubi's clinic, will be countered by the world of religion and the holy in Mecca, which will bring about a rebirth, both corporal and spiritual. Is it any wonder, then, that events and spaces seem to mirror one another in the autobiography? Leïla's desire to publicly assert her physical wholeness by baring her breast in the Casablanca airport must be set alongside her desire to almost stop every pilgrim on the streets of Mecca to declare God's existence. She practically ululates with joy in the streets of Mecca, a desire for a public expression of religiosity that harks back to the loud praying she and her husband had performed in the streets of Paris.

The transformation that took place in Leïla's body in Mecca moved her into the realm of the blessed. But the disappearance of the corporal manifestations of the cancer will not by any means imply the end of Leïla's journey. She will now begin a medical treatment on the advice of a European physician she trusts. She returns to Morocco and becomes ill again. This time, there is an operation (the narrator is particularly coy on details here), and Leïla goes in and out of a coma.

But then another religious intervention occurs. This event, consisting of a dream narrative with varying renditions, represents the culmination of the journey, bringing the spiritual in harmony with the corporal.

Leïla, in the middle of a "long sleep," as she calls it (and not a coma, as "they call it"), has a dream. She sees the Prophet wiping his hand on her hairless head. He enjoins her "in a warm voice" not to worry, since only good will come to her. He then presses hard on her head and she awakens in a bed sopping with perspiration. She is shaking with surprise and pleasure.[34] The dream leads her to think about Islam and her own role in it: had she lived at the time of the prophecy, she would have been one of the first to follow the religion, even going on the *hijra* and fighting in battles: "I would have endured all sorts of punishments" on the Islamic path.[35] She had been extremely sad, but the hand of the beloved (*al-habîb*) had stretched out to her after she had fallen asleep "on a pillow wet with tears of sorrow and pain."[36] She presses on her eyes to imprint on them forever the image she has witnessed. She awakens happy with her oneiric vision. The picture is there as though she had just seen it, and she begins to repeat the words of the Prophet. It is he who said, "He who sees me in a dream truly sees me, for the devil does not impersonate me."

The narrative continues. Leïla's bed and pillow are wet with perspiration. She hesitates but finally decides to awaken her husband. He turns on the lights in all the rooms and rouses everyone, thinking that this is the moment of separation. "Do not ask about the surprise that overtook them nor their great happiness," Leïla admonishes her readers, especially when everyone saw her walking. She relates the dream.

"I saw a light shining until it almost obliterated my eyes." Leïla ascertains that it is the Prophet. And because of what she knew from the books detailing the Prophet's life—that is, that the Arabs used to come to him from everywhere and from different classes, that he would address each individual according to his or her intellectual abilities and in the dialect which he or she understood, that he would lend an ear to the people and answer their questions, that they would not leave his presence until they were satisfied and content—because of all this, "I related to him the story of my illness . . . and my conflict . . . and my belief." The Prophet listens with great care until she finishes her words. Then he takes his "generous hand" and wipes it on her head from left to right, while ordering her to be patient and telling her that she will only experience what is good. Then he presses on her head and she awakens.

The all-around reaction to this dream is happiness. All praise the Deity and pray. Some spray rose water, others bring incense and perfume, still others try to get a blessing from the pillow. Leïla meanwhile is shaking and praising the Lord. She finally asks the family members to leave the room so that she can regain her strength. She then performs her ablutions and spends the rest of the night in religious activity until she falls asleep. How generous is God and how great, exclaims Leïla. She always remembers that God's mercy has no bounds, and His power no limits.

"Where is the beard that appeared on my face as a result of the great amount of cortisone?" No effect remained of it after her vision. Rather, "black shining hair grew on my head and my eyelashes and my eyebrows appeared . . . as though I had lost nothing." Leïla's hair emerges despite the chemotherapy, which, she argues, made this an impossibility. "It all appeared after my vision and on that same night, in other words after the dawn prayer." [37] Everything returned to what it was. How could it be otherwise, Leïla adds, since the Prophet had wiped his generous hand on her head?

The dream event with its miraculous component is narratively complex, being perhaps the most complex incident in the book. Like other episodes in *Do Not Forget God,* the narrative of the cure dream is laced with religious materials. The complexity of this oneiric experience comes not so much from the dream itself but from the way Leïla narrates it. The oneiric experience surfaces and resurfaces in the text, each time with variants, adding to its narrative complexity.

In the initial rendition, Leïla is in the middle of a "long sleep" (and not a "coma") and sees the Prophet wiping his hand on her hairless head. He enjoins her not to worry, since only good will come to her. He then presses hard on her head, and she awakens in a bed drenched with perspiration. She is shaking with surprise and pleasure.

Here, the miracle cure is made up of fairly straightforward events that seem to be taking place in their normal chronological placement within the narrative. The cancer patient is the passive observer. The only action she herself performs during the miracle cure, the only time she is the subject of a verb, is when she "sees." Even the words of the Prophet are mediated through a visual action: she does not hear them but sees the Prophet uttering the words of reassurance. Clearly, in this accounting of the event, Leïla is passive before the male religious figure.

The second account of the cure dream occurs in the middle of Leïla's musings about her state. Leïla falls asleep, and the hand of the beloved stretches out to her after she has fallen asleep. She has almost lost her vision because of her sorrow, and she begins pressing on "those two strong eyes" to imprint on them forever the image she has seen. She awakens happy with what she has seen in her dream. The picture is there as though she had just seen it, and she begins to repeat the words of the Prophet: "He who sees me in a dream truly sees me, for the devil does not impersonate me."

This second rendition of the dream is more complex than the first. Here, Leïla is an active participant in the oneiric experience. She presses on her eyes, in the same way that the Prophet presses on her head. The entire dream incident ends with the famous *hadîth* about the veracity of seeing the Prophet in a dream. (This *hadîth* was part of Karîmân's spiritual trajectory as well.)[38] Not only is the Prophet there in Leïla's dream experience, but the *hadîth* vouches for the authenticity of his presence.

The third retelling of the cure dream is the one Leïla saves for the assembled family after she awakens her husband and he, in turn, awakens the others. In this third version, Leïla provides even more details. This time, her knowledge of early Islamic history helps her in her interactions with the holy figure. The reader also learns as Leïla relates the story that the Arabs used to come to the Prophet from everywhere and from different classes and that he would handle their needs individually, and in a dialect they understood. They would not leave his presence until they were satisfied and content. Encouraged by all this, "I related to him the story of my illness . . . and my conflict . . . and my belief." The Prophet listens and then takes his "generous hand" and wipes it on her head from left to right, while ordering her to be patient and telling her that she will only experience what is good. Then he presses on her head and she awakens.

Leïla's role in the dream has evolved yet again. No longer a passive observer of the Prophet's actions (as in the first rendition) nor someone reacting to the actions of the Prophet (as in the second version), Leïla now interacts with the Prophet actively. She carries on a conversation with him, telling him her story. The linguistic problems that might have existed are eliminated in advance by the narrator: the reader has already been told that the Prophet spoke to each individual in a dialect he or she understood. The Arabs also did not leave the Prophet's company until they were satisfied. This, of course, is what Leïla will do.

For the contemporary Moroccan breast-cancer victim, satisfaction means the elimination of her illness. It should then, perhaps, not be a surprise that the third retelling of the dream event concludes with the happy reaction of the family members. More importantly, it signals a change in the corporal reality that is Leïla. The Prophet's hand on her head wipes out the side effects of the cortisone. Her "beard" is gone and her hair has resurfaced. "It all appeared after my vision and on that same night, in other words after the dawn prayer." [39]

The presence of the *hadîth* about seeing the Prophet in a dream, like the earlier intertextual materials from the Islamic tradition, testifies to Leïla's knowledge of that tradition. Seeing the Prophet in a dream is a sign of the dream's veracity. Dreams that occur at dawn are highly privileged.[40] She makes a point of telling her reader that after announcing her oneiric good fortune to her family, she performed the dawn prayer. The timing of the dream experience could not be better.

More importantly, cure dreams are not an unusual phenomenon in the Arabo-Islamic tradition. Most often, the Prophet effects a cure during the dream itself. To take but one example, the Mamlûk polymath al-Safadî (d. 764/1363) includes the following cure dream in his work on the blind, the *Nakt al-Himyân fî Nukat al-ʿUmyân*. Yaʿqûb ibn Sufyân related that he had been copying late one night and continued copying until the night came to its end. He suddenly became blind and could not see the light and began to cry more and more heavily because of this. In the process, he fell asleep and saw the Prophet Muhammad in a dream. The Prophet asked him why he was crying, to which he replied, "O Messenger of God, my vision has gone and I am grieved by what has escaped me concerning the writing of your *sunna*." The Prophet then told him to approach him, and he passed his hand over Yaʿqûb's eyes as if he were reciting over them.[41] Yaʿqûb awoke, his vision restored, and returned to his copying.[42]

This dramatic dream that cures its dreamer from blindness highlights a corporal element important for Leïla's oneiric experience. Normally, ailing body parts are touched directly by the holy figure effecting the cure, as in the dream al-Safadî relates. In a more contemporary example, Niʿmat Sidqî, whom we already met in connection with Karîmân Hamza, is also cured. In her case, however, the "signs" of her cure have a direct and mimetic relationship to her ailing body parts. Her case demonstrates, as well, a fascinating relationship between the punishment of the body—in that instance, the face—and modesty.[43]

Mimesis is more complex with Leïla. The male Prophet passes his hand on the female head and not on the original source of the malady, the breast. This modesty is absolutely essential, and the cure effected is governed by the modesty rather than by the original illness. After all, the elements that Leïla highlights as restored to their normal state are all part of her head: the returning hair and eyebrows, the disappearance of the beard. A cure has taken place through the Prophet's touch, a touch restricted to the secondary body parts affected by the treatment of the cancer. Modesty is linked, however, with a corporal shift from the original locus of disease, the breast, to another body part and one which is apparently cured not of the cancer but of the effects of the western medical treatment. In the process of curing her head, moreover, the Prophet also refeminizes Leïla by giving her back her hair and removing her beard (beards and bald heads are normally masculine characteristics). Spiritual purification dissolves the gender ambiguities created by western technology.

More importantly, the Prophet has also returned the ailing narrator to the realm of the human. Leïla's body in its pre-oneiric existence had been transformed into almost that of a nonsentient being. She notes that her legs had failed her and she was almost walking "on all fours." She was unable to speak due to pus and blood, so that her speech was turned into sign language. Her nails were falling off and her teeth were breaking.[44] The reference to walking on all fours and to the inability to speak is a sign that the narrator has been transposed from the realm of the human to that of the animal. The Prophet's appearance will change all that, and Leïla will return to the category of the human.

These dramatic alterations in the physical reality that is Leïla's body set her apart from her medieval predecessor, the blind scholar whose dream cure by the Prophet permitted him to return to his previous activity. Leïla's dream cure reinforces an aspect of her persona that she had acquired on the ᶜumra: a proximity to the holy. This time, it is her family members, rather than female fellow pilgrims, who attempt to derive blessings from her pillow.

Leïla's alterity, her difference, perceived as an ability to impart blessings, is not something that appears suddenly at the conclusion of the cure dream. The narrator had been careful to separate herself earlier from her family members. The setting of the nocturnal oneiric experience is very telling here. Everyone was worried about her health and afraid that she would not come out of her coma. She assures her reader that all seem to have forgotten that if there were anyone who would be eternal, it would have been the Prophet. But even he was not immune from death, the contemporary Moroccan woman asserts, having learned about his mortality from the Angel Gabriel. "The truth," she continues, "is that I was not in a coma as they called it . . . rather, as I said, I was in a long sleep."[45]

The distinction between being in a sleeping state (what she believes) and that of being in a coma (what they believe) is critical. Sleep is essential for the veracity of the cure dream that will follow. Leïla emphasizes the truth-carrying nature of her vision. For her, in fact, this is not even a dream or something imaginary but "the most truthful reality."[46]

In the spiritual journey, sleep functions as a marker to indicate the narrator's mental state. Leïla is not alone here in her chronic sleep problems. Her Egyptian coreligionist Karîmân faced similar problems on her spiritual journey, though without a dreaded disease.[47] Like Karîmân, Leïla's concern with this physical activity manifests itself from the beginning of the text. After the initial incident with the discovery of the breast abnormality, Leïla sleeps with the aid of sleeping pills.[48] When her family incites her to visit Dr. Yacoubi, her response is fear that her body part will be cut out: "Leave me alone. . . . I want to sleep."[49] Sleep evades her in Europe and she is forced to resort once again to the strongest sleeping pills.[50]

Following the first spiritual intervention in Mecca, after which the narrator undergoes more medical treatment, sleep once again escapes her. This time, however, she takes advantage of insomnia to spend her nights in prayer and Qur'ânic recitation.[51] She desires to stay awake at night in order to be alone in these calm hours, "and I would see no one but God."[52] It is prior to the cure dream that Leïla is finally able to conquer her sleeplessness: "I slept a deep, calm, and natural sleep, without sedatives or an injection. I slept a sleep the likes of which I had not slept since my earliest youth." The conquest of this chronic insomnia is due to the serenity in the narrator's belief in the Deity, providing her with an inner strength that allows her to face her difficulties.[53]

It should then not be a surprise that the Prophet should make his appearance at this juncture of the spiritual journey. But, interestingly enough, it is as though Leïla had been preparing herself carefully for this personal entrance by the Muslim holy figure in her sleep. Even before the cure dream, the contemporary Moroccan cancer victim had been following a type of popular religious practice, in which she heeded the Prophet's advice on how to handle pain. This includes the recitation of certain Qur'ânic *sûra*s three times into the palms of one's hand. This is followed by spitting in the palms lightly without leaving any saliva and then wiping the body with this. After presenting the formula, the narrator adds " . . . at the time of sleep."[54]

All these practices and corporal habits lead to the most momentous event in the spiritual journey, the cure dream. If nothing else, the multiple narrations of this episode testify to its importance. The final assimilation of Leïla to the rank of the holy in the third retelling is arrived at through the first and second tellings, which emphasize the sensory universe.

Observe for a moment the act of seeing. This sensory activity is central to the narrative. The multiple facets of the scopic and the gaze as these became part of the almost-daily world which the narrator inhabits are by now familiar. Her body is the object of multiple gazes: those of family members, those of the medical establishment, those of her co-religionists in Mecca. Leïla herself is, of course, not an unimportant player in the game of the gaze.

It is in the events surrounding the cure dream that this activity reaches its apotheosis. Before this event, Leïla's physical state is critical. Leïla looks at her family members to fully imprint their picture in her mind forever.[55] Not long after that, she will enter that deep sleep presaging the cure.

And the cure dream is predicated on the visual. The narrator confirms the existence of the Prophet through her ability to see him. More important is the presence of the *hadîth* in which the Prophet calls attention to the scopic: "He who sees me in a dream truly sees me. For the devil does not impersonate me."[56] The visual act is central to the veracity of the dream activity, which hinges on seeing the Prophet. When Leïla awakens, she is extremely happy by what "I have seen in my dream. . . . And the picture of what I saw was imprinted in front of my vision until it was as though I see it now."[57] The repeated allusions to the visual emphasize the pivotal nature of this act.

Sight plays a role even after the dream comes to an end. "My bed, and my pillow, everything is wet with perspiration. . . . Alone in this room, and in the dark of night . . . What do I say? Do I tell what I saw or not?"[58] Leïla, of course, will relate what happened, and this in multiple versions.

The domestic politics of the dream sequence are not without interest. Leïla is alone in her room during this momentous event. She does eventually awaken her husband, who will awaken the other family members. The cure through the dream, therefore, occurs between Leïla and the Prophet, between a diseased contemporary woman and the holiest figure in Islam. There is an undercurrent of eroticism in this encounter, as Leïla calls her nocturnal visitor "my beloved."[59]

But, this eroticization is not just that of the medical encounter but of another sort of encounter as well: the mystical encounter. This is by no means an unusual phenomenon in the contemporary discourses of women revivalists. Was not, after all, Karîmân's journey also imbued with this?[60] In Leïla's case, the at once mystical and medical eroticization is concretized heterosexually by the fact that a male Prophet, Muhammad, is curing a female believer, Leïla, in the same way that the maleness of Jesus is heterosexually joined to the Catholic nun, who becomes his bride and wears his wedding ring.

The miracle cure with the Prophet, like the onset of the cancer and the disappearance of physical symptoms, represents a phase in the development of the cancer. These incidents share many narrative characteristics, the primary of which is repetition. In the two incidents involving the discovery of the inflamed body part and the disappearance of the lumps, the exploration of Leïla's body is verified by multiple participants. In the dream event, Leïla's body is touched only by the Prophet; no human agents participate in the touching process. This is not insignificant and testifies to a change in Leïla's status. She has now been assimilated to the rank of the holy. Her relatives seek a religious blessing from the cushion and pillow on which she had been resting her head. But to arrive at this rank, Leïla's dream went through a repetitive transformation, leading to a final event in which she communicates directly with the Prophet.

The time markers labeling these stops on Leïla's cancer journey are also coded. The discovery of the abnormality in Leïla's breast takes place in August, the narrator using the western month. The two incidents involving religious interventions are labeled in their Islamic time frames: one during the ʿumra, the other during the month of Ramadân. No western month is alluded to here: the body purified through religion is defined by sacred temporalities. The experience in Mecca adds to this sacred element, Leïla's experience leading her to not know day from night.[61] Time loses its significance when it comes in touch with the numinous.

Having lived through this story, Leïla becomes a firm believer in God's power. In the closure of her narrative, she admonishes her reader that as long as this power is with him (masculine singular), "fill your life with hope, because God is with you." She closes with a familiar Qur'ânic image: "and the gates of heaven are always open to you . . . so do not forget God."[62]

These words of caution end the narrative, tying the story back to the title of the book. The end of the narrative, however, is not the end of the book, in the same way that the beginning of the narrative does not constitute the beginning of the book. The book that is the physical object in which Leïla Lahlou's story is embedded is a more complex entity. Just as Leïla's breast cancer must be arrived at through levels of medical examinations, so must the reader traverse layers of text before he or she encounters Leïla, the narrator. This is, of course, not dissimilar from Karîmân Hamza's work in which the first-person narrator had to also traverse male narrative gatekeepers before embarking on the recounting of her own journey.[63]

Dr. Mehdi Benaboud is the first textual sentinel whom the reader encounters in Leïla Lahlou's Arabic original. Benaboud's introduction follows the title page directly. Benaboud leaves no stone unturned as he details the stages of Leïla Lahlou's illness and recovery at the same time as he dances around what he himself calls "a deep medical problem."[64] Benaboud's introduction is followed by Lahlou's dedication of the book. Then follows another title page, this time with a verse from the Qur'ân, and still one more introduction, this by Leïla Lahlou herself.

Not so with the French translation. The gatekeepers in this instance are multiple and, what is even more interesting, of different sorts. After the table of contents, the work presents a segment of a speech by King Hassan II of Morocco, in which the royal leader quotes the Prophet on imploring the Deity and beseeches his nation to undertake this act one thousand times a day. Then follow the dedication of the work and the acknowledgments. These are succeeded by an extract from an interview with Leïla Lahlou done by Moroccan Radio and Television (RTM) in which she discusses her cure. Only after this does Benaboud make his French textual appearance. He is followed by a Qur'ânic verse (the same one that exists in the Arabic edition) and Leïla Lahlou's own introduction.

Gérard Genette, in his work, *Seuils,* has awakened critics to the importance of the various extratextual materials in which a narrative swims, including the cover and title of the work.[65] In Leïla Lahlou's work, part of this extra material surrounds the breast-cancer narrative that Leïla tells, redefining it and creating a discourse that transcends that of the narrator. What is the impact, in the French translation, of the various components of the work? The presence of the Moroccan ruler is certainly provocative. It is almost the verbal equivalent of displaying a picture of the political leader on the wall of one's office (a custom all-too-common in public offices and stores in the Middle East and North Africa). That this ruler should then be quoting a *hadîth* emphasizes his own role as religious leader: his title of *amîr al-mu'minîn* (the commander of the faithful) appended to his words in Leïla Lahlou's book would guarantee him that, in either case. What the *hadîth* also does is to place the royal figure and the breast-cancer victim in the same religious universe, that of Islam. When Leïla Lahlou then begins her words in the interview with a discussion of the Prophet Muhammad and his setting up the first medical facility in Islam, she effectively closes the circle and links herself to the world of Islam to which King Hassan II alluded.

These materials also testify to a visible presence of the Moroccan state in the French book. In the process, Leïla Lahlou herself becomes virtually a national object and monument through her interview with the state media. This entire affirmation of the entity that is Morocco reflects the phenomenon inside the journey itself. There, Leïla's medical existence in Europe is embedded within a discourse on her homeland: its beauty, its existence as a tourist site.[66] This embedding is a testimony to the transnationalism inherent in Leïla Lahlou's text.

The closing of the physical book echoes its opening—but as a contrast. If the book is preceded by religious validations, it is closed by medical documentation. And if the medical documents are linked largely, if not exclusively, to the West, the religion of the opening sections is associated with the Moroccan state.

One would not be doing Genette's observations justice if one did not attend to Leïla Lahlou's book cover. This cover represents a picture of the Ka°ba, crowded with Muslim worshippers, bodies bent in prayer. In the bottom left corner of the cover, and superimposed on the Ka°ba is a cameo, a sort of halo-medallion with Leïla Lahlou in it, the entirety floating over the holy space. But this is where the similarity between the cover of the original Arabic and that of the French translation ends. In the Arabic original, the author is wearing a less modest head covering than in the French translation: part of her hair, in fact, escapes the confines of its white covering. In this less modest portrayal, Lahlou is also wearing white sunglasses that match the color of the clothing. The glasses have a fade, permitting Lahlou's eyes to gaze directly at the reader. An ever so slight hint of makeup is there to add to this reasonably fashionable portrait. In the French translation, which is, of course, chronologically later, Leïla Lahlou dons a more conservative head cover, whose resemblance to the earlier one is only in its color: white. Her glasses this time do not have a fade and do not match the head cover. The pose is infinitely more modest, with Leïla Lahlou's eyes looking downward, away from the reader. The French Lahlou also appears older than her Arabic counterpart (Figures 5 and 6).

فلا تنسئ الله

Figure 5.   Cover of the original Arabic edition of *Falâ Tansa Allâh*.

These visual images are powerful, indeed, perhaps the most powerful
of the extratextual elements, precisely because of their placement as the
first component of the work encountered by the reader. The medical
documentation in the back pales by comparison. Medicine versus religion: religion will win. The visual element reinforces the verbal narrative here. And was not visuality a vital component of the work?

Figure 6.   Cover of *N'oublie pas Dieu*, the French translation of *Falâ Tansa Allâh*.

The two different pictures of Leïla Lahlou superimposed on the mass of Muslim pilgrims tell their own story. It is a story that emphasizes the verbal text that follows and in which the body and religion not only had pivotal roles but were intimately intertwined.

Leïla Lahlou, either with her eyes looking at the reader or with her eyes looking down, reminds the reader that the gaze is a vital component of her journey. As her body becomes the object of the scopic, be it in the medical or the religious environment, it becomes validated as a corporal entity, first diseased, then cured. Various people travel down the path of the diseased body and touch it, including members of her biological family and her spiritual one. Ultimately, however, it will be the Prophet's touch in the oneiric state that will be central, effecting as it does a cure of the dreaded cancer. In the process of this moving corporal odyssey, some body parts, such as the hair, disappear, only to reappear. As the narrator puts it, God gave her this and simply took it away.[67]

As Leïla muses about her lost hair, she notes that this is the test of belief. She was the one who was obsessed with her physical beauty and worried lest she lose one hair. Now, she prides herself on having a bare head, refusing to cover this head with anything.[68] In this obsession with her hair, Leïla comes close to Karîmân, for whom hair was a prized possession.[69] But whereas Karîmân's journey culminates with the covering of this body part, Leïla takes pride in having no covering on her head. This verbal assertion, interestingly enough, runs counter to the visual text that is the exterior of the book, in which Leïla's head is covered, be it in its Arabic or its French manifestation. But perhaps that is the privilege of the diseased body.

The narrator's religious zeal also translates itself into keeping the head bare, in the process going against all the religious injunctions that dictate the concealment of woman's hair. This zeal leads the narrator to muse that, had she lived at the time of the Prophet, she would have been one of the first to follow the religion and would have endured all sorts of punishments to this end.[70] The reader might wonder: is not cancer a punishment?

The illness, in fact, is also subject to mutation by means of the sacred geography that permitted the transformation of the body. Following the ᶜumra, the cancer can become a source of pleasure, a source of jealousy for others: "I found a pleasure and delight that if the patients who were with me in the hospital knew, they would envy me my cancer."[71]

With this, the narrator has redefined the illness as the privileged site of the religious experience, facilitating the final and most triumphant religious intervention, that with the Prophet. Just as with Karîmân, these changes are not arrived at easily.[72] Rather, they represent fundamental shifts in the two women's attitudes to and understanding of religion, shifts that dictate at the same time a redefinition of their previous secular way of life. Leïla speaks of opening the lock of secularism that had governed her intellect.[73] Her secular lifestyle was not too different from that of her Egyptian colleague, Karîmân: singing, beautifying herself, enjoying sports. Like many others, she thought that religion would deprive her of the world. The word here is *dunyâ,* the base world.[74] She ignored the pillars of Islam and knew only the fast, and even that was a fast without prayers.[75]

The spiritual transformation will redefine Leïla's existence. She now asks people around her to replace the tapes of Andalusian music with tapes of the Qur'ân.[76] Andalusian music is not alien to Moroccan culture but, rather, an essential part of it. Leïla's rejection of this music is a rejection of a relatively secularized aspect of her culture. Not only that, but her medical universe will be imbued with religion. Her radiology treatment in Paris after the *ᶜumra* is facilitated by prayer.[77] In its own way, this is not too dissimilar from the spiritual techniques Barbara Stone undertakes when facing treatment for her breast cancer.[78] In Stone's case, even her physician encourages the spiritual as a component of recovery.[79]

For Leïla, the medical itself becomes possible because of religion: she returns to medical treatment following the Prophet's advice.[80] The Moroccan narrator's position is concordant with most Islamic revivalist attitudes to medicine. In a contemporary religious work on medicine, *La Médecine à la lumière du Coran et de la Sunna,* the author, A. Taha, makes it clear that God is "the one who cures, but the physician and medical science represent the means."[81] Leïla would certainly agree with that, at least after she has experienced Muslim spirituality. After all, when medical treatment was initially proposed and she had not yet undergone her religious transformation, she refused that treatment, an un-Islamic attitude indeed.[82] In an interesting case of contemporary revivalist intertextuality, both Taha's programmatic work and Lahlou's first-person narrative exploit the same Qur'ânic verse from the Sûrat al-Shuᶜarâ': "And, whenever I am sick, He heals me."[83] For Leïla, this verse functions almost as a key to the entire work, appearing before her narrative even begins to unfold.

As the reader well knows, the healing came about through the intervention of the holy. It is as if Leïla seizes her ailing body and places it in the hands of religion, albeit allowing medicine to play its own game on the side. Along the way, her body has traveled continents, only to return to its original locus of illness, Morocco, where the religious cure will take effect. These geographic displacements, these journeys are all essential to the narrative that Leïla recounts. The religious pilgrimage is countered with scientific pilgrimages to the West, represented by France and Belgium. These pilgrimages involve travel from a kind of periphery, Morocco, to two different centers: a medical one in Europe and a religious one in Arabia. And yet all the types of geographies encountered—from the corporal through the sacred—were essential for the return to the original homeland.[84] After all, were it not for Paris, Leïla might not have heard the voice that incited her on the spiritual path. And were it not for the ⁽umra, the lumps might not have ceased to exist, or even more importantly, no cure dream might have taken place.

Prior to her spiritual awakening, religion for Leïla was "an invitation to living with the dead." [85] Her journey testifies to the opposite, yet she herself must almost cross into the world of the dead before regaining the world of the living.

All this, alas, was temporary. Leïla Lahlou would die of intestinal cancer in 1991, almost a decade after her miraculous cure. Her husband assured me, when I spoke to him in Morocco in 1996, that despite the pain of her last days, she retained her faith to the end. But while she retained her faith, her husband was injecting her pain-wracked body with morphine.[86] Medicine and religion would continue to be players on the corporal stage of Leïla's body until the actual demise of this female body.

CHAPTER SIX

Sacred Springs, Damaged Bodies

Leïla Lahlou and Karîmân Hamza effected their spiritual trajectories through both geographical displacements and corporal transformations. Whereas Lahlou's breast-cancer journey took her to Europe and to the holy sites of Islam, Hamza's spiritual travels involved displacements both in her home country of Egypt as well as to Mecca. Both Lahlou and Hamza were operating in a Muslim environment, in which they had to find their niche and intensify their religious commitment.

The religious transformation of Sultana Kouhmane, a Belgian-Moroccan Islamist activist, appears at the outset to be completely different. Her work, *L'Islam, la femme, et l'intégrisme: Journal d'une jeune femme européenne,* is written in French and published in Belgium.[1] This autobiographical saga narrated in the first person chronicles the story of a young woman who finds the Muslim path and enjoins others to do the same. Her work, setting itself as it does in a hostile environment, that of the Christian West, also functions as a guide for the Muslim way of life and an aggressive defense of Islam.

But this does not mean that the personal element is lacking. Far from it. Nor does it mean that the work diverges drastically from those of Lahlou and Hamza. Rather, the three spiritual sagas share many components, not the least of which is a fascination, when not an obsession, with the body. Female bodies and male bodies, healthy bodies and maimed bodies: they migrate geographically or metaphorically in this contemporary Francophone narrative. These bodies do not function in isolation but serve as a powerful physical testimony to the power of the Islamic tradition.

Sultana's autobiographical journey crosses religious and geographical borders.[2] Born to a Belgian Christian mother and a Moroccan Muslim father, Sultana grows up experiencing the racism of Belgian society. Her engagement and marriage to M. S. (with a few exceptions, that is how he is referred to in the text) lead her to a fully Muslim lifestyle. Along the way, Sultana will accompany her husband to his village in the Moroccan Middle Atlas, where she performs a pilgrimage to the local saint's tomb. In Brussels, Sultana and M. S. are instrumental in guiding several women on the correct spiritual path. Sultana's saga becomes the forum, as well, for discussions of, among other things, western society, western feminism, and the pitfalls of a secular society.[3] As such, the work testifies to an important gender component in the growing literature of a transnational Islamic revival movement.[4]

On its cover, *L'Islam, la femme, et l'intégrisme* attributes itself to two authors, Cheikh Mohammed Saghir and Kouhmane Sultana (an inversion not unusual in the North African onomastic system—her first name is clearly Sultana because she is addressed as such in a dialogue in the work).[5] Cheikh Mohammed Saghir's presence on the cover of the book complicates the textual issues and adds an element of ambiguity to the attribution of the text.

The work by Kouhmane shares the textual presence of the male gender with the works of Hamza and Lahlou. Suffice it to say that, normally, the male voices are confined to an introduction or an afterword. Their presence is then noted in the extra material but not as coauthors, as in this Belgian pamphlet, which itself features no introduction or epilogue. This certainly is the case with the work by the Moroccan writer, Leïla Lahlou, surrounded as it is by male voices, be they physicians or not, in both the prologues and the epilogues.[6] Then there is the highly unusual intertextual presence of Shaykh ᶜAbd al-Halîm Mahmûd, who repeatedly appears and reappears in Karîmân Hamza's work. There, the first-person narrator almost shares her narrative with selections from the works of her prolific male spiritual guide.[7] But neither Lahlou nor Hamza places the male as coauthor for the works by the women themselves.

What is most disturbing in this attribution of coauthorship to a male voice in the Belgian work is that it contests the first-person female narration in the "journal" itself. Nevertheless, the nature of the internal narrative substantiates its existence as a type of autobiography. The autobiographical pact is altered, but not completely eliminated, in this unusual text.[8]

Despite this ambiguity, however, the internal narrative tells a different story. The text is narrated in the first person. The M. S., who is called Mohammed in some instances (Mohammed Saghir, to be seen below), Sultana's husband, and who makes an appearance in the journey is not a coauthor in any sense of the term. Sultana does include a sort of sermon by Mohammed Saghir on political refugees at the end of the booklet. Directly after these words, she signs her name, "Kouhmane Sultana," thereby ending the narrative.[9]

In addition, the subtitle, *Journal d'une jeune femme européenne*, implies an intimacy created by the presence of this first-person narrator. Sultana repeatedly refers in her text to *"mon journal"* (my diary). This entity is something in which she feels the need to note her thoughts and her words. It also functions as the repository for other documents. As such, it is the place in which she records Mohammed Saghir's speech on political refugees, with which *L'Islam, la femme, et l'intégrisme* ends.[10] Is this journal the work that the reader is holding in his or her hands, or is the journal an altogether different text to which the reader has no access? The subtitle of the book, starting as it does with the word *Journal,* does not clarify the issue. Nor does Sultana the narrator. What is clear, however, is that as the first-person narrator who manipulates and redirects the words of others, including those of Mohammed Saghir, she holds primary narrative responsibility for *L'Islam, la femme, et l'intégrisme.*

In an exercise in literary history, which is not unimportant here, Mohammed Saghir resurfaces as the author of a pamphlet on AIDS, *Vaccin et Traitement Islamiques Anti-SIDA* (Islamic Anti-AIDS Vaccination and Treatment), on which more momentarily.[11] In this manual, he cites Sultana Kouhmane's work. In his literary universe, she becomes the sole author of *L'Islam, la femme, et l'intégrisme,* with himself as the individual who introduces her book.[12]

Of course, the reader of Kouhmane's text knows that there is no one introducing her work. Sultana delves at once into her first-person narrative on the page immediately following the internal cover page. No introduction is present, nor is Mohammed Saghir. The works by Karîmân Hamza and Leïla Lahlou demonstrated the importance of the materials surrounding the first-person journey.[13] In *L'Islam, la femme, et l'intégrisme,* a tension is created between some of this extratextual material and the narrative itself. These materials in Kouhmane's book include the actual book cover and an internal cover, both of which display the two names, Cheikh Mohammed Saghir and Kouhmane Sultana, with the male name preceding the female one.

In fact, as the reader discovers in Sultana Kouhmane's journal, authentication by the male gender is par for the course. Male religious authorities are very significant for Sultana, just as they were for her Egyptian and Moroccan coreligionists, when she embarks on the straight path. The problematic is set on the first page of the story itself.

Sultana begins her journey with the declaration that she had always believed that dreams related to the past and not to the future, until she dreamt the most decisive dream of her life. On a Thursday night, Sultana dreams of a male dressed all in white who approaches her calmly and gently. He has a long conversation with her, which she does not remember completely, and finally tells her that someone will come and transmit Islam's message to her and that this individual will not be a prophet. He enjoins her and her family to receive this individual. In the morning, when Sultana awakens, the words of the man "whom I believed to be the Prophet Mohammad" were still ringing in her ears, "and my lips were mumbling them in the manner of a child memorizing his history lesson." [14] Later in the day, she relates this dream to her parents and to a friend. Sultana retains the impression that she has really met the man.

A week later, Sultana has still not forgotten her dream. The reactions of her friend and parents vary. Her friend, more of a believer than Sultana, tells her that she will perhaps become "a true Muslim" and give birth to a child with a brilliant future, a prediction to reappear below.[15] The father takes the occasion to speak to his daughter of religion and belief. The mother, on the other hand, "Belgian and baptized Catholic," is very surprised to hear her daughter, who was otherwise uninterested in such questions, begin to talk about religious matters. She suggests going to a specialist, an Imam. Sultana is not opposed to the idea but has no desire to go to a mosque. For her, Islam means "integrism, terrorism, a backward movement." [16]

Nevertheless, Sultana and her mother go to the Brussels mosque to meet the Imam. He greets them in Arabic: *Assalamou Alaykome* (Peace Be Upon You), followed by a *Bismillahi Rahmani Rahimi* (In the Name of God, the Merciful, the Compassionate). (The two renditions into the Roman alphabet are the narrator's.)[17] The latter phrase surprises the two women, and the Imam proceeds to translate it for them. A conversation ensues between the male authority and the two females about religion. The Imam closes the episode with a discussion of the dream. First, he repeats to Sultana the Prophet's words in the *hadîth* that the individual who has seen the Prophet in a dream has truly seen him. Then the religious authority interprets the dream to the young woman: the Prophet has never lied. He only enjoins the good, so she should follow his orders. If he has promised her something, she should await it and not lose hope. The interview ends at this point with the Imam providing mother and daughter with written material on Islam, including a translation of the Qur'ân.[18]

What an auspicious beginning on the path to religious salvation! The incident starts with a seemingly simple oneiric experience and leads to the transmission of the popular *hadîth,* already familiar from Karîmân's and Leïla's texts. The appearance of the white-clad man whom the dreamer interprets as the Prophet is not insignificant. First, as the reader knows well, the appearance of the Prophet in a dream is possibly the most important sign for any dreamer, and in this case for the female dreamer in Belgium.[19] She is now a player in the complex world of Arabo-Islamic oneirocritics, just like her two geographically distant female colleagues, Leïla and Karîmân.[20]

There is a difference, however, between the three oneiric experiences. As literary and cultural critics know, the placement of an event in a narrative is of prime semiotic importance. Textual neighbors define and recast an event, endowing it with variant meanings. This is no different with dreams, which are, after all, privileged events in these spiritual journeys.[21] With Karîmân, the initial call was mediated not through a real oneiric experience but rather through a state from which she awakens. Her dreams occur later in her journey, after her spiritual quest has been set in motion, and help define her as part of Shaykh ᶜAbd al-Halîm Mahmûd's spiritual family.[22] For Leïla, the cure dream with the Prophet represents the culmination of a narrative concerned with breast cancer and a body in pain.[23] In Sultana's case, the dream is the first element the reader encounters. And this is not just any dream, but one with the Prophet. The dream opens Sultana's journey—both the spiritual journey and the textual journey that allows the reader to share the spiritual journey with the female hero. The dream continues to haunt the dreamer, and she repeats its message.

There are layers of significance to this oneiric arrangement. First and foremost, this opening incident in the saga immediately sets the religious context for what is to follow: the context is Islam without the shadow of a doubt. This is all the more important since the story unfolding before the reader is one that takes place in an alien environment, the Christian West. The linguistic factor is critical here as well: Sultana is Francophone and her cultural and linguistic background is far removed from the Arabophone and Muslim settings of Karîmân, on the one hand, and of Leïla, on the other. The appearance of the Prophet will neutralize all that and provide the female Belgian narrator with as much credence as her literary cousins from Egypt and Morocco.

The oneiric experience in Sultana Kouhmane's text signals a call to the religious path. This is not too dissimilar from the example of Karîmân, whose call comes from the venerable Shaykh ᶜAbd al-Halîm Mahmûd. Although Karîmân does not inform her reader specifically about her sleeping state, nevertheless she carefully indicates that she awakens after the call has been set in motion.[24] For Sultana, as with Karîmân, the call arrives through both visual and oral/aural means. Sultana sees the male figure and is able to interpret his appearance. She also signals the pivotal role that this event will play in her life. As she herself notes, she had always believed that dreams related to the past and not to the future, until this particular dream. Her future is then what is at stake, and the reader knows that this future will be immersed in Islam. If nothing else, the title of the book will have already indicated that. More importantly, the appearance of the male in the dream is augmented by an oneiric verbal injunction.

Like her literary cousin, Karîmân, Sultana repeats the message she hears. In her case, she has been reduced to a child memorizing a lesson, a transformation that denotes a type of rebirth, since it is as an adult that she will continue on her spiritual journey. Immediately after the meeting with the Imam, she speaks of her fiancé.[25] This is no child. But in reality her being turned into a child will facilitate the subsequent visit to the Imam. He will furnish her with what she is looking for: a "valid" (her term) interpretation of her dream.[26] Of course, this "valid" interpretation, which can only be had from the male religious authority, will be provided despite the fact that Sultana herself has already deciphered her oneiric experience. Her transformation into a child means that the Imam can more easily fulfill the role of spiritual leader and interpreter of the religious tradition. His valid explanation actually only confirms Sultana's interpretation. Had she not, after all, believed upon awakening that the man she had seen in her dream was the Prophet Mohammad?[27]

The image that the female dreamer uses as she is repeating the Prophet's words is that of a history lesson: Sultana must learn history, a task she will accomplish on her spiritual voyage. The final certification of the dream's meaning will not come about until the oneiric vision is officially linked to the tradition itself by a male religious authority, the Imam of the Brussels mosque.

This Imam stands out as the reader meets him. First, there is his linguistic register. The opening words he utters in Sultana's French text are basic greetings in Arabic. These words are alien to the two females, and the Imam translates them. True, Sultana is Francophone and this interlude makes the reader aware that her knowledge of Arabic must be virtually nonexistent. But more is at play here. The Imam's greeting is also a referent to a religious and cultural universe unfamiliar to the Belgian mother and her daughter. The situation is not dissimilar to that of Karîmân when she first heard Shaykh Mahmûd's phone greeting.[28] And then, of course, there was no difference in language, since Shaykh Mahmûd and Karîmân were addressing one another in Arabic.

In Sultana's example, the changing of linguistic fields is prevalent. The Arabic language places the Belgian male religious authority in a special universe. Not only is he then privy to a supplementary knowledge base, but it is this special linguistic base, the Arabic one, that permits him to link Sultana through the *hadîth* directly to the textual world of the Prophet, which is, after all, an Arabic one.

When the Imam relates to the young woman and her mother the words of the Prophet that he who has seen him in a dream has truly seen him, he does not identify the text by its technical name of *hadîth*. He simply tells them that these are the words of the Prophet. Later in her journal, as Sultana becomes more confident in her Islamic knowledge, she will begin using this Islamic terminology.[29]

The popularity of this *hadîth* was already apparent in the analyses of the accounts by Karîmân and Leïla. Striking here is its presence in a western, non-Arabic context. Once again, the Mamlûk polymath al-Safadî can clarify the issue. In his *al-Ghayth al-Musajjam,* he relates the following: a learned man was asked about the saying of the Prophet that when he is seen in a dream, he is truly seen, and how this could be, since the Prophet was seen in the same hour by many different people in many different places. The answer was given that Muhammad was like the sun, whose light covers many countries, East and West.[30]

The problem disturbing the medieval dreamer does not faze the contemporary Belgian female or her equally contemporary Imam. The two of them take it for granted that the man who appears to the young woman in a dream is the Prophet. The time-traveling and geography-hopping questions do not pose problems for them. But the well-educated reader of Sultana's journal may be familiar with the explanation provided by al-Safadî. East and West can easily come together through the oneiric experience with the Prophet.

The visit to the Imam provides an important textual closure to the dream incident with which the journal began. Sultana sees the Prophet in a dream and upon awaking "has the impression" that she has really met the man and that this was not a dream. But this impression does not become certainty until she has encountered the Imam. Only he, as the male religious authority with in-depth knowledge of the Arabo-Islamic tradition, is able to effect this transformation from impression to reality. In a sense, the Prophet, by becoming a reality, has also been transformed from a mere vision to a solid corporal entity through the male Imam.

Sultana's nightly vision and ensuing discussion with the Imam center on an aspect that was equally critical for Karîmân and Leïla: the visual. Not only does Sultana provide a physical description of the man in her dreams, but she then questions the Imam about seeing God.

I [*that is Sultana*]:   If God exists why doesn't one see him?

THE IMAM: Many things exist without the human eye being able to see them. . . . It is not that God does not exist, it is the human being who is incapable of seeing Him. God is too luminous to be seen by eyes and minds blinded by matter and limited in time and space.[31]

The religious leader in this extended conversation with Sultana and her mother delves into the importance of the visual, sealing his words with comments on the visual importance of seeing the Prophet in a dream and the truthful value of what the holy figure has transmitted to the young Belgian woman.

The male as purveyor of the Islamic religious tradition is not a phenomenon unique to the Belgian author. He was consistently present with both the Egyptian Karîmân Hamza and the Moroccan Leïla Lahlou. Interestingly enough, however, this phenomenon transcends writings by religiously minded female authors. It is also exploited by the anticlerical feminist physician-writer Nawal El Saadawi. The Egyptian El Saadawi is, of course, on the opposite side of the religious and cultural divide in the Middle East from that of the religiously minded women here. Yet, in some of her most recent fiction, she pits her female heroes against male upholders of the centuries-old Arabo-Islamic tradition, the *turâth*. This she does most eloquently in two of her latest novels, *Suqût al-Imâm* (translated as *The Fall of the Imam*) and *Jannât wa-Iblîs* (translated as *The Innocence of the Devil*).[32] These Saadawian female heroes emanating from the pen of a secularized feminist, unlike the narrators of the spiritual sagas, however, are not saved. Their ignorance of the Arabo-Islamic textual tradition spells their doom.[33]

To return to the Francophone journal: The Imam is the first real male religious authority (excluding the nocturnal vision) to make an appearance in Sultana's textual world. Soon, however, M. S., the young woman's fiancé and future husband, will enter the stage. He acts as Sultana's teacher and eventual guide on her journey. Like the Imam, M. S. appears at the outset to be particularly learned in the Islamic tradition, and this despite the fact that his linguistic presence remains Francophone, except for some stock phrases.

M. S. relates to Sultana the following anecdote. One of his Belgian friends, Pierre, an atheist though baptized a Christian, called him to continue a dialogue they were having on religion and the evolution of modern society. The first meeting had brought together individuals from different religious traditions. Expressing his intent to attend a second meeting, M. S. said, "I will be there *in cha Allah*." Pierre, for whom M. S. had already translated the Arabic expression as "if God wills it,"[34] said he would certainly be there, since his car was new and he himself was in excellent health. M. S.'s response: "Oh yes? I answered, repeating *in cha Allah—in cha Allah*."[35] During the week, however, Pierre had a car accident that damaged his vehicle and confined him to bed. He telephoned M. S. from the hospital. In the conversation with Sultana's husband that follows, Pierre ends all his phrases with *in cha Allah*. M. S. asks that his friend not make fun of him but then is told about the accident. The two conclude their dialogue with a profusion of *in cha Allah*s. The anecdote completed, M. S. proceeds to explain to Sultana that one's words will count with God sooner or later, and that everything is registered with the Deity. Pierre's accident, M. S. continues, was not a coincidence.[36]

This anecdote occupies the bulk of a chapter in Sultana's journal on "Chance and Providence."[37] Its telling by both M. S. and Sultana (she is, after all, the narrator of the text) is devoid of humor. Yet any reader with a superficial knowledge of the Islamic tradition (be it Arabo-Islamic, Perso-Islamic, or Turko-Islamic) will recognize the story immediately. It is none other than an extremely popular anecdote in which Juhâ, the wise fool, on his way to market, is asked where he is going, to which he replies that he is going to the market to sell his donkey. He is admonished to use the phrase "God willing" (*In Shâ'a Allâh*), but he shrugs it off. On the way to the market, he is accosted by robbers who steal his donkey. The next time he sets out to the market, he is once again asked where he is going. This time, he liberally sprinkles "God willing" after his every word.[38]

Turning the wise fool of the Islamic tradition into a modern-day western atheist is telling. The intertextuality inherent in this exercise alters the humor of the original anecdote. M. S.'s account of Pierre and the ubiquitous phrase foregrounds the theological aspect of the Juhâ anecdote. Both Juhâ and Pierre must encounter mishaps to be convinced that they should use the appropriate formula. In Juhâ's case, the use of the "God willing" is not a cultural and linguistic anomaly. Pierre, on the other hand, is a western atheist. His use of the phrase testifies to a change of attitude to God's will, as well as to a linguistic borrowing.

And this is where the observation about Pierre's being baptized a Christian comes into play. His misadventure, coupled with the religious attitude of Sultana's husband, seems to call attention to the superficiality of his atheism. One car accident and a little sermon from M. S. alter his attitude to divine providence.

The indirect comparison between Juhâ and Pierre is even more telling on the corporal level. Both the medieval wise fool and the twentieth-century atheist encounter mishaps that affect their means of transportation: in the case of Juhâ, his donkey, and in the case of Pierre, his vehicle. The anecdote leaves Juhâ's body out of harm's way: no sooner does he escape unscathed than he is on his way again to the market, having learned the spiritual part of his lesson. Pierre is not so fortunate. His misadventure leads to his being injured and confined to a hospital. His lesson in God's will comes about through an attack on his corporality. Spirituality and corporality are intimately linked in this contemporary universe. Spirituality necessitates a corporal transformation not unlike that observed in the case of Leïla, whose breast cancer in her body brought about salvation in her soul.[39]

The incident with Pierre reminds the reader, if he or she had forgotten it, that Sultana's spiritual journey is accomplished in an alien territory, that of the Christian West. The Morocco that is the land of Sultana's father is geographically present, but its appearance is carefully and strategically dosed. It is the country to which Sultana travels on her honeymoon, an incident that has critical ramifications for the narrator's spiritual journey, bringing together as it does geographical, corporal, and spiritual issues.

"It is my honeymoon trip and I am happy. We are, my husband and I, in the heart of the Middle Atlas." Thus does one of the central chapters in Sultana's journal begin. Sultana continues. Their stay has been organized in such a way that they can benefit from being in the middle of nature: the mountains, the forests, the water. Daily activities include mountain climbing, walks in the fields, reading, or generally talking alongside the great spring in the area. M. S. tells his wife that there are numerous springs inside and outside the village that help irrigate the fields.

Once this quick introduction concludes, Sultana declares:

> Finally, I realized myself what some Muslim sisters had told me in Europe: "Islam does not prevent its followers from fully and properly taking advantage of their life or the beauty of nature, or from tasting the pleasures of love and the brightening up of the body—as long as this stays within the frame of God's laws, outside of which pleasure often degenerates into delirium, honey into poison, freedom into a degrading servitude.["][40]

"Today," (Sultana's term, on which more later) M. S.; his niece, Aziza; and Sultana wake up early and head for Sidi Slimane, the mausoleum of the countryside. M. S. is a descendant of this marabout, but he often says "in Islam one is not obliged to be of noble birth to be noble of heart."[41] Arriving in the sanctuary, the narrator realizes that she is not tired but that she is perspiring and immediately wants to take a shower.

> As though he had read my thoughts, M. S. showed me with his finger something that was shining like a mirage under a tree. It is the spring of Sidi Slimane, which pours its limpid and cold water in a sort of little natural and wild swimming pool.
>
> Hidden by my own clothes stretched out by Aziza, I let myself go to the immaculate caresses of the blessed water of the spring. Washing my head and torso, I whisper the intention of purifying myself of all my sins that I committed when I was a slave of modern obscurantism and of the illusions of western feminism.
>
> A few meters from us, M. S. stands guard, assuring us from time to time that we are safe from all gazes, except perhaps those of the birds hanging on the branches that surround us and those of the angels, witnesses and protectors to whom God had entrusted us.
>
> The fact that my husband, whom I qualified one day as an integrist, permitted me to bathe myself in the wild, to make myself beautiful, forced me to question my preconceived ideas on the position that woman occupies in Islam.[42]

Islam, the reader learns, not only respects woman but assigns her the role of watching over life, peace, and love. Forcing a daughter to wed a man she does not love is a tribal custom and not an Islamic tradition. Woman represents half the human race: she is the mother of a man, his sister, his wife. Islam's injunctions to a woman that she cover "the charms of her body" are not there to denigrate woman but to protect her. "By protecting the modesty of woman, it is the unity of the family that one protects, it is the moral and spiritual future of children that one guarantees, it is the society in its entirety that one builds on solid foundations." [43]

Sultana explains that like the man, the Muslim woman has the right to live her life to the full, to learn, to express her opinion, to choose her mate, to pray, and to elevate herself to the highest level of spirituality. "The deadly fault committed by feminists is to have pushed woman to compete with man, to walk in lock-step with him in all the domains of life, to run after the mirage of equality on the altar of which she continually sacrifices her right to femininity and motherhood.

"It is not competition that must be there between the two sexes, it is complementarity." [44]

The comparison between the position of women in Islam and women in the West continues in Sultana's text. In Islam, woman is the axis around which gravitate the elements of a family; in the West, the family has lost that axis. In Islam, woman is a treasure jealously defended by the whole family. In the West, she is often reduced to a cheap piece of merchandise, manipulated by advertisements. The reader further learns from Sultana that there is no third sex in Islam.[45] Just as a man has no right to feminize himself, the woman does not have the right to masculinize herself. "In Islam, the woman has the right to swim, to bathe herself, but she does not have the right to bathe the community in sin and debauchery." [46]

Sultana here repeats that woman has the right to learn, to study, and to work in such a way that this contributes to the edification of society and not to the destruction of the family.

> How many men have forgotten their wife, their children, because of a naked leg that they met in a coed swimming pool?
> How many young women who had uncovered themselves in front of their father then found themselves involved in incestuous relationships with him? . . .[47]
> Some say that uncovering one's body does not lead necessarily to sin and debauchery. Possible. But one forgets that the world is not populated only by normal individuals. . . .
> To safeguard woman, Islam immunizes her with faith, vaccinates her against the false appetites of the flesh, and covers her with decent clothing that inspires respect and discourages devils.

> Through the institution of the veil, of clothing appropriate for woman, Islam seeks to prevent ill so as not to have to seek to cure it afterward.
>   Before converting myself completely to Islam, I thought that the religion was at the origin of the miserable conditions in which some Muslim women still live, until M. S. called my attention to the two following facts.[48]

The facts that M. S. tells Sultana will lead to the conclusion of the chapter. If the West could only progress after distancing itself from the Church, the opposite is true of Islam: when Muslims were attached to their religion, they were the masters of the world; when they distanced themselves from it, they lost control over themselves. Islam, as opposed to Europe, gave women the right to sign contracts and to manage their own affairs. The example here is that of Khadîja, the wife of the Prophet. Islam is against degradation, the depravation of morals, and the massacre of nature and humankind.[49]

This interlude in Morocco is rife with issues that form the backbone of Sultana's work: geography, the body, the holy, gender, Islam, and of course, the West. It is not that some of these major concerns only surface with this incident. It is, rather, that this will be the first occasion that Sultana takes to present her ideas at length.

The chapter bridging this range of topics is entitled "Woman and Freedom." And as with other chapters in the work, Sultana teaches her reader the lessons he or she needs through an example or a personal experience. In this case, it is her own trip to North Africa. This voyage to the Middle Atlas in Morocco represents Sultana's major geographical displacement, and it is, in the journal, the first and last time that she leaves her native Belgium. How interesting it should be then that this voyage spans both corporal and spiritual issues.[50] As the reader meets Sultana in this chapter, she is already in Morocco on her honeymoon. The reader knows by now that the happy couple had their wedding in the springtime. However, the actual wedding is not described, nor is the journey to North Africa.

It is the heterosexual couple that takes precedence here, in a triumphal declaration by the narrator that "It is my honeymoon and I am happy."[51] This happiness follows a period in which the narrator is extremely nervous and unhappy, due in no small part to the fact that she and her fiancé, despite the fact that they love one another, "have two different mentalities." He is an intellectual and an idealistic, practicing Muslim. She accused him of being retrograde and an integrist. He reproached her with the facts that "I smoked, and spoke to the men who visited my father." She, on the other hand, is naive, sentimental, spoiled, and used to the ease of life.[52]

Clearly, by the time the couple is in Morocco, these differences are resolved and Sultana is happy. Like her literary coreligionist, Karîmân, she
indulged in smoking, a habit that both must clearly break on their new-
found religious path.[53] Her discussion of women and their roles in the
context of the North African experience also suggests that her social interactions with men, the subject of M. S.'s disapproval, have also been
transformed.

The event in Morocco that involves the body purified has an immediacy for the narrator that is evident in her discussion of time. "Today"
is when the event takes place. Does this mean that the narrator recorded
her recollections in her journal on the same day that they occurred? It is
possible, but the reader is given no such indication. What is noteworthy
is the constant shift in Sultana's narration between the present tense and
the past tenses (be it the imperfect or the simple past). The event may
have been recorded on the day it transpired, but its narration shifts from
its existence in the past to its immediacy in the present. Complicating
the temporal dynamics is the insertion at strategic points in the narration of the event in the Middle Atlas of materials on Islam and women
(such as the words of Sultana's Muslim sisters in Europe) or on the
power of the Deity. The subject of "Woman and Freedom" is clearly a
momentous one.

This voyage in Morocco functions like a pilgrimage of sorts for Sultana. She becomes a participant in M. S.'s family history as she learns
about his being a descendant of the local saint. Even more important,
she partakes of the purification process at the spring with a female family member and not simply the husband. The niece, Aziza, is the one who
provides the first level of protection, as she holds the stretched clothing
meant to hide Sultana. The husband stands guard a few meters away.
His gaze is clearly averted from the female body, as the homosocial unit
of the two women takes primacy in this event. Only the birds and the
"angels" can see Sultana's naked body.

The vocabulary Sultana uses for this act is interesting indeed, smack-
ing as it does at once of the sensual and the corporal. The water caresses
the narrator's body as she lets herself go. But no sooner does the narrator express this sensuality and corporality than she moves immediately
into the domain of spirituality. Still in the water, she washes her head
and her torso, a bodily act that is immediately linked to her purification
from her sins as a "slave of modern obscurantism and of the illusions of
Western feminism." The echo of Christian baptism here needs no com-

mentary, signaling as it does once again the importance of the West in Sultana's journal.[54]

The geographical location of this event in Morocco is crucial in defining it as a pilgrimage of sorts. It is the first place in the work that Sultana speaks of a total conversion to Islam.[55] And like the narratives of spiritual transformation by Karîmân Hamza and Leïla Lahlou, that of Sultana Kouhmane also needs a journey to a holy place. For Karîmân, who is geographically closest of the three women to the holy places of Islam, this represents a pilgrimage to Mecca. For Leïla, coming as she does from North Africa, the journey to the holy sites represents a *ᶜumra*, or little pilgrimage to Mecca. Sultana, who is half-Belgian, is culturally the farthest from the Muslim holy places. Her pilgrimage is instead accomplished by a journey to a saint's tomb in Morocco. What is critical is the actual displacement itself, a move away from one's home country to a geographical site that can function as the "other" and in which one can experience the holy.[56]

Equally profound here is the issue of water. The Moroccan breast-cancer victim, Leïla, spent her days in Mecca on a restricted diet but drinking copiously from the holy water of Zamzam, a liquid she then shares with her husband in the hotel room. The purificatory rite for her involves the holy liquid coursing through her body and bringing an end to her physical lumps.[57] For Sultana, the water is equally important: she even calls it *l'eau bénite de la source* (the holy/blessed water of the spring).[58] But, in her case, the water is not ingested. It washes over her body, purifying her of the sins of modernity and feminism. And *l'eau bénite* is the term used for the water in a baptismal font.

The movement from corporality to spirituality is a constant in this incident. Woman's body and its uses and abuses become the link between secular and religious lifestyles. The imagery the narrator exploits to express societal problems and solutions is not only corporal but attached indissolubly to the female: "In Islam, the woman has the right to swim, to bathe herself, but she does not have the right to bathe the community in sin and debauchery."[59] Sultana, who has just immersed herself in the holy water of the spring can then take her action, generalize it, and move it from the domain of the body to that of society. Swimming and bathing can now eloquently refer to the act of bathing the entire community in "sin and debauchery." How interesting it then becomes to remember that the Moroccan Leïla goes from the act of swimming in public to the bath in her home where she will discover the abnormality in her breast.[60]

Although Leïla the narrator makes no moral linkage between the baring of her body and the disease in her breast, Sultana contrasts the debauchery of the public pool with the purification of the holy spring. The swimming female body, like the puffing body in Karîmân's spiritual journey, lurks behind these moralistic discourses. "How many men have forgotten their wife, their children, because of a naked leg that they met in a coed swimming pool?" wonders Sultana.[61] What a fascinating construction! The men are led into forgetting their family by a naked leg met in a coed swimming pool. To add to the moral horror of the incident, the family is not mentioned as a unit, but its members, a wife and a plurality of children, are listed clearly. The naked leg (in French, *une jambe nue*) stands separate from the body to which it is attached and becomes the physical part that leads the men to perdition. The men meet this leg, expressed in the French with the verb one uses normally to meet people (*qu'ils ont rencontrée*). The leg obviously is the appendage that stands for the entirety of woman's body and its power when it is naked.

Interestingly enough, if one were merely to follow the logic of the French language, it would be equally easy to read the naked leg as a male leg and not as a female one. In that case, the seduction would go beyond the woman herself to include any human body. Obviously, however, Sultana wants her reader to assume it is the female body that is the problem here and not simply any body; otherwise, would she have necessarily spoken of "a coed swimming pool"? The swimming female body will come to the surface again below.[62]

This potential sexual ambiguity is something that the text ventures into just prior to the possible dangers of the seduction. The narrator states that "there is no third sex in Islam." Any act of denaturation is an abomination. Just as a man does not have the right to feminize himself, a woman does not have the right to masculinize herself.[63] These comments, which at first glance are not terribly explicit, in fact allude to what amounts to a gender crossing of sorts. They would be familiar to the reader as a recasting of the Prophetic injunction that shuns the crossing of gender boundaries. Sultana does not indicate her sources here. One of the most famous Prophetic *hadîth*s states that the Prophet cursed the men who resembled women and the women who resembled men.[64] Even without direct attribution, this discussion brings the narrator fully into the contemporary Muslim debates on men and women and the proper bounds between them. This debate also touches on issues of crossdressing. Marjorie Garber has eloquently elaborated the discourses of transvestism and cross-dressing in the West, at the same time demonstrating their cultural power.[65] There are, of course, many examples of transvestism on the part of both genders, predominantly from the medieval period of Arabo-Islamic civilization. And all this despite the fact that the Prophet Muhammad himself admonished against this practice. Today, the issue is alive and well not only in secular texts but in contemporary religious discourses as well.[66] Sultana's adducing this is not so unusual in a work in which she is seeking to lead women (and men) on the proper religious path.

But it is not simply an uncovered female body in a swimming pool that can be the source of a potential disaster in a nuclear family. "How many young women who had uncovered themselves in front of their father then found themselves involved in an incestuous relationship with him?"[67] In this instance, social control is in the hands of women. After all, it is the women who are not covered in front of their fathers who run the risk of incest. The message here is the same as that with swimming: covering the female body is essential for the well-being of family and society.

All this Sultana explains as she is herself swimming and baring her body in a spring in Morocco. In her case, however, she is protected from the public gaze by two gatekeepers: the female relative, Aziza, and the husband, M. S. She sets the example here: Islam does not forbid women to enjoy these corporal pleasures, but these pleasures must be had in a protected and controlled environment.

The medical imagery associated with women's role in Islam is powerful indeed. The corporality that is inherent in any medical project, and hence in medical imagery, surfaces here. Islam "immunizes" and "vaccinates" woman against the false appetites of the flesh.[68] As Sultana makes extremely clear, religion and corporality are a powerful duo, here as elsewhere in the journal.

For Sultana, the subject of women in Islam is intimately tied to that of women in the West and from there to that of western feminism. Throughout her journey, she points to the pitfalls of the secular lifestyle and the noxious effects of western feminism. The purificatory rite in Morocco, performed on her honeymoon, functions almost as a corporal denunciation of the western way of life, in which, as Sultana puts it, woman is reduced to cheap merchandise.[69] The objectification of woman in the West is precisely what Sultana wishes to counter with her own sanctioned display of her body in the Moroccan spring, a display seen only by the birds and the angels.

Oddly enough, birds and supranatural beings are precisely what one encounters when one ventures to the site of Sultana's pilgrimage. I decided to investigate the site myself on a visit to Morocco in 1996. The spring, with its attendant saint's tomb, is a fascinating place.[70] Sidi Slimane is located in the heart of the Middle Atlas. When I attempted to get more geographical precision about the "Ben Tatou Mountain," to which Sultana refers in her description of the site, I got absolutely nowhere. Even specialists in Moroccan geography at Moulay Ismaïl University in Meknes insisted that no such mountain existed. Perhaps an attempt at geographical precision is vain here, since autobiography, like all literary texts, is a construction, and as I have shown elsewhere, the narrator of an autobiography is under no obligation to present the truth, whatever that may be.[71]

But what makes the site so interesting is its spiritual heterosexuality. As one wanders up a hill toward the sanctuary of Sidi Slimane, one crosses beautiful Moroccan countryside. A river flows below the sanctuary, and cats dot the walkway to the famous tomb. But Sidi Slimane's tomb is not alone here: next to his mausoleum lies the tomb of the female Lalla (Saint) ᶜA'isha al-Sudâniyya.[72] According to local lore, she liked to stay in caves by the water and was a female spirit. Sidi Slimane himself supposedly controlled birds and jinn. The entire location in which this male-female saintly couple operates functions as a pilgrimage site for the area. Lalla ᶜA'isha may come out at night and is said to visit individuals who choose to spend the night at the site. I was told that this was not her grave but simply her "place." Historically, she is said to have been a contemporary of Sidi Slimane. The spring emanates from the second cave, where Sidi Slimane himself lived.

But the spring today is a complicated structure. The river flooded in the early 1960s and the area was built up. There are currently two swimming pools, one for males and one for females. Caretakers keep the location clean. The water in the pools that flows from the Middle Atlas mountains is limpid and cold. The curator of the site is Ahmad ibn al-Belriti. His son, Abdel Aziz al-Belriti (that is how his name is written on his national identity card) was my guide on this extraordinary visit. When I asked him about the tree, he pointed out to me a thick fig tree, which he said had been there long before the two swimming pools were built.

Moroccan friends who have grown up and lived in the area confirmed all that the official guide had told me. Amina Bouchakor explained that her grandmother used to take her to the site as a child and she swam there. Around 1966, the swimming pool was built. Abdallah Malki also swam there around the same time. Amina added that many still believe that Lalla ᶜA'isha comes out at night.

The legendary pair of Lalla ᶜA'isha and Sidi Slimane is a heterosexual couple whose presence in the site mirrors that of the contemporary heterosexual couple, Sultana and her husband, who visit the site on their honeymoon. A woman friend, still single, laughingly confided to me that she had been sent to the shrine to pray for a husband. Though she went to pray, she did not marry. Sidi Slimane's control over birds and jinn is not insignificant here. His namesake, the Prophet Solomon (Slimane is the North African pronunciation of Sulaymân, Solomon) is also credited with control over these two groups of creatures.[73] That it should be the bird and the "angels" who watch Sultana bathe her body then takes on that much more importance. Angels would seem to stand in for the jinn, controlled by Sidi Slimane in this most important geographical locale for the Muslim visitor from Belgium.[74]

Though numerous elements of this complex site do, thus, surface in Sultana's account, one has been completely suppressed: the presence of the female sacred. In context, this is stronger than Karîmân's occultation of famous female Sufi saints, like Râbiᶜa.

More importantly, the North African locus serves as the land in which Muslim values and customs are honored. Sultana explains one of the possible Muslim lifestyles, that involving polygamy. The reader learns about this in a chapter titled "Pourquoi la polygamie?" (Why Polygamy?). Sultana is by now, as she herself declares at the beginning of the chapter, a sincere believer who cannot ignore the Qur'ânic laws, which she did not accept only to comply with those that interested her. It is not normal for her anymore, she continues, that a Muslim would fast during the month of Ramadân without performing the five daily prayers or that one would perform the pilgrimage while continuing to "drink and fornicate." Islam is not only a religion and rituals, she informs her reader, it is a global and coherent lifestyle. But she had been naive and a victim of anti-Islamic propaganda. She could not understand why Islam, a fair and just religion, had instituted polygamy, until she heard the following story.[75]

Ali, a friend of Sultana's husband, is twenty-five years old and works in Rabat. His wife, Khadija, is very beautiful and very pious. They are happy despite the terrible accident that left Khadija half paralyzed. Ali was faithful to his wife until one day Sultana overheard him complaining to her own husband of his sexual frustrations. "A young man in good health is too weak to resist temptation." She continues that if her husband were an atheist or a secularist, he would have advised his friend to take on one or two mistresses while keeping his wife, or even to separate himself from her to choose a healthy wife, or even to divorce her and no longer think about marriage. A life of sexual irresponsibility would be more in keeping with what modern civilization is attempting to institute while feeding people "with wine and drugs." Instead, Sultana's husband tells Ali to control "the call of the flesh" by fasting from time to time and to tell nothing to Khadija, who would herself come to understand that a man "does not merely need tenderness and affection." Three months later, Khadija suggests to her husband that he look for a second wife, who could give him the healthy pleasures "and legitimate children," to which he had a right. Fidelity, goodness, and chastity win out over temptation and egoism, the narrator of the work continues. Now Sultana understands why Islam instituted the "law of polygamy" without forcing everyone to submit to it. She sees the virtues of this system and concludes that it is far from being one that despises woman and turns her into an object of pleasure or simply a breeder of illegitimate children. Now she also understands why prophets were polygamous and why their wives were happy. Woman's role in this area, she concludes, is central.[76]

The first-person female narrator of this journal seems much more comfortable teaching her lessons to the reader through anecdotal examples. The incident with Ali and Khadija, like that with Pierre, is a case in point; however, the episode with Pierre was presented by Sultana's husband, whereas that of the married couple is restricted to Sultana's narration. This is not a textual coincidence: the topic is an intimate one and perhaps the lesson, aimed at the female gender, is better handled through direct narration by Sultana. It is also quite possible that M. S. might not have discussed this issue with his wife. Does she not, after all, learn of Ali's sexual frustrations by overhearing him speaking to her husband about them? This type of narration is not unique in the journal: the account of a woman afflicted with AIDS whom Sultana guides on the right path is also related without male narrative intervention.[77]

But the subject of polygamy is not just more intimate than that of divine providence (the example with Pierre). Polygamy is also highly problematic. Sultana herself recognizes this at the beginning of the chapter. As a sincere believer, she declares that this is an area that she must not occult in her religion. Anti-Islamic propaganda notwithstanding, she believes she must also justify this practice to her reader. What better way to do this than through an example?

And what an example are Ali and Khadija! First, they are two of the very few characters in the journal who possess actual names, rather than simply initials (Z. is the friend to whom Sultana relates the dream, M. S.

is the husband). The attribution of names is highly significant in a text in which most characters receive their onomastic identity through initials. Attaching names to the members of this heterosexual couple endows each of them with a more solid identity, transforming them into real individuals in the narrative. This attribution of personhood, to use Phyllis Trible's term, is crucial for the illustration of the extremely sensitive topic that is polygamy.[78]

Three months after the overheard conversation and M. S.'s advice to Ali to fast, Khadija counsels Ali to take a second wife. Did Ali follow M. S.'s advice not to speak to Khadija of his sexual needs? The reader assumes this is the case and that Khadija, being the pious wife she is, is simply following the Islamic precept that allows men to have more than one wife.

Certainly, the case seems to be important for allowing Sultana to understand the importance of polygamy in Islam. By writing about this incident, however, she has done more than explain her own process of coming to grips with this thorny area. She has also inserted herself into one of the liveliest areas of discussion in Islamic revivalist discourse today. Pamphlets and books extol the virtues of the multiplicity of wives (ta'ad-dud al-zawjât). Religious pamphlets on this important topic abound in the specialized bookstores all over the Arab world, North Africa, as well as in European capitals with significant Muslim populations. Some of the booklets are even distributed free in the streets of Fez today (except to the unsuspecting individual who will pay for them).[79]

The geographical placement of this anecdote is also crucial. The narrator is careful to tell the reader that Ali "works in Rabat." Is the reader to understand that the couple lives in Morocco? Most likely. Obviously, this would simplify matters enormously. Polygamy would be much easier to maintain in North Africa than in Europe. This in turn would transform Morocco into the locus where it is possible to live fully according to Islamic precepts. Sultana is not off the mark here. In Morocco today, polygamy provides the setting for lively debate. A recent conference in Rabat on the subject of polygamy brought together religious authorities and academic specialists to discuss this practice, which is not illegal in that North African country.[80]

But more is at stake here than simply the question of a multiplicity of wives. An intricate game of sexual politics is being played out in the entirety of the chapter. The story of Ali and Khadija is embedded within extra-anecdotal material. The opening section preceding the dramatic story is a global defense of Islam as a way of life, in which polygamy is but one element. The closing section following the anecdote is directed to the status of women in Islam and a general justification of polygamy. The opening section, in its absence of specificity, stands as a mere *entrée-en-matière* for the anecdote. The material following the story of Ali and Khadija is much more striking. Polygamy, the reader learns, is essential. If Islam had not foreseen it, "male believers would have found themselves in an impasse, especially after a war that would have spared the women or in a society in which the number of men is inferior to that of women, or still in serious cases like that of Khadija and Ali." [81] More importantly, a woman, instead of "limiting her role in the family to giving pleasure and a child to a man," should help "propagate the light of the divine message." Woman's role in this area is central and irreplaceable. [82]

Sultana unwittingly engages here in a dialogue with other Muslim women who also address the problem of polygamy and social justice. The debate on polygamy is, in fact, a transnational one and stretches beyond the geographical borders of North Africa. [83] Aihwa Ong, for example, discusses the position of the Sisters in Islam in Malaysia vis-à-vis this practice, noting that, "They reinterpret polygamy not as a right, but as a responsibility to ensure that socio-justice be achieved for orphans. . . . Allah indicated polygamy as the solution to this particular problem of war orphans and widows." [84] Going further, Ong notes that the Sisters in Islam "conclude firmly, that there is no basis in the *Qur'an* 'to say that polygamy is Islam's solution for men's alledged[ly] [sic] unbridled lust.'" [85]

Whether the Sisters in Islam would agree with Sultana is a matter of interpretation. Her plea, interestingly enough, is also in contradistinction to other tendencies common today in Moroccan society. Fawziyya al-Ghisasi, the Moroccan convener of the recent conference on polygamy, informed me that the response of most Moroccan women to the question of polygamy is to stipulate in the marriage contract that should the husband take on another wife, divorce from the first wife will ensue. In fact, this is acceptable in accordance with Moroccan social and legal norms. [86] Seen against this background, Sultana's plea is that much more eloquent—and urgent.

Perhaps more interesting is what Sultana's position on polygamy tells about corporal gender and sexual dynamics. Men are victims in a society in which polygamy does not exist. The narrator's vocabulary is extremely telling. The men are labeled as the believers (*les hommes croyants*), whereas the women earn no such label. They are just women (*les femmes*). Not only that, but the women are responsible for maintaining the polygamous situation, for "propagating the light of the divine message." [87]

This concluding discussion illustrates only too well some of the sexual politics of the couple, Ali and Khadija. Ali is painted by the narrator as the victim of this strange union. He is the one who remained "faithful and devoted to his wife." Yet his fate is sexual frustration. In addition, he must cheat this natural corporal appetite of the flesh by denying another: that for food. The reader of this pithy moral tale assumes that Ali follows M. S.'s advice to fast for the three months before Khadija finally sees the light and enjoins him to take another wife. This second wife, as the narrator puts it, will be able to give him "the healthy and pure pleasures and the good and legitimate children to which he had a right." [88] Note the gender here: the male has the right to the pleasure and the children, not the female. And, of course, Khadija did exactly what Sultana is advising women: she suggested to her husband the second wife.

Other gender politics are at play here. Reverse the dynamics of the heterosexual couple and look at Khadija for a moment. The "terrible accident" that ruins the sexual life of this otherwise perfect couple is not specified. Yet, this unspecified misfortune makes "all conjugal life" impossible, according to Khadija. Did she confide this information in Sultana? The reader assumes so, though he or she never overhears Khadija speaking to Sultana (as Sultana herself overhears Ali speaking with M. S.).

This silence that textually afflicts Khadija is portentous. She does not seem to suffer, nor does she express any sexual frustration. True, she is half paralyzed and her corporality is restricted by that. But the reader is not told why sexual intercourse is impossible for the couple. Certainly, paralysis, here partial paralysis, does not necessarily preclude sexual activity in a woman. Is Ali unwilling to have sexual intercourse with his wife? This is yet another silence, though a different anecdote on physical disability and eroticism raises the question. In either case, the position of Ong's "Sisters in Islam" has a greater consistency. A Muslim woman whose husband was rendered conjugally unfit would not have the recourse of a second husband—only the choice between resignation and divorce.

Woman's body is as problematic for Sultana as is the entire issue of polygamy. The case of Ali and Khadija confirms the outcome of another failed heterosexual relationship discussed in the journal. In it, a young—and beautiful—woman is abandoned by her fiancé because she now limps. Her physical injury was caused by being hit by a "hooligan" at a sports event. She had accompanied her fiancé to the stadium only because he had managed, by repeatedly dragging her with him to these events, to instill in her "this modern insanity which is the love of a sport." But this fiancé, who had initially felt sorry for her and who pretended to really love her, was unable to put up with a disabled woman, given his attachment to evenings of dancing and to what M. S. calls "coed games." This young woman visits M. S. to seek a conversion to Islam.[89]

This story of the Belgian woman converted by M. S. is related directly by him to Sultana. As is common with Sultana's narrative, the setting may be as significant as the story itself. "That evening my husband came home later than usual." Thus does this story begin. Sultana has no doubt in her husband's fidelity, because she knows that if a younger and more beautiful woman were to offer herself to him, his own values would keep him from giving in to her. Before she can ask him why he is late, he tells her: "It is a very beautiful young woman. . . ." "What?" replies Sultana.[90] But her husband reassures her and begins the narration of Catherine's story (for that is the young woman's name).

Part of the interest of this story lies in its corporal politics. Sultana sets up the possible competition between herself and a nonexistent beautiful young woman in the opening introduction. It does not matter if such a woman offers herself to her husband, he will not be tempted. Nonetheless, when M. S. opens the dialogue, even before Sultana asks him the reason for his tardiness, with the phrase, "It is a very beautiful young woman," the reader is not quite sure where the story will lead. The reader is, however, reassured, in the same way that Sultana is, as the story unfolds. The potential threat posed by the young woman's beauty is effaced by her physical handicap.

The corporality here is not the domain of Catherine alone. After M. S. has concluded his story, he goes to eat and sleep. Sultana, however, says that she was not sleepy. "I have nausea. The case of this young woman made such an impression on me that I began to shake. That could have been me."[91] The male narrator, once his role as religious guide is complete, can proceed to the fulfillment of his bodily needs, food and sleep. That is not what happens to the female listener. Her reaction to the story is physical: not only is she nauseated and unable to sleep, but her body shakes as well. It is the possible identity between herself and Catherine that is in question here.

Once again, corporality and spirituality come together. As the husband explains it to his wife, Catherine was greatly influenced by this incident that befell her, not only physically because of the handicap, but morally because she no longer has confidence in the love of men or in modern civilization. The maiming of the female body will translate here into a recourse to religion. Important as well is the dissolution of the western heterosexual couple, whose existence was based on sexual pleasure and immorality. Catherine, like her textual sister, Khadija, is silent. Her female voice is transmuted into that of the male, as her narrative of conversion is related by the male voice that was instrumental in setting her on the right path.

The reader discovers, as the narrator of the journal does, that for this victim of male sports violence, the religion of the Prophet Muhammad is more than a spiritual force. It is also a physical life-giving force: had this young woman not embraced religion at the hands of M. S., her fate would have been suicide, a destruction of her bodily entity. But Sultana's role is more than simply that of a listener. She takes the occasion to denounce western mores and values, praising Islam's attitude to sports and a healthy body. Violence in the sports stadium is compared to violence in the broader political arena. This conversion incident is telling for the larger corporal and spiritual agenda that Sultana elaborates in *L'Islam, la femme, et l'intégrisme*. Woman's body becomes a pawn between a modern society breeding all sorts of ills and the spiritual world of Islam.

What more eloquent way to interrogate this nexus than through an incident exploring AIDS? Like other victims, Madame Y., the AIDS victim, receives a full chapter in Sultana's journal. Y., HIV-positive, was born a Muslim and has given birth to a normal baby with no sign of the virus, and this despite the fact that she herself saw the first signs of the disease appear on her own body. Y. had followed an anti-AIDS treatment during her pregnancy and now "is completely cured." Sultana remembers the conversation she had with Y., and she transcribes it for the sake of the reader with a simple "here it is." The rest of the chapter is then devoted to a dialogue between Y. and Sultana. The reader discovers through this dialogue that Sultana was the only person who knew Y.'s dark secret. Y. was fairly pessimistic about her prognosis, but Sultana encouraged her, leading her down the religious path.

Y.: People say that AIDS in incurable. I still hope that the physicians will end up finding a cure.

I [*that is Sultana*]: One must hope in God. You're a Muslim, right?[92]

And later, as Sultana tells Y. that it is possible for her to redo her life, Y. asks:

Y.:   Is it possible? I am condemned and even if medicine were to discover
        something against AIDS, I will not be there to profit from it.

I: What do you know about it? I see that you still don't consider God's ab-
        solute power in the world. Medicine and technology only realize what He
        permits them to realize.

Y.:   But can He cure me from AIDS?

I: Of course He can. It is He who created you, it is He who tries you now,
        and it is He who will punish you if you continue to ignore Him or cure
        you if He wishes.[93]

As the dialogue draws to a close and Sultana seems to have instilled her
message in Y., the latter asks her friend to lend her a Qur'ân and a
prayer book. Sultana hands these to Y., enjoining her to keep them for
herself and for the father of her child.[94]

    Y.'s interchange with Sultana is rife with corporal issues. The AIDS
victim is concerned about her bodily cure, while her friend is concerned
with her spiritual well-being. In fact, when Y. inquires about medicine
and its possible discovery of a cure, Sultana responds with the religious
cure that will be effected by the Deity. Woman's body is pulled between
the poles of religion and medicine.

    Timing here is as crucial as it was in other incidents Sultana relates.
The chapter with AIDS is entitled "*Le SIDA: Qui est responsable?*"
(AIDS: Who is Responsible?). The chapter immediately begins with Sultana and her husband "on this afternoon," constantly praising the Deity. This is the sole appearance of the husband in the chapter, as he exits the narrative to give his place to the AIDS victim. When Y. appears,
she is described as "a Muslim by birth," who has just given birth to a
healthy child. She did not "contaminate" her child, "she who had even
seen appear on her body the first symptoms of the terrible illness."[95]
This introduction to the woman who will inhabit this extended chapter
with Sultana makes it clear that Y.'s body had already been ravaged by
AIDS. What the specific symptoms are the reader is not told. Simply put,
Y. followed the anti-AIDS treatment during her pregnancy and is con-
sequently completely cured and her child safe. The actual appearance of
the AIDS symptoms on the woman's body renders the cure that much
more dramatic.

    The structure of the chapter itself speaks just as eloquently to the cen-
trality of this subject. The extremely brief introduction with Sultana and
her husband singing God's praise leads directly into the story of Y. First
the reader must be assured of the happy outcome before the dramatic dialogue between the two women actually takes place. Sultana remembers

"today" this conversation that took place three months ago. This conversation will then occupy the rest of the chapter. Y.'s opening lines are crucial: "Listen Sultana. You are the only one who knows that I have AIDS. You, you know how to keep a secret. I have confidence in you and I know that you can help me." [96] Sultana will most certainly help her friend. The guarding of the secret, however, is a different matter altogether, as the reader of the journal discovers.

No summary, no moral conclusion closes this chapter. AIDS, it would seem, needs no such epilogue. It is a dramatic enough illness that its mere example suffices. It is also a medical condition that can speak as eloquently to the corporal reality of the individual afflicted with it as it can to the social and modern ills that bring about this condition. Sultana's act of saving Y. does not come about easily or without a refutation of the non-Islamic lifestyle.

I [*that is Sultana*]:   You watch television?

      Y.:   Yes, why?

      I: A film or a serial takes certainly more than a quarter of an hour of your time? Well, it often takes less than fifteen minutes to do one's ablutions and one's prayer.

      Y.:   You are right, I was crazy and God punished me. [97]

As the dialogue develops, Sultana emphasizes again the contrast between Islam and the West. Discussing the fate of the child in all of this, Sultana explains to Y. that the child suffers the consequence of the actions of his parents through "the chromosomes of his father and the belly of his mother," an interesting conjunction of male transmission with the female uniquely as carrier. This applies as much for drinking alcohol as it does for smoking cigarettes (the smoking female body rears its ugly head again). "If she [the mother] listens to Bob Marley, he [the fetus] listens to Bob Marley with her; if she listens to a psalmody of the holy Qur'ân, he listens with her." [98] As Y. leaves Sultana, she receives a copy of the Muslim holy book. The elaborate discussion with Sultana will not have been in vain.

But these ills of the modern world do not explain how AIDS was transmitted to Y. If her having AIDS is not kept secret, how she got AIDS remains a mystery. She alludes to the punishment of God, and that is the only cause that the text acknowledges.

Mohammed Saghir, in his pamphlet on AIDS, can perhaps shed some light on this dilemma. Before he delves into the question fully, he notes that an HIV-positive individual, after developing the illness, "followed the Islamic treatment and is now, thanks be to God, completely cured." [99] The male speaker gives no name, nor even an initial. Is he referring here to Y.? Quite possibly, though not necessarily. If he is addressing that case, then the cure would be thanks to religion and not to the medical treatment Y. was receiving.

It is really more the discourse underlying Saghir's discussion that is crucial. The subtext there is homosexuality as primary cause for this deadly illness. Imam Mohammed Saghir is not alone in this reading. In a fascinating work, *SIDA: Les religions s'intérrogent,* religious authorities representing diverse traditions gathered in Paris to discuss AIDS. Among them was Dalil Boubakeur, a physician and the rector of the Institut musulman de la Mosquée de Paris. In his opening statement, he states clearly that "I exclude here contamination by blood transfusion, which does not enter into the frame of a religious debate. We are talking about drug addiction, homosexuality, and the type of heterosexuality considered illicit in Islamic law." [100]

This juxtaposition of medicine and religion throughout Sultana's discussion is not without consequence and stands in contradistinction to the opening segment of the story in which the first-person narrator of the journey was quick to inform the reader that this female AIDS-victim had followed *"le traitement anti-SIDA"* (anti-AIDS treatment). Medicine, it would appear at first glance, provided the actual cure.[101]

Leïla Lahlou's case does not go unnoticed in the Belgian discourses on medicine and religion. Mohammed Saghir speaks of her in his book on AIDS. In praising the curative powers of the waters of Zamzam, he mentions Leïla's experience and her cure from her cancer, noting at the same time the existence of her book, *Do Not Forget God.* Cheikh Mohammed Saghir speaks of the Moroccan breast-cancer victim only as "Leyla" and not as Leïla Lahlou, making her identification for the uninitiated reader that much more difficult (although he does mention the title of her book).[102] But Mohammed Saghir warns his reader that another individual did the same thing as Leïla and was completely unsuccessful.[103] Saghir does not mention the Prophet Muhammad's nocturnal visit to the Moroccan breast-cancer patient, which obviates the need for any other religious text. Y.'s exit from Sultana's narrative is accomplished with a Qur'ân, much as Sultana exited the mosque in the opening chapter with the same book, but in her case given to her by the Imam of the Brussels mosque. The holy book in both instances in the Belgian journey marks a new and religious lifestyle. In its own way, this is not too dissimilar to what happens to Leïla, for whom the beginnings of the spiritual quest in Paris signaled the need to purchase a copy of the Qur'ân.[104]

For Sultana's reader, Y.'s adventure must sit alongside other corporal adventures, like that of Catherine. In fact, these stories about maimed female bodies make it clear that Sultana's "journal" is more than simply an account of a personal spiritual trajectory. Its neopatriarchal (and contemporarily common) deference to male religious authority is re-inforced (dare one say fleshed out?) by a phallocentric sexual politics and an overwhelming sense of female corporal fragility.

Sultana has been textually assimilated to the religious tradition by the conclusion of her narrative. She quotes liberally from the Qur'ân, that book that was handed to her and her mother in the opening pages of the journal by the Imam of the Brussels mosque. After the initial dream in which she saw the white-clothed figure, she had repeated the figure's words like a child "memorizing his or her history lesson." By the end of the narrative, Sultana seems not only to have memorized this history les-son but to have inserted herself in the history of Islam in the West and the larger discourses on woman and the body.

The last words uttered in Sultana's text are those of Mohammed Saghir, the *conseiller pédagogique* (pedagogical counselor) at the Centre Islamique de Belgique. But her name, Kouhmane Sultana, appears as the signatory of his words.[105] Male and female come together at the end of *L'Islam, la femme, et l'intégrisme.*

This is but a transitory state, however. Mohammed Saghir was in-deed in reality Sultana Kouhmane's husband. The happy heterosexual couple whose life on the religious path is portrayed in Sultana's journal no longer exists, however. Sultana and her husband were divorced and he left Belgium to reside in Tangiers, Morocco. She remained in Bel-gium, but her current whereabouts are, unfortunately, not known.[106]

CHAPTER SEVEN

The "Integrated" Body

Although Sultana's geographical travels extend to North Africa, her narrative of spiritual rebirth is primarily set in the West—in other words, in a non-Moroccan, non-Muslim environment. Her spiritual autobiography is imbued with this hostile environment, and in fact, all the episodes in Sultana's life in one way or another speak to the West. Be it the dream incident, the conversion of Catherine, or Sultana's own pilgrimage to Morocco, all these events involve a commentary on the West. None, however, delves into the everyday life of a Muslim woman in the West, the subject of this chapter.

The spiritual journey by Sultana Kouhmane is far from being the only contemporary text that deals with the pervasive racism of European society, especially with regard to its immigrant populations. One of the most eloquent writers to deal with this topic is the Moroccan author and French Goncourt Prize winner Tahar Ben Jelloun. His *Hospitalité Française* (French Hospitality) is a denunciation of French attitudes to immigrants. More recently, he has authored an articulate pamphlet on the topic, *Le racisme expliqué à ma fille* (Racism Explained to My Daughter).[1] Julia Kristeva and Jacques Derrida have also analyzed the dilemmas of having foreigners living among the European populations.[2] That this racism is a consistent part of the immigrant experience can be seen in the fact that it transcends the theoretical works and rears its ugly head in works of popular culture as well. The comic strips of the French Beur Farid Boudjellal are an excellent example of this.[3]

This problematic issue of racism is a thread that runs consistently through the societies described in these works, and, of course, in that of Sultana Kouhmane. Yet, Ben Jelloun and Boudjellal write from a secular point of view, whereas Kouhmane's journey is on the opposite side of the cultural divide. To take but one example, Ben Jelloun qualifies the integrists as "fanatics," whereas Sultana dances around the concept of integrism, redefining it and stretching its conceptual borders.[4]

One of the most interesting chapters in Sultana's journey involves reminiscences of her childhood. These memories of a not-too-distant past are localized in the school system and are crucial because they move from strictly personal and educational issues to more global social concerns, extending to male-female relations and woman's position in Islam and the West, topics dear to the narrator. As such, these recollections function as an excellent example of Sultana's repeated verbal play based on the word, *intégrisme:* on the one hand, *intégrisme,* with its meaning of integrist, implying a religious traditionalist and, on the other, *intégrisme,* meaning integration into European society. The analysis of these childhood incidents will be enriched by other materials in Sultana's journal that deal with the everyday life of Arab immigrants in the West.

The chapter of poignant childhood memories comprises seven incidents that in one way or another involve Sultana's education. They begin with her mother's attempt to register her daughter, who bears a Moroccan name, in a Belgian school. This finally successful struggle to penetrate the Belgian educational system is followed by episodes in the school itself. Here, Sultana treats her reader to different narratives starring herself and her young female companions, as well as school officials. The individual stories are sometimes followed by a brief summary and social commentary, despite the fact that a longer conclusion ends the chapter.

The process of memory in this segment of the journey is fascinating. Sultana declares that she does not know why, on a certain evening, she remembered her life as a student. "I did not like school so much and it is only today that I am beginning to understand why it was so."[5] This initial dislike sets the context for the totality of events that follow.

In addition, the process of memory and narration produces a great deal of tension. This is apparent on the verbal level of the text. The narrator, for example, uses the present tense at times to express the time of the narration itself; that is, when she is an adult looking back at her childhood. At other times, the present tense is used for the events described in the incidents themselves. This tension extends to the conclusions following most of the incidents. The reader is never sure whether the conclusion, or the moral presented after the individual events, was drawn by Sultana the child or Sultana the adult. While it is much more likely that it is the adult speaking here, nevertheless this uncertainty adds another level of tension in the text.

The opening sentences for this series of analepses create a chronological disjuncture in the telling of the adventures. The events have clearly taken place in the past, but nowhere are they narrated previously, nor will they be subsequently. Thus, they function as completing analepses. In their present textual location, they materialize long after Sultana has "totally converted" to Islam and has wed M. S.[6] This is not unimportant, since her adult religious transformation to Islam colors the reading of these childhood incidents.

The dislike for school is in the past tense. Sultana, in fact, uses the imperfect, alerting the reader that this dislike did not represent an isolated occurrence, but rather a continuous state. This past tense, however, is itself embedded in two presents. On the one hand, there is the present of the evening (*ce soir*), during which the act of remembering is initially engaged. On the other hand, there is the present of today (*aujourd'hui*), which signals the act of understanding for the narrator's dislike of school.[7]

Once this chronological disjuncture is established, the narrator informs her reader, "Here is, therefore, how the few bitter memories that describe the condition of the young Muslim female in Brussels in the 80s unfold often in front of my mind."[8] These "few bitter memories" that "unfold" do so in a quasi-cinematic manner, like the shots of a film. Sultana's narrative camera zooms in and out as each incident takes center stage only to disappear and permit the following event to unfold. The characters starring in these incidents divide themselves into good guys and bad guys. The narrator, her family, and her friends represent the forces of good, there to battle the forces of evil, represented by various Belgian officials. These childhood episodes group themselves, thereby permitting a more detailed examination of the narrator's role and its evolution. An interesting game with voices surfaces.

In the first incident, the reader watches as the mother tries to register her young daughter in a Belgian school. The narrator immediately moves back in time, and dramatically does so in the present tense. "I am ten years old and we have just moved."[9] With this simple declaration, Sultana has transformed herself into a child, whose mother is searching for a school in which to place her children.

Once this introduction to the first incident is complete, then begins a dialogue between the mother and the school official:

MOTHER [*by telephone*]: Good morning, I would like to register my daughter in your school.
SECRETARY: Yes, ma'am, there is no problem. What is your name?—Mrs. X—and that of your husband?—Mr. X—and of your daughter?—X—Ah! I note that they do not have Belgian names!
MOTHER: No, sir, they are Moroccan.[10]

The Moroccan identity causes a shift in the voice of the official. This the narrator clearly indicates: "the voice had changed." This changed voice can then hesitate about the matriculation of the student after having initially declared that there was no problem. Now the question of the student's placement plays an important role. When the mother identifies the year in which her daughter should be inscribed, the secretary can assert that there is simply no place for the young girl in school.

Sultana's mother is intent on discovering whether this refusal is based on space or on national identity. She calls fifteen minutes later and asks about registering Sultana's twin cousins who are the same age as she. But they are Belgians.

This time the dialogue is just as interesting as it was earlier:

MOTHER: Hello! Good morning, I would like to register my two sons in your school, please.
SECRETARY: Yes, ma'am. Your name please and those of your husband and your children.
MOTHER: Belgian names.
SECRETARY: Yes, there is no problem.[11]

The mother is then invited to fill out the necessary forms for the Belgian youngsters.

But when the mother appears in school, it is to register her daughter. The mother tells the story upon her return to the house. She had confronted the male official, revealing to him that she was the individual who had called soon after his refusal to register her daughter with the request for the enrollment of the two sons. This confrontation, related by the mother, also surfaces in the form of a dialogue between herself and the secretary. Her final words to the Belgian official sum up the situation: "It is true that it is preferable to enroll two Belgians rather than one Moroccan. In either case, I will not leave your office as long as she is not registered!" [12] The result of the ensuing discussion is that the girl is enrolled in the school, but she is made to repeat a year. "All this because on my card it was written: Moroccan nationality." [13]

Thus ends the first remembered school incident from Sultana's childhood. Perhaps most striking is the fact that the major part of this incident reaches the reader through the form of a dialogue between the mother and the male school official. The narrator initially indicates that the opening conversations between her mother and the school official took place on the telephone. What this means is that Sultana was not a participant in the interchange. It is possible that she overheard the conversation on a telephone extension, but as the incident develops and the mother returns to relate her success to the family, it becomes clear that that is most likely not the case.

That these are reconstructed conversations becomes more evident when one looks at the official's comments as they are transmitted in the narrative. In a rather coy manner, the text reveals in the first interchange the absence of names for the protagonists. They are all transformed into an X: be it the mother (Mrs. X) or the father (Mr. X) or the daughter (X). These substitute-names, furthermore, appear in the dialogue within the space dedicated to the school official. That the mother may have uttered these "names" is possible, given the dashes preceding and following each of the Xs. It is equally possible, however, that the school official may have been simply repeating the mother's words within his own part of the dialogue (the secretary is a male, a fact that emerges later in the incident).

This onomastic absence calls attention to the precarious nature of the identity of the protagonists. It is the school administrator who concludes in the first chat about registering the young girl, "Ah! I note that they do not have Belgian names!" The mother then counters that they indeed are not Belgian, but Moroccan. The reader, of course, remains in total ignorance as to what these names might be. Simply, he or she is aware that these are foreign names, a fact that seals the fate of the daughter, Sultana.

The transparent racism of the Belgian school system does not deter the insistent mother, however. She uses a ruse, that of pretending to enroll Sultana's cousins, in order to uncover this racism. In this ruse, which also unfolds through a dialogue, the mother provides the school official with Belgian names. This time, however, there is no need for the X. The male secretary concludes immediately that the names are Belgian.

What is the function then of the X in the first exchange? Is it simply a literary flourish? That is, of course, a possibility. But more lurks behind the use of the simple initial. The anonymity of the individuals is but one factor. An X suggests unknowableness, foreignness—eventually alienation. The Belgian names do not need this metamorphosis and redefinition into an algebraic sign: they are recognized immediately by the secretary as being Belgian.

Names, the reader understands, are an important factor in instigating a racist reaction, even by someone in a position of social authority, such as a school official. The recognition of the inherent racism in this incident is done on two levels by the two females involved, on one hand, the mother, and on the other, the daughter. In her last interchange with the secretary, the mother draws the first conclusion. "It is true," she says, "that it is preferable to enroll two Belgians rather than one Moroccan." [14] The narrator of the journey herself then draws the conclusion once again, when she notes: "All this because on my card it was written: Moroccan nationality." [15]

The gender element may not be accidental here. The victimization of the female is accomplished for the benefit of males. Once again, as it was with the racism, it is the female speakers who call attention to the gender of the cousins. The first-person narrator speaks about "my twin cousins (male)." [16] Then the mother, addressing the secretary, says "my two sons." [17] Interestingly, the male secretary does not pick up on this gender component. When he asks for the names of the parties involved, he says "your children," [18] leaving the question of gender aside.

The mother may have succeeded in registering her Moroccan daughter in the Belgian school near their home. But the young girl pays for this success: she is made to repeat her last year in school. The racist Belgian educational official has, in a sense, won the battle here.

The battle with the school system in this incident is really only the beginning. The second incident Sultana recalls also involves her placement in a school. The camera follows the young girl as she is becoming older and encountering more difficulties. This time, she is twelve years old and the orientation of her studies is in question. Her teacher, for one, has advised that the young girl follow a scientific track. When the mother goes to the appropriate school, she has a run-in once again with a school official. In this case, however, it is the director of the establishment. After the male official sees the identity of the mother and daughter, a dialogue ensues in which he suggests registering the young woman in a vocational track. The mother replies, "Surely not. Her previous teacher never counseled me to register her in a vocational track." She then lambastes this move with strong vocabulary:

> One does not condemn a student to go into a vocational track without giving him the chance to realize his potential in the field of studies that he prefers.
> You either register her in the technical sciences or I will register her in another establishment.
> Now I understand why three quarters of the children of immigrants are in vocational school.
> Often non-European parents who come to register their children do not understand French well. And you tell them anything to justify the disorientation of their children.[19]

The mother, as in the previous incident, has the last word. And what a word this is! First, it is a powerful attack on an educational system that "condemns" a student to a vocational career without providing that student with the opportunity to succeed elsewhere. Condemnation speaks a host of ideas that extend from the mere registration in a given school system to a career option that will have major consequences in one's life. Is it a wonder, then, that the mother should threaten to move her daughter to another school if she is not placed in the right track?

This is the point, however, where the narrative moves from the personal to the general: the situation of immigrants in a European society. Now, the mother argues, she understands why the majority of the children of immigrants are in vocational studies. This understanding comes about because the future of her own daughter is under threat. Had she been like the "non-European parents who come to register their children" and who "do not understand French well," she would have been fooled by the school officials.

This vigorous attack on the Belgian school system and its treatment of non-European parents is delivered not by one of the non-European parents but by Sultana's mother, who, as the reader remembers, is Belgian. The authority of her voice is that much greater. When the secretary confronts the mother in the first incident, noting the non-Belgian names, he separates her from her husband and the daughter: "Ah! I note that they do not have Belgian names!" It is the *they* that is critical here, isolating the foreigners from the Belgians. But, fortunately for the daughter, the mother is not cowed by the male representatives of the Belgian educational system. She confronts both of them with the racism of their society, of which, of course, she herself is a member. The reader does not discover the ultimate outcome of Sultana's registration in this incident. But, in a way, it becomes almost secondary to the major point of the story, which is to expose and combat European racist attitudes to non-European immigrants.

The mother proves to be an important voice in these dialogues. Yet once Sultana is in school, she herself will become a participant in these reconstructed dialogues. The following incident acts as a bridge, as it were. Here, Sultana will enter the text as speaker at the same time that the mother exits that role. The presence of the two female speakers, mother and daughter, signals a transition in the text.

Sultana returns to school after a week's illness to discover that she faces an examination for which she is unprepared. She requests a delay, which the teacher refuses with the response that Arabs only come to school for the welfare payments. Sultana is extremely angry and declares to the teacher that she does not have the right to tell her this. A few days later, her mother calls the school because of some problems Sultana is having with a boy of whom she is afraid. This time the dialogue is between the mother and the director of the school. The conversation starts out over the young man who is bothering the daughter and quickly moves to the earlier accusation made by the teacher. The director, clearly ill at ease, asks Sultana's mother to reveal the name of the teacher, given that such judgments should not be made in his establishment. The mother provides no such information, and her statement is categorical: he is the director and he should concern himself with the behavior of his teachers in the same way that he concerns himself with the behavior of his students. Besides, she adds, she promised her daughter that she would not say anything further about this incident. The upshot of the story for Sultana: after this, people are surprised that the children of immigrants prefer to hang out in the streets rather than going to school.[20]

Once again, the mother comes to the rescue. She, better than the daughter, is able to confront the Belgian educational system. While Sultana attempts to face down the teacher, the mother goes directly to the school director. A clear hierarchy prevails. Not only that, but the mother steps in when the matter concerns a boy who appears to be harassing her daughter.

From this subject, the dialogue between the two adults—the mother and the director—then moves to the topic of Arabs and welfare payments. The sentence addressed by the school teacher directly to Sultana is repeated with some changes by the mother. The teacher had said to Sultana, "*On sait très bien que vous les Arabes vous ne venez à l'école que pour les allocations*" (One knows very well that you, the Arabs, you only come to school for the welfare payments). In repeating this statement within quotes in her own dialogue with the director, the mother says: "*Nous savons que les Arabes ne viennent à l'école que pour les allocations*" (We know that the Arabs only come to school for the welfare payments).

When the teacher uttered those words that provoked the narrator's anger, she set up a distinction between the speaker and "you, the Arabs." When the mother picks up the statement, she turns it into the first-person plural, *we*. Of course, in theory, the mother is seemingly doing nothing but repeating the words of the teacher, since she clearly states that this is a judgment made by teachers against their students. But in fact what the mother has done is to redirect this statement, making it without question the belief of the teacher. The recasting of the phrase moves the subject from the impersonal *one* to a more specific *we*. Yet both renditions are global in their assessments and once again castigate the Belgian educational system. As this incident with the teacher indicates, Sultana is reasonably well settled in school. The mother's voice, so critical in the first childhood memories, can now disappear, as the young Sultana herself takes over the process of negotiating her relationship with the Belgian instructional system.

The next incident stars Sultana and a substitute art teacher. For introductions, the students had to write their name, their address, and their nationality. As the teacher calls out the names, the students stand to identify themselves.

"What a scene she made when she arrived at my name," Sultana explains as the dialogue begins between herself and the substitute teacher. The latter wants to know the "true nationality" of the student. Sultana replies that it is what she has written on the paper: Moroccan. The teacher believes that the student is making fun of her, to which the young girl replies, "No. But I do not see what difference it makes to you that I be Moroccan or Belgian." The teacher responds that the girl had better have her identity card or else she will be taken to the director's office. "The entire class was laughing because they all knew that I was telling the truth. Often before knowing my nationality, people believe that I am Belgian." It is when they become aware of her true nationality that "most of them completely change their attitude toward me." Sultana continues: this is painful for "an adolescent" and provokes a desire to revolt against the social order. "Which explains in part, but does not justify, delinquency in the nonpracticing Muslim immigrant circles."[21]

The moral of the story, provided for the reader by Sultana herself, goes beyond the classroom. The action of a substitute teacher is able to transport the narrator from the school environment to that of society in general and juvenile delinquency in particular. Sultana, an adolescent in the event itself, can speak to the behavior of other adolescents, whose desires are to revolt against society. The narrator walks the line between what she calls "explaining" juvenile delinquency and justifying it.

Localizing this problematic behavior becomes all important. Sultana is careful to qualify the circles in which delinquency takes place: "nonpracticing Muslim immigrant circles." Key here is practicing versus nonpracticing Muslim immigrants. These childhood memories surface textually after Sultana's complete conversion. Religion would seem to be the antidote to these social ills. With this concluding aside, religion enters the childhood memories. The earlier incidents presented conclusions that applied to the life of immigrants, regardless of their religious background. The incident in which Sultana becomes a major player is also the one that opens up the issue of religion. It is perhaps not an accident that this is also the incident in which the Christian mother makes her last appearance in the dialogues.

Once the reader is transported to the universe of Islam, other issues can surface. The next childhood memory involves a Moroccan friend of Sultana: "But she, she already practices her religion very well and comes to the lycée wearing a head scarf. I should say that I admire her a lot, because here in Belgium it is already difficult to be a Moroccan girl, but wearing a head scarf is surely even more difficult." The young girl's story, told in her own words, follows this brief introductory setting. "The girl: 'You know S., this morning the director was near the door of the school and when I wanted to enter she stopped me.'" The director informs the student that as of today, she no longer wishes to see her wearing a head scarf; otherwise she can remain at home. The young girl tells Sultana that she was very surprised that the school director would tell her this, because, "If I put on a head scarf it is not to follow fashion but to hide my hair because God does not want us to provoke the other sex." She continues by noting that in front of her was a girl who had a cap, a strange haircut, and "multicolored hair." This student gets no blame from the female school director, nor does she receive a "sermon." "Why are we judged according to our clothing and our colors?" Z.'s "calvary," a term that will return momentarily, reminds Sultana of the adventures of her friend Fatima-Zohra when she was a student in a primary school in Brussels.[22]

The story of Z., for that is how the young veiled girl is referred to, leads without commentary to the next incident, that with Fatima-Zohra. But, unlike the narrator, the critic should alight for a brief moment at this particular childhood memory involving Z. There is no dialogue here, simply Sultana's introductory words followed by Z.'s narration of her adventure, addressed to S. The female school director speaks, but her words are embedded within Z.'s narration and, hence, subject textually to her interpretation. This comes without much ado: why should the young Muslim girl be subjected to this treatment when other girls, who are clearly described as being outside the norm ("bizarre haircut, multicolored hair"), are left to do as they please? The cultural distinctions are made quite clearly: the demeanor of the observant young Muslim girl is pitted against the outlandish bearing of her peer, whose nationality remains unspoken.

The perception of harassment on Z.'s part goes uncommented on by the narrator, though it is clear that she holds her childhood friend in high regard. Her initial comments speak to this. Not only does her friend already practice her religion "very well," but Sultana respects her a great deal because to the difficulties of being a Moroccan she adds those of wearing a head scarf.

The vestimentary decision is explained by Z.: this is not a question of fashion but of religious duty. The Deity is the ultimate authority here, whose desires are fulfilled by the female's modesty, a modesty linked without a doubt to the "other sex." The responsibility for provoking the other sex becomes the domain of the female: it is her behavior and her comportment that are subject to restraints. Just as with polygamy discussed earlier, the female gender holds the larger share of responsibility for maintaining the social order and keeping temptation at bay.[23]

This brief adventure that Z. has with the Belgian educational system leads to a more dramatic story, this one starring another friend of Sultana. Fatima-Zohra is the hero of this episode, which she has related to Sultana. Fatima-Zohra has no speaking voice; simply her story is transmitted to the reader by Sultana herself.

Fatima-Zohra, like the other students in school, was supposed to go swimming. "Despite her young age, she was already a believer and practicing." She preferred to stay in school rather than to amuse herself with her colleagues. "For her, the essential was to go to school clean and ready for study." Moreover, Fatima-Zohra "agrees with her mother that coed swimming leads the individual, as well as society, in the long run, to problems of mores that are much more important than the muscular strength and immediate pleasure that swimming provides."

Fatima-Zohra was left in the classroom with another student (who was being punished for a completely different reason) and the instructor, who gave the two girls a writing exercise as punishment. The other girl began crying, and her punishment was eliminated. Fatima-Zohra, who does not cry easily, simply asked that she be excused as well. Her request was refused, and when she handed in her work at noon, she wrote on the paper, "I do not go swimming with the others because God does not wish it." When she returned to the school that afternoon, the instructor was awaiting her and sent her to the corner, where she had to keep her hands raised in the air for the remainder of the afternoon.[24]

This adventure, starring a young Muslim girl in the by now familiar Belgian school system, seems to need no commentary. Instead, Sultana narrates it herself and leaves the conclusion for the reader to draw. The favoritism of the school system is all too apparent. The initial punishment consisting of a writing exercise (it is defined as such by the narrator: "*une punition écrite*") might at first glance seem arbitrary and unjust; however, it pales by comparison to the young girl's being placed in a corner with her hands in the air all afternoon.

This corporal punishment is inflicted on the same body part, the hands, that are responsible for writing the note about not swimming. This is semiotically significant. The essential symmetry set up between the writing body part and the punished body part is not dissimilar to the phenomenon discussed earlier with regard to Niʿmat Sidqî and female adornment. There, the face that was bearing the forbidden makeup was meted out justice by the Deity in an interesting system of equivalences.[25] Here, of course, the Deity is not the one sitting in judgment. Instead, it is the nonreligious school system, represented by a male instructor.

This does not mean that religion plays no role in this case. Far from it. In fact, it is adherence to religious precepts that leads the young girl to suffer the corporal punishment of the school system. She refuses to swim with the others "because God does not wish it." By inserting the Deity in this discussion of a school activity, Fatima-Zohra has placed herself in the same universe as Sultana's other school colleague, Z., who dons the veil because God does not want women to provoke the opposite sex.

The student who refuses to participate in coed swimming is quite young, a point that Sultana emphasized in the beginning of her narration of the incident. Yet despite her young age, the girl is precocious and mature, preferring to remain at school rather than "having fun with the children of her own age." She was already a practicing believer. More importantly, she "agrees with her mother" on the question of coed swimming and its moral dangers. This agreement moves the child directly into the world of adults, again underlining her maturity.

Fatima-Zohra's separation from her peers is also evident in the way she interacts with the male teacher, the one who metes out punishment. Rather than crying and manipulating him through emotion, as the other student does, Fatima-Zohra simply requests that she be excused from the written assignment. Despite his refusal, which she deems unjust, she continues to do the work.

This exemplary female is an ideal spokesperson against coed activities that are perceived to be dangerous to the moral health of the community. Swimming is a topic that Sultana had already warned her readers about, when she so eloquently spoke about the possible seduction of a male by a naked leg.[26] Swimming was also an important component in Leïla Lahlou's breast-cancer journey, a journey with which Sultana's husband was familiar.[27] And did not Sultana herself partake of this activity in Morocco when she dipped her body in the spring in the Middle Atlas?[28] But Sultana's experience was not coed swimming. The purificatory exercise in Morocco involved only two women, Sultana and her sister-in-law, Aziza, both protected from the prying eyes of the opposite sex by Sultana's husband.[29] Fatima-Zohra's narrative and her assessment of coed swimming go to the heart of male-female relations. It is not only modesty through the head scarf that will govern these relations. Coed activities, like swimming, are examples of daily and dangerous temptations.

The last incident that leads Sultana to her conclusions on women in Islam and the West is perhaps the most eloquent of the childhood memories. One day, begins Sultana, she had a Dutch class, and the teacher did not stop looking at her and walking around her seat. Last week, he had given her the answers on the "interrogation" and before that had proposed private classes to her. This she had refused, having heard a lot of "bizarre stories" about teachers and students.

After the Dutch class, a student from the class came to Sultana and said to her:

THE GIRL:	Well, S., you are lucky!
I [*that is Sultana*]:	Ah yes! And why?
THE GIRL:	Come on! You are not going to tell me that you did not notice that the teacher has a weakness for you.

<table>
<tr><td>I [that is Sultana], playing the ignorant:</td><td>Ah! I did not notice. And besides what do you want that to change in me?</td></tr>
<tr><td>THE GIRL:</td><td>You are joking or what? Precisely, that can change a lot. In either case if he walked around me like that, me, to have a successful year, I would give in to him. I would even go so far as to sleep with him if that was necessary.</td></tr>
</table>

Sultana sums up the dialogue: "I found her words so stupid and ridiculous that I preferred to go and leave her with her ideas of a future liberated woman."

The incident does not stop here. The girl loses no time, and a week later, seeing that Sultana was not responding to the teacher's advances, she put it in her head to go after him herself. Since he did not take the first step, she did. Sultana wishes to tell her reader how this girl performed this act.

> She dressed in a big décolleté and put on makeup, something that she was not in the habit of doing.
>
> | GIRL: | Sir, please come and see, there is something that I do not understand in this text. |
> |---|---|
> | TEACHER: | Two minutes, I am coming. |

The girl proceeds to provoke the teacher by tossing her head back. He does not delay in his response, "caressing her hair." The other students are surprised both at the girl's audacity and at the teacher's insolent behavior. Sultana notes that this incident took place many years ago "but it is only now that I understand why a young Muslim girl who respects herself insists on keeping her scarf on her head." [30]

This is perhaps the most complex of Sultana's childhood memories and says a great deal about the exploitative nature of the heterosexual school environment. The incident brings together a variety of characters, including Sultana, the teacher, and other students as well, among them the female seducer. In the beginning of the episode, Sultana is the object of attraction. By the end of the story, she has not only categorically refused this role, but she has also handed it to someone else. In between, however, she has a chance to play coy with her school colleague and to describe the latter's manipulations of the situation. In the first dialogue, Sultana enacts the role of the ignorant female, while signaling the reader that she was quite aware of the teacher's intentions all along. It is her absence of interest in this game of seduction that spurs the other student to declare her intentions to manipulate the teacher, if need be with sexual favors, in order to successfully complete her school year. And this is, of course, precisely what she sets about doing.

Interestingly, the first signs of seduction consist of corporal items of female adornment. The young student dons a décolleté and makeup. These are the things that Muslim injunctions about modesty warn about: indecent dress and makeup. This is not to say that the male teacher is by any means innocent. Quite the contrary: he had already been painted by Sultana in her opening words as someone who is ready to abuse his situation of authority, going so far as to offer her private lessons. She is smart enough to reject these. Female adornment is what permits the other student to set the trap for the male teacher. Not only does he fall into this trap, but he caresses the student's hair in front of her peers. The reader does not know the outcome of this liaison, but perhaps it was already alluded to by the student herself when she admitted that she would exchange sexual favors for success in school.

Time is not unimportant here. The narrator lays out the teacher's advances to her one after another, with time breaks between these actions. Her colleague, intent on seducing the teacher, also waits one week before she undertakes her seduction. Her request to have him explain something to her, the act that sets in motion the seduction, is met with the teacher's response, which he begins with a time reference as well: "Two minutes." But where no time delay exists is in the teacher's immediate conduct toward the student seducing him: "He noticed very fast that she was trying to provoke him. He did not delay in answering her call, by caressing her hair."

The surprise that the other students evince toward this action might be potentially shared by the reader. But Sultana's point does not go unheeded. It is possible to escape abusive situations such as this, even though they may recur over and over, as the teacher's repeated overtures to her testify. But once a woman's behavior has set something in motion, as with female adornment, then the male's response is immediate. Unlike Sultana, who rejects the sexual overtures of this male teacher, he himself does not think twice about his potential entrapment by the young girl. He simply dives in and caresses her hair in front of the students.

What a testimony this story is for Sultana's religiously conscious readers! Before the act of seduction itself, Sultana had walked away from this potentially abusive situation and declared that she preferred to leave her colleague "with her ideas of a future liberated woman." Is the reader to understand that this is how "liberated" women behave? Sultana's conclusions would suggest an affirmative answer. Once again, the time element is inserted. The narrator assures her reader that this event occurred years ago "but it is only now that I understand why a young Muslim girl who respects herself insists on keeping her scarf on her head." Hence, it is not coincidental that it is the student's hair, rather than an arm or a shoulder, that the teacher touches. And with this epiphany, Sultana can embark on a discussion of woman's role in Islam and the West.

Woman's position in Islam is contrasted with that in the West, and specifically Europe. The reader is quite aware that this is a topic dear to Sultana's heart. Woman in Europe gives up more than she receives, while pretending to be happy and free. In Islam, woman, in order to "guard her honor, her faith, and her integrity," can sacrifice everything: studies, a degree, work. That is because her liberty does not reside in appearances but in her ability to say no: "no to being a woman-object, a slave to modern blackmail, disguised in perfidy, and to social conditioning more enslaving than imprisonment in a penitentiary."

For Sultana, the lures of modern secular society—a discotheque, a park, flowers, laughter, music, dance—are there to be attacked, since they function basically to turn woman into a "slave." "A sheep that one fattens in a beautiful pasture is not free. The rose on which flies and filth land cannot have a beautiful spring or a beautiful smell." One must not listen to those who say that Islam wants woman to be ignorant and confined to her job as a housewife. "This is what Islam forbids woman to learn: the art of stealing her neighbor's man, the weaving of nets of debauchery, and the sacrificing of children to the golden calf and to the dragon of feminism." In her private life, says Sultana, a Muslim woman relaxes, plays, sings, dances with her husband, studies, teaches, gets angry, and so on. To veil oneself, to remain serious, to escape temptation is "to defend oneself against the breakers of couples, to push away evil, and to defend one's conjugal palace and spiritual kingdom; it is to refuse slavery and the submission to the infernal mesh of the outside—only to obey the Creator, Master of the Worlds." [31]

Sultana begins with a revolt against the sexual exploitation of the school environment with which most feminists (and probably most women) would sympathize. But the Belgian narrator turns this into an attack on feminism and the liberated woman. She does this by reversing discourses of public and private space, inside and outside, open and closed, freedom and confinement. The western stereotype of Islamic marital customs sees the woman's role as inferior and concretizes the idea of imprisonment through the symbol of the harem—a subjugating,

enclosed space. Of course, Sultana ennobles woman's space by calling it
a "conjugal palace." It is the outside, the world of work, or of public
leisure, that becomes for her the space of unfreedom, of "slavery." Sultana even uses, to stress the lack of freedom in this outside world, a western image of absolute confinement, the "penitentiary." No longer is it
the home that is the prison—an image very common in contemporary
secular writings in Arabic, as in Raymonda Hawa Tawil's title, *My
Home, My Prison,* or in the powerful short story by Ihsan Kamal, "A
Jailhouse of My Own." [32] Now it is the public, nondomestic, space that
is compared to the prison.

Sultana's revaluation of space is concretized in a striking image: the
infernal mesh of the outside (*l'engrenage infernal de l'extérieur*). Normally, *engrenage* implies a crowded space. It is a claustrophobic image,
but here it is associated with the exterior, which would normally imply,
if not freedom, at least openness and the absence of physical constraint.
Neither Karîmân Hamza nor Leïla Lahlou made such a clear reversal of
the valuations of private and public space.

Sultana is closer to Karîmân and Leïla when she places her emphasis,
as she had earlier, on the health of the heterosexual couple. Veiling protects from the "breakers of couples," just as it permits the defense of the
"conjugal palace." This vision of the couple conforms to the one that
emerged from the analysis of the body above: the health of the heterosexual couple is in the hands of the woman. [33]

This concluding material appended to Sultana's childhood memories
serves to redefine the totality of the incidents and to transform the experiences of a schoolgirl into a generalized commentary on women in Islam and the West. The culmination of this recasting is to define various
zones, or geographies if one will, in the experience of the female Muslim living in the West and of her "integrated body." These zones include
the social, the corporal, the sexual, and of course, the religious.

The social zone is perhaps the most easily defined. The young girl's
social environment is that of the Belgian school system. Here, all the authority figures are painted as hostile to Islam and to immigrants. And
these authority figures run the gamut from the schoolteacher to the
school director. The male teacher is abusive, and the female teacher,
racist. The school administration fares scarcely better.

The incidents involving the registration of Sultana in the school system teach an interesting lesson. Both parties misrepresent the reality
to further their goals. The school administrator claims that there is no

space for the young girl in the educational establishment when he becomes aware of her Moroccan nationality, only to change his mind when he hears of the possible matriculation of Belgian nationals. The mother, to unmask him, does not hesitate to call immediately after his initial refusal and to change the national identity of the potential students. This game of deliberate misrepresentation on the part of both adults is one whose lessons do not go unnoticed by the narrator.

This disguising of the truth is not unique in Sultana's spiritual journey. In a chapter on political refugees, the narrator relates the case of Ahmed, an Arab who has been living in Brussels for many years and who considers himself a member of Belgian society. His attempts to rent an apartment are what is under discussion. He would call, and when asked his nationality and the number of his children, he would tell the truth, hence finding himself without a place to live. "Until the day he decided to lie on the telephone." Then follows a dialogue with Ahmed and a landlord. When asked how many people are in the household, Ahmed replies this time, "My wife, myself, and four little dogs." When the landlord discovers that the household contained four children and not four dogs, the affair almost ends up in court.[34] Ahmed's story is about more than racism. It exposes the western preference for pets over people. The reader knows already that, in an Islamic worldview, valuing dogs over children is especially outrageous.

Ahmed's case is the last one in Sultana's journey and is followed directly by Mohammed Saghir's words on political refugees, a section that forms the closure to the spiritual journey. The narrator presents Ahmed's case sympathetically. When she introduces the dialogue he has with the landlord, she clearly states that he could not find a place to live "until the day he decided to lie on the telephone." The lesson here is the same as the one with the mother, except here the lying is not disguised but rather fully displayed to the reader of the journey. Both Ahmed and Sultana's mother are combating the racism of Belgian society. The moral of both stories is that if one must resort to lying in order to accomplish this, so be it.

But Sultana's mother is more than simply someone who misrepresents the reality to register her daughter in school. She is a strong character who battles the educational system on more than one occasion. At the same time, she is someone who is not Moroccan, but Belgian, a position that permits her greater access to the social structure of her native country, whose rules and regulations she seems to understand and manipulate quite well. Unlike her, Ahmed, the Arab in search of a living space, needs to call several times before he finally decides to lie about his family in order to find an apartment.

The mother, because of this liminal position, can more fully negotiate the social zone between Morocco and the West. After all, it was the mother's idea to go and seek the Imam's help in the opening chapter of Sultana's journey after the fateful dream. The narrator could not have put it more clearly, noting that her mother, "Belgian and baptized a Catholic . . . was also the first one to have the idea to speak to someone who was a specialist, that is, an Imam." [35] And, of course, the reader knows the importance of this visit in Sultana's life. [36]

Like the other zones, the corporal zone is a recurring one in the journey. The various manifestations of the body have been amply discussed above. [37] The childhood memories are further testimony to some of the links already seen between corporality and sexuality. Clear is the fact that these zones involving the body have to be controlled from an early age. Sultana's young colleagues who suffer at the hands of the school system do so because they have chosen to follow Islamic precepts of dress and demeanor in a hostile environment. The reason they have chosen this way of life is precisely to guard against the ills of the modern secular western lifestyle.

But this does not mean that the environment in which Sultana is operating on an intimate level is purely Islamic. The mother's allegiance to Christianity acts as a background to the discourse of Islam in Sultana's journey, echoing, at the same time, a Christian layer in the text. This appears in the first pages of the journey when one of Sultana's friends interprets her opening dream by telling her that she will become a "true Muslim" and that she will give birth to a child who will be someone in the future. [38] This last prediction, while not unknown in an Islamic context, has obvious Christian resonances. The narrator does go with her husband and some friends to Brugmann Hospital to watch a film on conception and pregnancy, but this possibility in her life ends here. This is the same hospital that Leïla visited for her cancer treatment. [39]

This Christian substratum is also present on the verbal level of the text. Z.'s run-in with the director of the school who forbids the head scarf is described as a "calvary." [40] It is true that the French word *calvaire* is more common in everyday parlance than its English equivalent. But this does not eliminate its Christian semantic basis. The different zones, ranging from the corporal to the spiritual, testify to the complexities of Sultana's journey and the testimony it sets forth of a Muslim minority having to survive in a racist western environment dominated by Christian cultural discourses.

But more than survival is at issue, the reader discovers. The mission of *L'Islam, la femme, et l'intégrisme: Journal d'une jeune femme européenne* is much more broadly defined and can be seen, in an ironic twist of language, as a "civilizing mission." Sultana tells her readers that God has permitted Arabs to come to Europe to work and, more importantly, "to make known the true face of Islam to those who do not know it or fear it, thus transmitting the Islamic message, which alone can exorcise modern society." [41]

This is certainly a serious mandate for the Muslim living in the alien environment of the West. And it is, ultimately, the task that Sultana has set for herself. The entire discourse of enslavement functions as a guide to the ultimate liberation of the modern woman through Islam, a liberation that can only be sustained within the heterosexual couple and with the support of a masculinized religious tradition.

CHAPTER EIGHT

Geographies of the Sacred

In her fascinating *Writing a Woman's Life,* Carolyn G. Heilbrun notes that there are four ways to "write a woman's life." The first of these entails a woman's telling her own life, writing her autobiography.[1] *Medicines of the Soul* has traveled primarily autobiographical roads, built by women telling their stories, and all in the first person.

The tellers of these stories emerge from different continents and speak different languages. Nevertheless, their journeys converge in odd and interesting ways, in the process engaging different discourses. These discourses span at the same time the medical, the corporal, the spiritual, the political, and the geographical and are, of course, deeply gendered. For the Egyptian Karîmân Hamza, the Moroccan Leïla Lahlou, and the Belgian Sultana Kouhmane, the body comes together with the soul to forge memorable narratives of redemption and spiritual fulfillment. In this process, all three women will cross various sorts of boundaries and borders, including linguistic and geographical, on their life-fulfilling sagas.

As with all autobiographical ventures, the literary operation of telling involves first and foremost a complex of narrative techniques that play in one way or another with time. The process of memory is one that allows the three women to look back at their lives as nominal or secularized Muslims whose spiritual quests will end in a religious conversion. The narration of the tales diachronically follows the actual transformation, in a strategy common in all three autobiographical projects.

Each of the three female heroes of these dramatic narratives, in her own way, begins her spiritual journey with a lack. The journey functions as a rectification of this lack. For Karîmân and Sultana, the lacks are less dramatically corporal than social and psychological. The shadow of suicide looms large in these journeys, and that would entail corporal destruction. Suicide is forbidden in Islam and is a serious sin.[2] The spiritual redemption that these potential suicide victims undergo saves them from eternal perdition. For Leïla, breast cancer is the additional danger that must be conquered.

At the same time, all three narrators experience a deeply significant transformation in their knowledge of their Islamic religious tradition. Beginning from a position of what could be seen as unawareness and unfamiliarity with Islam, Karîmân, Leïla, and Sultana are transformed into quasi authorities on their religious traditions. These changes and transformations might lead one to think that a *Bildungsroman* is in progress in these highly complex narratives. A female *Bildungsroman,* however, entails many other features that one does not encounter in these works. Nor do these journeys purport to be fictional in any way, an important literary fact that adds to their drama.[3] Nevertheless, there is indisputable development and progression in the lives of the heroes, evident attempts at finding self-fulfillment in a universe in which such a spiritual quest is by no means easy.

One of the central elements in all three sagas is the body. In fact, the three narratives link the other central element, the spiritual, to the corporal, in the process defining the spiritual through the corporal. The most dramatic example of this is, unquestionably, that of the Moroccan, Leïla. The breast cancer places her body at the foreground of the journey, and the reader watches as the mutating female body is ravaged by the disease and its medical treatment, only to be cured at the end by the spiritual intervention of the Prophet.

Along this curative journey, Leïla's body takes on various dimensions, intersecting with other discourses, primary among which is the religious. The physical entity that is the female body acquires significance in the opening of the journey. It is perhaps no accident that the saga begins after the exposure of this body in a swimming environment, a locus of whose moral dangers the Belgian, Sultana, amply warns her reader.

But there is more to Leïla's body than just this initial exposure. The body exposed and analyzed functions as a recurring topos in *Do Not Forget God.* Leïla's desire to publicly bare her body at the airport in

Casablanca was discussed. Of course, this desire was expressed in the context of a breast-cancer odyssey and as a means of revealing the fact that her body remained intact after the European medical journey. Nevertheless, such an exhibitionist desire would certainly run counter to the covered body advocated in Karîmân's story. The freedom from corporal constraints that Leïla's desire expresses is obvious in other parts of the breast-cancer narrative. The body touched and the body explored are other manifestations of this.

Leïla's entire discourse of body and shame intersects in provocative ways with the corporal discourses of her two coreligionists. For her, the breast becomes like any other body part that is examined without shame or embarrassment. The fixation on body parts is not unique to the breast in Lahlou's book. The body and the transmutations it undergoes traversing the domains of religion and medicine were analyzed. Nevertheless, there are other body parts that bring the Moroccan saga within the same universe as that of Karîmân or even Sultana. Hair is one of the dramatic elements here that receives a great deal of attention. Leïla's hair is restored to its previous state by the Prophet Muhammad during his oneiric intervention; therefore, the visibility of this body part, its ability to be the object of the gaze, is primary. The opposite is the case for Karîmân, for whom the hair, her pride and joy, must be covered and shielded from view. And the hair as temptation was key in Sultana's odyssey.

This entire game with the gaze and the body being played in these three journeys adds another dimension to the scopic regimes in which the three women are operating. Normally, the position advocated by Karîmân and Sultana would take precedence, that woman's body should be hidden. And this, of course, is the visual message that the covers of Leïla Lahlou's book also promulgate, with the two different pictures of the hero with her hair concealed. Leïla's textual message, however, is different. Clearly, a diseased body can inflect the scopic regime dominant in the culture.

Leïla's corporality is subject to the vicissitudes of medicine and religion. The case is expressed a bit differently by Karîmân Hamza, for whom the body itself as a sum of parts is not so much transformed and mutating as it is an object that must be hidden from view. While Karîmân's body also is subject to changes, these alterations remain, at least on the level of the narrative, external, as the emphasis in Karîmân's journey centers on a movement from unveiling to veiling. And the covering was not easily had but represents a corporal battle between the female narrator and male authorities.

For Sultana, the complexities of the body are there as well. In her case, however, she diverges from her Egyptian and Moroccan literary cousins. Whereas for Leïla and Karîmân, the corporal element focused essentially on the narrator and her body, for Sultana the corporal involves a multitude of bodies. True, the body of the narrator is the one that is purified in a dramatic visit to a spring in Morocco. But in Belgium, other bodies vie with that of the narrator. Here, the bodies are most often diseased bodies, such as that of the AIDS victim, or otherwise sickly bodies, such as that of Khadija, a damaged body that eventually leads to her husband's taking another wife.

Sultana's diseased bodies also play an ambiguous game with medicine, a game that would not be unfamiliar to Leïla. After all, the AIDS victim is afflicted with a physical illness, much as the Moroccan breast-cancer victim is. And for her, as for Leïla, religion competes with medicine. These tensions between the religious and the medical operate beyond the narratives themselves. A Moroccan friend, Amina Bouchakor, told me of the case of a colleague who was afflicted with breast cancer. Amina mentioned that everyone recommended to the breast-cancer victim that she read Leïla Lahlou's book with its spiritual cure to make her feel better. When I mentioned to Amina that Lahlou herself had died of another cancer, she responded by telling me that this colleague had also died of her cancer.[4] When I related this anecdote (without names, of course) in response to a question following a public lecture at al-Akhawayn University in Ifrane, Morocco, a member of the audience, an Egyptian physician living and practicing in Morocco, expressed her dismay. For her, breast cancer was a concrete illness, and she considered it irresponsible to allow cancer victims to live under the illusion that they might become cured through some kind of religious intervention.[5]

But, of course, narratives of spiritual redemption, such as the three at hand, are operating under different rules than those applied by the physician who engaged me in this conversation. The breast cancer in Leïla's journey functions like the possible suicide in Karîmân's text or like the AIDS in Sultana's work. All three corporal threats intensify the redemptive power of religion and spirituality.

This particular aspect of the narrative of spiritual transformation in which illness is an instigator to the religious path is not a peculiarity of the texts analyzed in depth. Shams al-Bârûdî had the same experience, which she defines as a punishment, as did the famous actress and singer Shâdiya, who also took up the veil.[6] And do not forget that classic text by Ni^cmat Sidqî in which these same motifs of corporal punishment and spiritual salvation operate.

The female body is what defines these transnational narrators and permits them to become players in the highly charged arena of gender politics in contemporary Islam. When they begin on their spiritual journeys, all three women demonstrate a lack of knowledge of their complex Islamic religious tradition. All three must come to terms with (or at least work with) male figures who seemingly hold the keys that unlock the secrets of this knowledge. Interestingly enough, this aspect of gender politics unites the three female believers across continents and languages. In Karîmân's case, her entire spiritual and corporal transformation had to be mediated through the male gender. Not only is Karîmân's mentor on the path a prominent male religious figure, but the medieval models who function as signposts on the spiritual road are also men. Certainly, female mystics could have been adduced here, but they were not.

The gender politics in Karîmân's case are complicated by the presence of the male as father figure. But not to worry here. For the narrator to finally—and fully—integrate herself into the religious community, both her biological paternity and her spiritual paternity must be eliminated, as both her biological father and her spiritual father die before the end of the narrative.

Of course, Karîmân, the hero of the spiritual journey, is not the first female literary character who must kill the males in her narrative in order to achieve independence. This construct exists in other texts in the Arabic literary tradition, but these texts emanate most often from more secularly minded writers. The Palestinian female poet Fadwâ Tûqân, in her autobiography, would be an eloquent example here, as would the Egyptian ^cAbla al-Ruwaynî.[7]

The male gender, as it turns out, is equally important for both the Moroccan narrative and the Francophone Belgian one. In Leïla's case, the female body becomes a pawn in the game of gender politics. The physicians whose medical advice Leïla seeks are all men. And the named physicians in the appended medical documents are also of the male gender. But even more important, the spiritual leader who teaches the breast-cancer victim the intricacies of her own Muslim tradition in Mecca is a male, the Imam of the mosque. True, once Leïla has assimilated the tradition, she is able to pass it on to her women coreligionists in Mecca, but she cannot do this without the teaching of the male first. Of course, the ultimate gender politics in Leïla's case are those of her cure through the intervention of the male prophet, Muhammad.

Leïla's case is not dissimilar to that of the Belgian Sultana. Sultana also receives her religious training from men. Not only does the male Prophet appear to her in a dream, but the Imam of the Brussels mosque is instrumental in interpreting this oneiric vision and setting her on the correct path. He is followed by Sultana's fiancé, who soon enough becomes her husband. And like Leïla, Sultana will learn to transmit religious teachings to other women, such as the female AIDS victim. Sultana's body is purified at the spring of a male saint, whose female companion has disappeared from view.

But above all else, the three narratives of spiritual salvation share a common gender problematic: the textual presence of the male voice in the first-person narrative by the female. On the most obvious level, all three works contain either an introduction, an epilogue, or both by male writers. The three first-person sagas of spiritual deliverance must share the limelight with men. In Karîmân's case, this was not only in the presence of an introduction and an epilogue but in the heavy intertextual presence of her male mentor, Shaykh ᶜAbd al-Halîm Mahmûd. His literary voice appears in the segments from his works that the narrator weaves into her own story. With Leïla, the multilayered introductory sections in the Arabic and French texts were complicated by that alternate medical narrative composed of documentation from male medical specialists, all writing in French. Here, as well, Sultana does not escape the gender web. The last chapter in her short book is by the male Cheikh Mohammed Saghir, otherwise known as M. S. in the text, who is her husband.

Just as the intertextuality with the male voice unnecessarily complicates Karîmân's narrative, so it is with the use of the male gender in the title of Leïla Lahlou's book. In the case of Sultana, the presence of the male extends to the title page of the work itself. Remember here that were it not for a publisher who insisted on a change of title, Karîmân Hamza's book would have foregrounded her male mentor on its cover page.

This heavy presence of the male voice is not necessarily a given in works by Islamic revivalist women telling their lives, or more correctly their spiritual transformations. The case of the actress Shams al-Bârûdî is an eloquent counterexample to these three works. Her pamphlet detailing her religious odyssey is introduced by Zaynab al-Ghazâlî, the female spiritual and literary foremother for all these texts. Not only that, but Zaynab al-Ghazâlî links her protégée to the famous medieval female mystic Râbiᶜa al-ᶜAdawiyya.[8] This powerful female personality was, of course, completely absent from Karîmân's mystical journey.

So why this need for male validation? On one level, one can argue that this question is culturally determined and not specific to the three cases or their spiritual quests. After all, there are other women writers who receive their seal of approval from men introducing their texts and even comparing them to male giants in the field. This is the case, once again, with the Palestinian poet Fadwâ Tûqân, whose autobiography was introduced by the prominent Palestinian male poet Samîh al-Qâsim and compared in the process to that classic modern autobiography by the Arab world's leading modernizer, the Egyptian Tâhâ Husayn.[9] Whatever the cultural baggage that may be carried by women writers in the Middle East and worldwide, it is certainly made heavier in the case of these religious writers. Their right to speak and tell their lives is unmistakably sanctioned by their male coreligionists. The entire question of the literary agency of the revivalist Muslim woman would seem to be tied to that of the male.

But there is, in fact, more at stake here. All three female protagonists are involved not only in gender politics that deal with male-female roles, woman's clothing, and so forth, but with more global and cultural gender politics that go to the heart of what defines contemporary Islamic discourses and political struggles. Evident also was the crucial role that the Arabo-Islamic textual tradition, lovingly known as the *turâth*, or heritage, plays in all three of these works, even in that by the Francophone Sultana Kouhmane.

The textual presence of the males testifies to the power and strength of this heritage. Not surprisingly, this heritage, handed down through the centuries, concentrates heavily on the male gender. This does not mean that the female component is absent, simply that the male voice is the one that negotiates and largely interprets this tradition for the female. That it should then be the male Imam in the Brussels mosque and the male Imam in the Meccan mosque who transmit this knowledge to Sultana and Leïla, respectively, should subsequently not be a cause of astonishment. Rather, the shock would have come had the opposite been the case, had a woman been the official transmitter of this high Islamic culture.

The identical situation vis-à-vis the *turâth* then obtains with all three women writers. Each must negotiate the complexities of this tradition of which she is initially innocent. The spiritual journeys function as a way of acquiring a knowledge of this heritage, knowledge that is indispensable for the change that each woman undergoes from nominal Muslim to devout believer.

This complicated relationship between women and the *turâth* must also be seen in the larger context of contemporary women writers and not merely Islamic women writers. The literary undertaking of, for example, the feminist physician-writer Nawal El Saadawi demonstrates a similar attempt to digest and reformulate the complex tradition, but in her case from a more secularly oriented (if not anticlerical) point of view. Her attempts to recast and rewrite the *turâth* amount to nothing short of the creation of an alternate feminist theology and mythology. And this she does in several of her works.[10] The agenda of the revivalist writer is, of course, radically different from that of a secularist writer like Dr. El Saadawi. Nevertheless, the gender politics are not dissimilar, in that for both the secular and the religious writers, control of the *turâth* is in the hands of the men who use it and disburse it to the women as needs be.

But the rich legacy of premodern Islam was not as univocal and certainly not as narrowly gendered as these revivalist texts might lead one to believe. True, the masculine dominated, as it has in all the Abrahamic religions. Alongside the dominant masculine traditions, however, were important feminine components of the religious life that ranged from the spiritual borderlands of folk religion through some of the most elite manifestations of the classical Islamic experience. Many of these elements still survive in Muslim religious practice today. But it is precisely this female Islam to which the three revivalists do not turn.

On the contrary, one almost has the impression that these three authors feared that their messages would be tainted by too great an involvement with this female side of the Islamic tradition. By telling their stories publicly and in more or less literary form, and by taking leadership roles of greater or lesser importance, these women certainly argue for, and contribute to, a visible and active role for their gender in the Islamic revival movement. Yet they do so through a masculinized version of their own tradition and under careful male guidance.

The point goes beyond gender politics. It should serve as a reminder that the Islamic revival is not simply a resurgence of earlier forms, a return to a past or to an authentic tradition, whatever that might be. What one calls a tradition or a heritage, spiritual or otherwise, is a series of choices, a construct, serving present purposes, including gender purposes.

Perhaps one of the most provocative ways in which the religious tradition appears in these women's stories of conversion is through the medium of dreams. And these are not just any dreams but ones in which male authority figures play an important role. The Prophet is primary here. The appearance of Muhammad, be it to the Egyptian Karîmân or the Moroccan Leïla or to the Belgian Sultana, is not a problem. How the Prophet can transcend geographical zones and borders in the oneiric state was a topic that had already fascinated medieval Muslim writers. In the context of the women religious writers, the appearance of the Prophet is but a spiritual sign of that crucial phenomenon.

As with other dream narratives, the precise location of the oneiric story in the unfolding of the narrative is extremely significant.[11] For Leïla, the cure dream with the Prophet represents the culmination and the successful resolution of a battle with breast cancer, functioning as the authentication of her entire journey. For Sultana, the opposite situation applies. Instead of ending the narrative, the dream with the Prophet opens it. The dream for the Belgian writer is the invitation to begin the journey on the spiritual path. For Karîmân, dreams are also a source of validation and, therefore, occur after the spiritual transformation has been initiated. Her dream, for example, with Shaykh ᶜAbd al-Halîm Mahmûd will signal her full integration into the spiritual family. The three women writers are, of course, not unique in their vision of the Prophet. Shams al-Bârûdî in her narrative also speaks of a dream in which the Prophet appears to her.[12]

Ibrâhîm ᶜIsâ, in his work on the veiling of former actresses and entertainers, has a skeptical attitude to the presence of dreams in many of the stories involving a religious transformation among the rich and famous.[13] Whatever the validity of ᶜIsâ's criticism, the oneiric experience remains an extremely important component of these spiritual narratives.

More importantly, the dream stories allow the women religionists to play on the high cultural register along with their male colleagues. The Prophet not only endorses the female sagas but, in the process, enables them to become major contenders in the creation of a contemporary revivalist discourse. All three women, no matter what the country, can then partake of the all-important activity of religious propaganda for Islam.

This participation also exploits another current in Islam, the mystical one. Karîmân showed the intricacies of this system and its paramount importance in her spiritual trajectory. But Islamic mysticism is not restricted to the Egyptian activist. This is a component of the spiritual that has an uncanny ability to, once again, transcend national and linguistic borders. Ibrâhîm ibn Adham, who was so instrumental in setting Karîmân on her journey, resurfaces in other texts by Muslim women of the revival. Both he and Karîmân's other important male mystic, al-Fudayl, make an appearance in Shams al-Bârûdî, in a text of advice as she is explaining to her reader about these two dramatic conversions.[14] Ibrâhîm's most dramatic role, however, is when he emerges in the autobiographical saga by Amatullah Armstrong, an Australian woman convert to Islam.[15]

These stories of spiritual transformation are a powerful articulation of the multilayered ways in which Islam functions in today's transnational world. Karîmân's saga, which seems to be superficially about dress, embodies in reality a strong Sufi content. Its mysticism emanates from the high Islamic tradition, drawing on some of the major names of this spiritual current. Sultana's journey to the spring in the Middle Atlas also reflects a mystical trend, that of a saint-worship often associated with Sufism. But her Sufism is closer to folk religion, to Moroccan maraboutism, with its pagan pre-Islamic substratum. At the same time, this recourse to the tomb of Sidi Slimane omits the female component, that of Lalla ᶜA'isha. Leïla also has a recourse to a spring, but hers is that of Zamzam, the water source fully monotheized and integrated into the orthodox Islamic religious system. The echoes of mysticism in Leïla Lahlou's spiritual saga are more subtle but still significant: the references to the *hâtif* and to the spiritual category of the *habîb*, or beloved.

From Egypt and Morocco to Saudi Arabia and from Belgium to Morocco, the examples affirm a yearning to be integrated into a largely masculine sacred. Yet this sacred, when combined with gender, yields results different from the highly legalistic theology of other, more conservative, revivalist sources like the Hanbalî Ibn Taymiyya (d. 728/1328) or his more popular successor, Ibn Qayyim al-Jawziyya (d. 751/1350). These materials are extremely popular in Islamic circles today and serve as foundations for much of the revivalist written corpus. The female religiosity of these spiritual autobiographies would appear to be quite distinct from the legal injunctions of these conservative thinkers and their modern disciples. The eloquent women of the contemporary Islamic revival may well be acting under the influence of male thinkers, but the gender element permits an interiorization of the journey on a much more mystical level.

This mystical bent in an otherwise heavily legalistic revival is highly suggestive. Is one, in fact, looking at a female contemporary spiritual revival distinct from the male one? If so, then this female component would be drawing part of its inspiration from Sufism, which has been considered by some scholars to be more open to women than the more orthodox, legalistic tradition.[16]

Whatever the validity of this assessment, it remains that the mystical is one of the ways that helps define gender in the contemporary Islamic revival. As Karîmân, Leïla, and Sultana become increasingly integrated into contemporary Islamic discourses, they find themselves crossing different types of boundaries, in the process becoming immersed in different geographies. The geographies in question range from the sacred through the medical to the touristic.

All three journeys begin with some type of physical displacement, an environmental break from the earlier life that leads to the new religious path. For Karîmân, it is the entry into the religious institute; for Leïla, it is the medical clinic that heralds the diagnosis of breast abnormalities; and for Sultana, it is the Brussels mosque. In the process of religious transformation, all three women will transit in and out of these different loci. Karîmân's odyssey begins in a religious institute, an environment alien to the young woman. In the process of her religious transformation, the reader will watch her move within different geographical and religious spaces, including the pilgrimage to Mecca.

Travel for a woman is not an automatic given on the cultural map of the Arab world and North Africa today. It is an inherently problematic, if not dangerous, activity that must be performed under certain conditions, such as with a legally sanctioned guide. The issue of the traveling woman receives a great deal of attention from contemporary religious thinkers and legists, who warn their readers about the moral dangers of woman's traveling alone.[17] And not surprisingly, it is handled in provocative ways by a secularist writer like Nawal El Saadawi.[18] Some of the flavor of moral danger associated with female travel comes out in the travel advice book of Rabîᶜ ibn Muhammad al-Saᶜûdî, who effectively compares the moral dangers of travel (for males) with those of female adornment.[19] Needless to say, for the three born-again women, travel in the spiritual journey is done according to social, religious, and cultural norms. All three women perform their geographical displacements in the company of the appropriate guides, such as a husband. Yet the mere fact of making these journeys, talking about them at length, and making of them a source of personal authority and validation implies a measure of cultural boldness.

For Leïla, the travels of the body will involve three continents: Europe, Africa, and Asia. In fact, the ideological tension between western medicine, on the one hand, and the Islamic miraculous, on the other, is concretized spatially through what are virtually two different pilgrimages. The first is a set of journeys to the high places of European medicine; the second, a voyage to the holy places of Islam. The geographical focal point, the place where the two journeys are connected, is Paris, the western city in which the hero sees the Ka^cba in front of her. Both itineraries are journeys from a periphery to a center: one, technological, the other, spiritual. Morocco, in this scheme, is the space where modern western medical culture and Islamic culture overlap.

By comparison, Karîmân's and Sultana's trajectories are simpler. They both move from a less to a more Islamic locus. With Sultana, this is obvious, since she goes from a western Christian country, Belgium, to the Muslim one of Morocco. Karîmân, like Leïla, already lives in a Muslim country. Both feel the need, however, to travel to Mecca in Arabia, one on the pilgrimage, and the other on the *^cumra*. This testifies to the spatial aspect of the religious, fundamentally transnational, quest. After all, Karîmân could have gone on a pilgrimage to the mosques of Cairo as a mark of her devotion, something quite common among Muslims who visit or live in Egypt. By the same token, Leïla could have made a pilgrimage to a Moroccan saint's tomb, like the one Sultana visited. For these narratives, spiritual transformation dictates physical displacement.

This religious geography can be conceptualized as being one of three zones: (1) the West, (2) North Africa and the Middle East, and (3) Mecca. The first zone, the West, is un-Islamic and potentially anti-Islamic. The second, North Africa and the Middle East, is a contested space of secularism and religion. The third, Mecca, is a pure space of the sacred.

It would be a mistake, however, to see these valuations as fixed. In the geo-semiotics of the transnational religious revival, signs must be understood by their syntax—that is, by their positions in a sequence. If Morocco is a zone of relative secularism for Leïla, it is one of pure Islamity for Sultana. Nonreligious or westernized aspects of Moroccan culture are simply invisible in her account. In the trip to Sidi Slimane, one does not traverse any modern cities, one simply arrives at the site.

In this system of sacred geography, the holy is translated into a place to the south for Sultana and to the east for both Karîmân and Leïla. In a sense, this recapitulates a very traditional Islamic geography in which the territories to the north and west of the Islamic world are zones of nonbelief.[20]

This geography has been modernized in a number of interesting ways. First of all, it resolves itself essentially into a direction rather than a location. One moves from the periphery of the sacred toward its center. If one starts in Morocco and Egypt, one goes to Mecca. But if one starts further on the periphery, that is in Europe, the same spiritual result can be obtained through a trip to Morocco. (The same phenomenon is there with the Australian, Amatulla Armstrong, in her travels to North Africa.)²¹ Leïla's starting point is Sultana's goal.

Most important, this Islamic geography has adapted to the present transnational world. It is a transnational geography of religion. First of all, Islam is within the West, so that Europe, for example (though the same could be said of New Jersey), is both a place outside the Dâr al-Islâm and a locus of Islamic activity. But spaces of more or less sacrality (or more or less secularism) exist within Muslim countries. Karîmân crosses into a new world when she goes to the district of al-Husayn in Cairo, previously a foreign land to her. The same could be said of the unspecified locus in Morocco where Leïla went swimming. In effect, the old division of Dâr al-Islâm and Dâr al-Harb is repeated in microcosm inside both the Islamic world and the non-Islamic world.

As the only one of the three born-again women to go from a Muslim country to Europe, Leïla also participates and even glories in another transnational geography, that of tourism. For Sultana, by contrast, tourist Morocco is nonexistent. One would never guess from her account that the site of Sidi Slimane lies close to the two great tourist cities of Meknes and Fez.

These complex geographies are complemented by an intricate geography of language. There are linguistic-geographical zones that intersect, and there are linguistic usages within each of these zones that help demarcate the spiritual. On the most obvious level, there is the zone of Arabicity, which is that of Arabic and the Arab world, and the zone of French, which is Francophone. Karîmân, for example, remains both linguistically and geographically within the zone of Arabicity. Leila, who is bilingual, navigates both zones, the Francophone zone (through Morocco, France, and Belgium) and the Arabic zone, since she travels to Saudi Arabia as well when she performs the ᶜumra. Morocco functions as the zone of linguistic intermixing, producing both Francophone and Arabophone results. Hence, the French translation of Leïla Lahlou's book takes on greater "Moroccanity," if one can call it that, in order that it be brought back within the fold of Leïla's native Morocco. This is partly the result of the political and cultural blessings the work receives from the King of Morocco and the country's media organizations. Sultana, like Karîmân, works essentially in one language zone, but in her case it is the Francophone. The bilingualism of Belgium surfaces only in a brief reference to a class in Dutch.

These geographies are clearly interlocking. Yet, the East/West division, or the Dâr al-Islâm/non-Dâr al-Islâm division, is not identical to the linguistic division. Sultana penetrates into the space of Islam, but this is also a part of the space of the French language. These multiple geographies remain mediated by language. This is what permits Morocco, which is not the center for Leïla in her journey, to become the center and the "source" (in its dual meaning, including that of the "spring") for Sultana. At the same time, the imbrications of the sacred and linguistic geographies can permit the discussion of Leïla's breast-cancer journey by Sultana's husband in his Francophone book on AIDS, published in Belgium but distributed there and elsewhere.

The linguistic usages within each of these geographical zones add a complexity to all three of the spiritual journeys. In Karîmân's case, the heavy use of the religious intertext, with its quotations from the Qur'ân, the *hadîth,* and so on, facilitates the coexistence of the classical and the modern literary levels of the Arabic language. These levels signal the presence of another cultural and religious plane, to which the female hero must aspire and which the reader knows she will eventually attain. The levels of language are also tied to an intricate game of religious politics. When the young woman first hears the Muslim greeting from ᶜAbd al-Halîm Mahmûd, she is taken aback, for that is not the cultural and religious universe in which she has been circulating. She will, however, learn these usages.

Complicating this linguistic situation in Karîmân's journey is the presence of the dialect. This particular level of Arabic emanates from the discussions the narrator has with individuals who are calling into question her spiritual transformation, both her female friends in the social club of which she is a member and the aggressive interlocutor in the religious establishment. What this means is that the physical location in which the dialect is spoken is not nearly as important as what its existence speaks to: a level of disbelief in, and mocking of, Karîmân's spiritual journey. Of course, in contemporary literary Arabic texts, most conversations are transcribed in the literary language. The presence of dialect in a text creates a multilingual situation with multiple referents that echo other divisions, in these cases the religious and the secular.

In Leïla's narrative, the Moroccan dialect makes no appearance whatsoever. The dialogues between the family members, for example, in reality surely took place in dialect. Nevertheless, they are transcribed in the literary form of the Arabic language, in conformity with standard literary usages.

Where Leïla's linguistic games appear more distinctly is in the mix of Arabic and French. This is, of course, not at all atypical of the North African literary and cultural situation. On the other hand, Leïla does gently poke fun at the accents of the non-Arabic-speaking female Muslim women in Mecca when they attempt to utter Arabic words. In such a context, the reader understands the high value that is placed on the language of the Qur'ân. Leïla's narrative exemplifies the hybrid and multilingual nature of North African culture, especially when this culture comes face to face with the Arabo-Islamic tradition.

For Sultana, as well, there is a bilingualism. But for her, this bilingualism manifests itself in the unfamiliarity of a religious language spoken and pronounced in a French environment. This is exactly what occurs in the Brussels mosque, when the Imam greets Leïla and her mother with the traditional Muslim greeting. This is similar to Karîmân's situation when she first hears this greeting. But for the Egyptian convert, the salutation, despite its cultural foreignness, is understandable since it is delivered in Arabic. For Sultana, the Arabic, despite its simplicity, is completely opaque and must be translated for her by the male religious authority.

This transnational world is a postimperial one, in that many—but not all—transnational forces reflect the history of European imperialism in the Muslim world. And, as the cases show, other factors, like language, are frequently more important than former imperial relations. The link between Belgium and Morocco, key to Sultana's text and vitally present in Leïla's, is one based on language alone. Belgium is one of the few European states never to have had any imperial involvement in Morocco, a country variously occupied by the French, the Spanish, the English, and the Portuguese. Leïla moves effortlessly between Morocco, Belgium, and France. No one ever seems to suggest that she consider medical treatment in the United States, Britain, or Germany, for example. Francophonia is more powerful than previous imperial connections (though, in the case of Morocco, the imperial connection is directly related to the linguistic one). That is why it seems more accurate to characterize this geography as transnational than postcolonial, a concept whose applicability to the world of Arabic letters is problematic to say the least.[22] The transnational nature of these geographies of movement stands out even more clearly when compared with the nationalism-creating itineraries sketched in Benedict Anderson's provocative *Imag-*

ined Communities. These Muslim women's itineraries show the impress of those Anderson identifies with the pre-modern "religious community"—with the significant difference that the center is no longer a place but only a direction. Yet these three spiritual itineraries follow neither an imperial nor a national pattern. They are of our postnational age.[23]

The linguistic issues raised in the three transnational spiritual autobiographies represent a phenomenon linked to the differences between the religious and the secular lifestyles. The transition between the two lifestyles is obviously critical to the entire enterprise for the three born-again women, as is the denunciation of the secular way of life. The "before" and "after" literary pictures of these three lives are not that dissimilar. Both Karîmân and Sultana smoked cigarettes. That activity was central in Karîmân's saga. In Sultana's case, her fiancé reproaches her for smoking and she, in turn, accuses him of being backward and an "integrist."[24] Both Karîmân and Sultana also spoke of their household pets.

Fundamentally, however, for all three born-again women, the transition can be defined as being essentially one that moves from the pleasures of the secular life to those of the religious life. All three women must abandon secular delectations and replace them with religious ones. Music, literature, clothing: all three women forsake the secular cultural products and promote the religious ones. Music is perhaps the element that best symbolizes these transformations, transcending as it does national and linguistic borders. When Sultana counsels the religious listener against the music of Bob Marley, she has clearly made a choice. Or when Leïla requests that the tapes of Andalusian music be replaced by tapes of the Qur'ân, she has made the same choice. But what she casts off is different: her rejection of Andalusian music is a rejection of Moroccan culture, whereas Sultana's rejection of Bob Marley is a rejection of western culture.

What is referred to in Morocco as Andalusian music bears a special relationship to Moroccan national identity today. Moroccans see Islamic Spain as representing an earlier phase of their own history. In fact, as often as not, the same groups ruled in what is now Morocco and what was then Islamic Iberia. A public performance of Andalusian music (like one I attended for the coronation anniversary of Hasan II in March 1998) is an elite and official cultural event equivalent to a staging of the Ring Cycle at Bayreuth. In rejecting this, Leïla is rejecting a large part of her largely Muslim national heritage and identity. The Islamic revival is not a return to the past or a defense of local authenticity against an encroaching western-inspired otherness. Islam, too, is a transnational movement with universal ambitions, and a revivalist can move away from his or her local, historically Muslim, culture just as much as from that of the West.

The enjoyment of the religious life is advocated by all three narrators. Adhering to Muslim practices does not necessarily translate into the casting aside of the pleasures of the flesh, the reader is assured. Sultana makes it clear to her reader that an alternate world of enjoyment exists. Simply, it exists in the home, where a woman can dance, sing, wear makeup, and so on.

In her defense of these pleasures, Sultana uses another spatial distinction: that between the home, where woman can partake of these activities, and the space outside the home, where men mingle with women, a situation fraught for Sultana with moral danger. This moral danger is not insignificant when the issue of veiling arises, as it does with the modest Muslim girls in the Belgian schools.

But veiling is essential to Karîmân's narrative. In her case, however, her transformation involves not only a movement from unveiling to veiling but also a movement from the private to the public, in which she becomes a visible and recognizable personality. In a sort of ironic twist, if Karîmân's journey were a western narrative, one would argue that it is a text of liberation, in which a woman narrator finds a public voice and place. This is precisely, in fact, what Shaykh Muhammad al-Ghazâlî had warned Karîmân Hamza about: criticism of her lifestyle would be leveled at her not only from the secularists who would oppose the wearing of the veil by women but by the more conservative religionists who would oppose the appearance of a woman on television. For Sultana, the veil reinforces, or carries to the outside world, spatial segregation of the sexes. For Karîmân, it is a visible obedience to God's command but also a sartorial transformation that facilitates her new, highly visible public role.

For Leïla, the politics of veiling are almost inconsequential, despite the book cover. Her body, rather than being veiled, is in fact involved in a continual process of unveiling. This is because her corporal entity functions as the battlefield of religion versus science, finally to become the space of the miracle cure and the holy.

No more eloquent reminder can be had for the fact that these spiritual sagas are imbricated, willy-nilly, within the politics of the contemporary religious revival. And this politics is not simply the religious politics of the religious revival. The politics of governments, nations, and states find their way into the spiritual narratives. Karîmân's increased involvement in the religious way of life translates itself into an increased

politicization in her text. The introduction to her book by Muhammad
ᶜAtiyya Khamîs speaks of the need for women like her who can undertake the battle against imperialism, Zionism, and communism.[25] She
herself, in the midst of the 1967 War, decides to embark on a discussion
on the Jews.[26]

But by far the most eloquent of the three narrators on the political
arena is Sultana. Her existence in the West means that, for her, defense
of Islam and Muslims is a continuing necessity. She not only addresses
herself to Middle Eastern politics such as the Israeli bombardment of
a Muslim area in South Lebanon but lances into the western media for
their minimal reaction toward the event, especially when compared to
their response to various explosions in the French capital. All this, for
Sultana, translates into a negative attitude to Muslim integrism.[27]

Of course, the image of Islam in the West is not a new topic.[28] More
interesting is the fact that Sultana is willing to delve into the highly
charged arena of sectarian politics. Certainly, she assures her reader,
Muslims hold French hostages in Lebanon. "But it is Christian Maro-
nites" who are responsible for an attack in Paris. In the course of the
same discussion, she asks why people confuse Arab and Muslim, when
"Islam has nothing to do with Arab nationalism." [29]

The political positions in Sultana's narrative reflect a strong anti-
western position, directed not only to the Europe she inhabits but to the
United States and the Soviet Union as well. The Americans are condemned for their attacks on Iran while at the same time selling the Ira-
nians arms when they came to fight Iraq. The Soviets, on the other hand,
fare no better, because they pretend to defend the oppressed populations
of the world while at the same time selling irradiated milk from Cher-
nobyl to Africans.[30] These positions are, of course, not necessarily coter-
minous with, and restricted to, a contemporary Islamic perspective. In
fact, they might just as easily represent a secularist Arab position as a religious Islamic one.

Sultana's involvement in these political discussions speaks to the pre-
eminence of the global and its various political currents. A transnational
Islam means that bodies and religions are enmeshed in geographies. It
does not simply mean that ideas and people travel; it means that these
cultural formations have a geographical, spatial dimension that reaches
beyond national or civilizational boundaries. This transnationality is
not only a factor for people in transitional environments like bilingual
Morocco or Muslim communities in Europe. It has become inherent in
all areas of Islam, so it can be found by implication even in Karîmân's

use of the dog, a flexible animal that crossed the boundaries from western pet to Sufi symbol.

Nevertheless, the agendas of the three spiritual sagas are not identical. Karîmân engages in her battle with almost no reference to western feminism. For Sultana, by contrast, this is a powerful issue that surfaces again and again in the journey. The complexities of female homosocialities also differed between Leïla's account and Karîmân's, and this despite the fact that both narrators were engaged with the identical religious activity, a pilgrimage to the holy places of Islam.

When these female sagas of redemption are set in the larger context of the Islamic revival, it becomes that much more critical to heed Jean-Noël Vuarnet's words in his *Extases Féminines*. The French critic underlines the necessity of distinguishing between the female mystical and the male mystical: "Men and women are perhaps not transmitting exactly the same thing. At least it is not to the same ears that men and women address themselves." [31] In fact, these gender differences are clear if one looks at the accounts of spiritual transformation from nominal Muslim to religious Muslim in which men are the central figures. These may be narrated in the first person, as in the case of Mohamed Ali Gerbaoui, or transmitted by an outside narrator, such as the stories related by Shaykh ʿAʾid ibn ʿAbd Allâh al-Qarnî. The gender component is extremely significant, as are the public-private distinctions.[32]

The three women writers in the transnational Islamic revival tell different and yet convergent stories. Woman's body is a central component of religious transformation, whether this body be located in Egypt, Morocco, or Belgium. All three women struggle with the corporal, as they progress along the spiritual path. They also share a sacred geography, one whose origins lie in medieval Islam. Spiritual salvation lies to the south and east, toward (but not necessarily in) that Islamic heartland which is Arabia. Spiritual danger (the modern forms of which are secularism and materialism) likewise has a physical locus, those lands to the north and west, which are Europe. For Karîmân, for Leïla, and for Sultana, it is their own bodies that must travel to sacred spaces, in physical journeys that seal the corporal and the spiritual.

Notes

INTRODUCTION

1. References to the specific works under discussion will be found in the chapters below.

2. Natalie Zemon Davis, *Women on the Margins: Three Seventeenth-Century Lives* (Cambridge and London: Harvard University Press, 1995), pp. 1–4.

3. See Michael M. J. Fischer and Mehdi Abedi, *Debating Muslims: Cultural Dialogues in Postmodernity and Tradition* (Madison: University of Wisconsin Press, 1990).

4. Fedwa Malti-Douglas, *Woman's Body, Woman's Word: Gender and Discourse in Arabo-Islamic Writing* (Princeton, N.J.: Princeton University Press, 1991); Fedwa Malti-Douglas, *Men, Women, and God(s): Nawal El Saadawi and Arab Feminist Poetics* (Berkeley and Los Angeles: University of California Press, 1995).

CHAPTER 1

1. Karîmân Hamza, *Rihlatî min al-Sufûr ilâ al-Hijâb,* 1st ed. (Cairo: Dâr al-Iᶜtisâm, 1981); Karîmân Hamza, *Rihlatî min al-Sufûr ilâ al-Hijâb,* 2nd ed. (Beirut: Dâr al-Fath lil-Tibâᶜa wal-Nashr, 1986). Unless otherwise indicated, references are to the second edition. Laylâ al-Hulw, *Falâ Tansa Allâh* (Casablanca: Matbaᶜat al-Najâh al-Jadîda, 1984); Leïla Lahlou, *N'oublie pas Dieu,* trans. Mustapha El-Kasri (Casablanca: Imprimerie Najah El Jadida, 1987); Cheikh Mohammed Saghir and Kouhmane Sultana, *L'Islam, la femme, et l'intégrisme: Journal d'une jeune femme européenne* (Brussels: Edition Al-Imen,

1991). On the inversion of Kouhmane Sultana's name to Sultana Kouhmane, see chapter 6.

2. The Rushdie case has generated a great deal of literature. See, for example, Lisa Appignanesi and Sara Maitland, eds., *The Rushdie File* (London: Fourth Estate Limited, 1989); Nabîl al-Sammân, *Hamazât Shaytâniyya wa-Salmân Rushdî* (Amman: Dâr ᶜAmmân lil-Nashr wal-Tawzîᶜ, 1989); Saᶜîd Ayyûb, *Shaytân al-Gharb: Salmân Rushdî, al-Rajul al-Mâriq* (Cairo: Dâr al-Iᶜtisâm, [1989?]); Malise Ruthven, *A Satanic Affair: Salman Rushdie and the Rage of Islam* (London: Chatto & Windus Ltd., 1990); M. M. Ahsan and A. R. Kidwai, eds., *Sacrilege versus Civility: Muslim Perspectives on The Satanic Verses Affair* (Leicester, U.K.: The Islamic Foundation, 1991). These works cover different perspectives and most include citations of other works as well as a chronology of the Salman Rushdie affair. More recently, Wendy Steiner, in a highly provocative and fascinating book, has set the Rushdie affair in the larger context of the contemporary debates on culture and art, including that generated by the work of Robert Mapplethorpe (*The Scandal of Pleasure: Art in an Age of Fundamentalism* [Chicago and London: University of Chicago Press, 1995]).

3. See chapters 7 and 8.

4. Elizabeth Alvilda Petroff, *Body and Soul: Essays on Medieval Women and Mysticism* (New York and Oxford: Oxford University Press, 1994); Paula M. Cooey, *Religious Imagination and the Body: A Feminist Analysis* (New York and Oxford: Oxford University Press, 1994).

5. The Houston-based *Arab Times,* to take but one example, regularly advertises these cassettes, as well as those of other preachers, to its readers.

6. A casual glance at any library catalog will show this to be the case. See also, for example, Yvonne Yazbeck Haddad et al, eds., *The Contemporary Islamic Revival: A Critical Survey and Bibliography* (New York: Greenwood Press, 1991). This work has been updated. See Yvonne Yazbeck Haddad and John L. Esposito, eds., *The Islamic Revival since 1988: A Critical Survey and Bibliography* (Westport, Conn.: Greenwood Press, 1997). The Fundamentalism Project from the American Academy of Arts and Sciences has already generated a series of volumes with studies that touch on various aspects of Islamic fundamentalism. Some of them will be of interest here. See, for example, James Piscatori, "Accounting for Islamic Fundamentalisms," in *Accounting for Fundamentalisms: The Dynamic Character of Movements,* ed. Martin E. Marty and R. Scott Appleby, The Fundamentalism Project, vol. 4 (Chicago and London: University of Chicago Press, 1994), pp. 361–373.

7. John L. Esposito, *The Islamic Threat: Myth or Reality?* (New York and Oxford: Oxford University Press, 1992).

8. Samuel P. Huntington, "The Clash of Civilizations?" *Foreign Affairs* 72, no. 3 (1993); Samuel P. Huntington, *The Clash of Civilizations and the Remaking of World Order* (New York: Simon & Schuster, 1996). The responses to Huntington's thesis came both after his article and in reviews of the book. See, for example, Fouad Ajami, "The Summoning," *Foreign Affairs* 72, no. 4 (1993); Roy P. Mottahedeh, "The Clash of Civilizations: An Islamicist's Critique," *Harvard Middle Eastern and Islamic Review* 2 (1996): pp. 1–26; Shahid Qadir, "Civilisational Clashes: Surveying the Fault-Lines," *Third World Quarterly* 19,

no. 1 (1998). For some of these complexities, see also Akbar S. Ahmed, *Postmodernism and Islam: Predicament and Promise* (London and New York: Routledge, 1992); Benjamin R. Barber, *Jihad vs. McWorld* (New York: Times Books, 1995).

9. See, for example, Leila Ahmed, *Women and Gender in Islam: Historical Roots of a Modern Debate* (New Haven: Yale University Press, 1992). See also the collections, Nikki R. Keddie and Beth Baron, eds., *Women in Middle Eastern History: Shifting Boundaries in Sex and Gender* (New Haven: Yale University Press, 1991); and Yvonne Yazbeck Haddad and John L. Esposito, eds., *Islam, Gender, and Social Change* (New York: Oxford University Press, 1998). The work by Khadîja Sabbâr, *al-Islâm wal-Mar'a: Wâqiᶜ wa-Afâq* (Casablanca: Ifrîqiyâ al-Sharq, 1991), contains materials on women and Islam as well as Moroccan case studies. Though some might wish to disagree with some of its points, the work by Fatima Mernissi, *Beyond the Veil: Male-Female Dynamics in a Modern Muslim Society* (Cambridge, Mass.: Schenkman, 1975), is nevertheless a classic. See the more recent Yamina Benguigui, *Femmes d'Islam* (Paris: Éditions Albin Michel, 1996); and the bilingual *Femmes et Islam/al-Nisâ' wal-Islâm,* collection under the direction of Aïcha Belarbi (Casablanca: Editions Le Fennec, 1998). See also, for example, Deniz Kandioyti, ed., *Women, Islam and the State* (Philadelphia: Temple University Press, 1991); Chandra Talpade Mohanty, Ann Russo, and Lourdes Torres, eds., *Third World Women and the Politics of Feminism* (Bloomington: Indiana University Press, 1991); Margot Badran, *Feminists, Islam, and Nation: Gender and the Making of Modern Egypt* (Princeton: Princeton University Press, 1995). See also Beth Baron, *The Women's Awakening in Egypt: Culture, Society, and the Press* (New Haven: Yale University Press, 1994). The linked issues of nationalism and feminism are also investigated in Kumari Jayawardena, *Feminism and Nationalism in the Third World* (London: Zed Books, 1986).

10. For a discussion of some of these discourses, see Malti-Douglas, *Woman's Body, Woman's Word,* pp. 3–4.

11. For some western-language works, see, for example, Sherifa Zuhur, *Revealing Reveiling: Islamist Gender Ideology in Contemporary Egypt* (Albany: State University of New York Press, 1992); Arlene Elowe Macleod, *Accommodating Protest: Working Women and the New Veiling and Change in Cairo* (New York: Columbia University Press, 1991); Judy Brink, "Lost Rituals: Sunni Muslim Women in Rural Egypt," in *Mixed Blessings: Gender and Religious Fundamentalism Cross Culturally,* ed. Judy Brink and Joan Mencher (New York and London: Routledge, 1997), pp. 199–208. Elizabeth Fernea's film, *A Veiled Revolution* (New York: First Run Icarus Films, 1982), is similar to many of these studies, since it concentrates on interviews with individual women who have chosen to veil themselves. Another example of works centering on the veil is Hinde Taarji, *Les Voilées de l'Islam* (Paris: Éditions Balland, 1990).

12. Fedwa Malti-Douglas, "Views of Arab Women: Society, Text, and Critic," *Edebiyât* 4 (1979): pp. 256–273. See also, *Woman's Body, Woman's Word,* p. 3.

13. This literature is enormous and only a few examples will be provided. See, for example, Muhammad ᶜAtiyya Khamîs, *Fiqh al-Nisâ' fî al-Salât* (Beirut:

Dâr al-Qalam, n.d.); Muhammad ᶜAtiyya Khamîs, *Fiqh al-Nisâ' fî al-Zakât wal-Siyâm* (Beirut: Dâr al-Qalam, n.d.). These volumes are in the series Dalîl al-Mu'minât.

14. Once again, this literature is enormous and only one example will be provided: Mohamed Menfaa, *Femmes Eternelles,* trans. Mohamed Benhamza (Paris: Al Qalam Éditions, 1992).

15. As with the previous reference, this literature is, once again, enormous and only a few examples will be provided: Jamal A. Badawi, comp., *The Muslim Woman's Dress* (Plainfield, Ind.: MSA-Women's Committee, Muslim Students' Association of the U.S. & Canada, n.d.). For a work illustrating what the veil should look like, see, for example, Hassan Amdouni, *Le Hijab de la femme musulmane: vêtements et toilette,* 2nd corrected ed. (Brussels: Édition Al-Imen, 1993).

16. Once again, this literature is enormous and the bibliographical references abound. I have provided only a few examples and have attempted to restrict myself to some of the works by fairly famous religious authorities today. See, for example, Muhammad ibn Sâlih al-ᶜUthaymîn, *Min al-Ahkâm al-Fiqhiyya fî al-Fatâwâ al-Nisâ'iyya* (Fez: Maktabat wa-Tasjîlât al-Hidâya al-Qur'âniyya, 1991); Mûsâ Sâlih Sharaf, *Fatâwâ al-Nisâ' al-ᶜAsriyya* (Beirut: Dâr al-Jîl and Cairo: Maktabat al-Turâth al-Islâmî, 1988); ᶜAbd al-ᶜAzîz ibn ᶜAbd Allâh ibn Bâz, *al-Rasâ'il wal-Fatâwâ al-Nisâ'iyya* (Riyadh: Dâr al-Watan lil-Nashr, A.H. 1410). Other references can be found in the notes above and below, as well as elsewhere in this book.

17. See, for example, Muhammad Mahmûd al-Sawwâf, *Zawjât al-Nabî al-Tâhirât wa-Hikmat Taᶜaddudihinna,* Silsilat al-Mar'a al-Muslima, vol. 3 (Cairo: Dâr al-Iᶜtisâm, 1979); Muhammad Fahmî ᶜAbd al-Wahhâb, *al-Harakât al-Nisâ'iyya fî al-Sharq wa-Silatuhâ bil-Istiᶜmâr wal-Sahyûniyya al-ᶜAlamiyya,* Silsilat al-Mar'a al-Muslima, vol. 7 (Cairo: Dâr al-Iᶜtisâm, 1979); Muhammad Fahmî ᶜAbd al-Wahhâb, *al-Sayyida Zaynab: ᶜAqîlat Banî Hâshim,* Silsilat al-Mar'a al-Muslima, vol. 9 (Cairo: Dâr al-Iᶜtisâm, 1980); Ahmad ᶜAbd al-Hâdî, *al-Umm fî al-Qur'ân al-Karîm,* Silsilat al-Mar'a al-Muslima, vol. 10 (Cairo: Dâr al-Iᶜtisâm, 1980).

18. ᶜUmar Sulaymân al-Ashqar, *al-Mar'a bayn Duᶜât al-Islâm wa-Adᶜiyâ' al-Taqaddum,* Silsilat Rasâ'il ilâ Ukhtî al-Mu'mina (Kuwait: Maktabat al-Falâh, 1984).

19. See, for example, Khamîs, *Fiqh al-Nisâ' fî al-Salât;* Khamîs, *Fiqh al-Nisâ' fî al-Zakât wal-Siyâm,* both in the series Dalîl al-Mu'minât.

20. See Valerie J. Hoffman-Ladd, "Polemics on the Modesty and Segregation of Women in Contemporary Egypt," *International Journal of Middle East Studies* 19, no. 1 (1987): pp. 29–42; Barbara Freyer Stowasser, "Religious Ideology, Women, and the Family: The Islamic Paradigm," in *The Islamic Impulse,* ed. Barbara Freyer Stowasser (Georgetown University: Center for Contemporary Arab Studies, 1987), pp. 262–296; Sanâ' al-Misrî, *Khalf al-Hijâb: Mawqif al-Jamaᶜât al-Islâmiyya min Qadiyyat al-Mar'a* (Cairo: Sînâ lil-Nashr, 1989). See also Fedwa Malti-Douglas, "An Anti-Travel Guide: Iconography in a Muslim Revivalist Tract," *Edebiyât* n.s. 4, no. 2 (1993): pp. 205–213; Fedwa Malti-Douglas, "Faces of Sin: Corporal Geographies in Contemporary Islamist Dis-

course," in *Religious Reflections on the Human Body,* ed. Jane Marie Law (Bloomington: Indiana University Press, 1995), pp. 67–75; Fedwa Malti-Douglas, "Pamphlets and Tracts," in *The Encyclopedia of the Modern Islamic World,* ed. John L. Esposito, vol. 3 (New York: Oxford University Press, 1995), pp. 299–300.

21. For an example of poetry directly addressing the woman, see Ahmad Muhammad al-Siddîq, *Qasâ'id ilâ al-Fatât al-Muslima* (Amman: Dâr al-Diyâ' lil-Nashr wal-Tawzîᶜ, 1984).

22. For more Francophone materials, see, for example, the publications of Édition Al-Imen in Brussels and those of Éditions Tawhid in Lyon, France. Other Belgian publications will appear in the analysis of Sultana Kouhmane. For the Éditions Tawhid, see, for example, Hani Ramadan, *La femme en Islam* (Lyon: Éditions Tawhid/Euro-Médias, 1991); Malika Dif, *Être Musulmane, Aujourd'hui: Position juridique de la femme musulmane selon l'Islam* (Lyon: Éditions Tawhid, 1996).

23. See Allen Douglas and Fedwa Malti-Douglas, *Arab Comic Strips: Politics of an Emerging Mass Culture* (Bloomington and London: Indiana University Press, 1994), pp. 83–109; Fedwa Malti-Douglas, "Children's Books and Cartoons," in *The Encyclopedia of the Modern Islamic World,* ed. John L. Esposito, vol. 1 (New York: Oxford University Press, 1995), pp. 98–103.

24. See, for example, Abdelhamid Bouraoui, "Note sur la production culturelle en Tunisie: Les éditeurs et leur production," in *La Dimension Culturelle du Développement* (Tunis: Centre d'Études et de Recherches Économiques et Sociales, 1991), pp. 217–223. It was clear at the conference at which this contribution was presented (conference on "La dimension culturelle du développement," held by the Centre d'Études et de Recherches Économiques et Sociales in Tunis in November 1988) that the Tunisian phenomenon was not peculiar to that country but was common to the region.

25. See, for example, *Voices of Resurgent Islam,* ed. John L. Esposito (New York and Oxford: Oxford University Press, 1983); Gilles Kepel, *Le Prophète et Pharaon, Les mouvements islamistes dans l'Egypte contemporaine* (Paris: Éditions La Découverte, 1984); Emmanuel Sivan, *Radical Islam: Medieval Theology and Modern Politics* (New Haven and London: Yale University Press, 1985); Bruce B. Lawrence, *Defenders of God: The Fundamentalist Revolt Against the Modern Age* (San Francisco: Harper & Row Publishers, 1989); Gilles Kepel, *La revanche de Dieu: Chrétiens, juifs et musulmans à la reconquête du monde* (Paris: Éditions du Seuil, 1991).

26. Cf. Muhammad Iqbâl ᶜArawî, *Jamaliyyat al-Adab al-Islâmî* (Casablanca: al-Maktaba al-Salafiyya, 1986), pp. 223 ff. ᶜArawî's work is an interesting study of Islamic literature. He also recognizes the dichotomy between what he calls "Arabic literature" and "Islamic literature" and the critics' tendency to leave the Islamic corpus by the wayside. His conclusions on the relationship between the two literatures are, however, different from mine.

27. Taslima Nasreen, *Femmes, manifestez-vous,* trans. Shishir Bhattacharja and Thérèse Réveillé (Paris: des femmes, 1994); Taslima Nasreen, *Lajja,* trans. C. B. Sultan (Paris: Éditions Stock, 1994). An interesting collection of documents addressed to Taslima Nasreen by writers in her support is in *Chère*

Taslima Nasreen . . . (Paris: Stock Reporters sans frontières, 1994). Khalida Messaoudi, *Une Algérienne debout* (Paris: Flammarion, 1995). The death threat in Arabic, followed by a French translation, is on pp. 251–253. For a discussion of the Nawal El Saadawi case, see Malti-Douglas, *Men, Women, and God(s),* pp. 11 ff. See, also, Yâsir Farahât, *al-Muwâjaha: Dr. Nawâl al-Sa^cdâwî* (Cairo: al-Rawda lil-Nashr wal-Tawzî^c, 1993); Fedwa Malti-Douglas, "As the World (or Dare I Say the Globe?) Turns: Feminism and Transnationalism," *Indiana Journal of Global Legal Studies* 4, no. 1 (Fall 1996): pp. 137–144. On Nasr Hâmid Abû Zayd, see, for example, Rif^cat Fawzî ^cAbd al-Muttalib, *Naqd Kitâb Nasr Abû [sic] Zayd wa-Dahd Shubuhâtihi* (Cairo: Maktabat al-Khânjî, 1996).

28. See Hamza, *Rihlatî,* pp. 225–226; Najîb Mahfûz, *Awlâd Hâratinâ* (Beirut: Dâr al-Adâb, 1967), translated as Naguib Mahfouz, *Children of Gebelawi,* trans. Philip Stewart (London: Heinemann and Washington, D.C.: Three Continents Press, 1981); ^cAbd al-Hamîd Kishk, *Kalimatunâ fî al-Radd ^calâ Awlâd Hâratinâ: Najîb Mahfûz* (Cairo: al-Mukhtâr al-Islâmî lil-Tab^c wal-Nashr wal-Tawzî^c, 1994). See also Muhammad Jalâl Kishk, *Awlâd Hâratinâ fîhâ Qawlân* (Cairo: Matâbi^c al-Zahrâ' lil-I^clâm al-^cArabî, 1989). I have dealt with some of these issues in Fedwa Malti-Douglas, "Binding Religion and Politics: The Relationship between Islam and Literature," *The World and I* 12 (1997): pp. 68–75.

29. Najîb al-Kîlânî, *al-Islâmiyya wal-Madhâhib al-Adabiyya* (Beirut: Mu'assasat al-Risâla, 1983), pp. 117 ff. See also, Najîb al-Kîlânî, *Afâq al-Adab al-Islâmî* (Beirut: Mu'assasat al-Risâla, 1985).

30. Al-Kîlânî, *al-Islâmiyya,* p. 118.

31. Najîb al-Kîlânî, *Rihlatî ma^ca al-Adab al-Islâmî* (Beirut: Mu'assasat al-Risâla, 1985). The work also contains some important interviews with the author.

32. Sayyid Qutb has always attracted the attention of scholars writing on the Islamic revival. See, for example, Yvonne Y. Haddad, "Sayyid Qutb: Ideologue of Islamic Revival," in *Voices of Resurgent Islam,* ed. Esposito, pp. 67–98; Shahrough Akhavi, "Sayyid Qutb: The Poverty of Philosophy and the Vindication of Islamic Tradition," in *Cultural Transitions in the Middle East,* ed. Serif Mardin (Leiden and New York: E. J. Brill, 1994), pp. 130–152; Shahrough Akhavi, "Sayyid Qutb," in *The Encyclopedia of the Modern Islamic World,* ed. Esposito, vol. 3, pp. 400–404. For the relationship between Muhammad Qutb and his more famous brother, Sayyid Qutb, see, for example, Olivier Carré, *Mystique et Politique: Lecture révolutionnaire du Coran par Sayyid Qutb, Frère musulman radical* (Paris: Presses de la Fondation Nationale des Sciences Politiques et Éditions du Cerf, 1984), p. 36.

33. John Millington Synge, *Riders to the Sea* (Boston: J. W. Luce & Company, 1911).

34. Muhammad Qutb, *Manhaj al-Fann al-Islâmî* (Beirut and Cairo: Dâr al-Shurûq, 1983), pp. 212 ff.

35. Qutb, *Manhaj al-Fann,* pp. 222–227; the quote is on p. 227.

36. See, for example, Carré, *Mystique et Politique,* pp. 7–40. See also Akhavi, "Sayyid Qutb," p. 131.

37. See Susan Rubin Suleiman, *Authoritarian Fictions: The Ideological Novel as a Literary Genre* (New York: Columbia University Press, 1983); Muhammad Ra'fat Sacîd, *al-Iltizâm fî al-Tasawwur al-Islâmî lil-Adab* (Cairo: Dâr al-Hidâya lil-Tibâca wal-Nashr wal-Tawzîc, 1987). See also, in addition to the works cited earlier, Muhammad al-Hasnâwî, *Fî al-Adab wal-Adab al-Islâmî* (Beirut: al-Maktab al-Islâmî and Amman: Dâr cAmmâr, 1986), which includes a fascinating interview with the author, a creative writer himself. See also Hânî Fahs, *Nahw Adab Islâmî Haqîqî: Masrah* (Beirut: Dâr al-Balâgha, 1986). This last work, although it is about the theater, nevertheless has some interesting observations on the issues of decor, clothing, etc. See also cImâd al-Dîn Khalîl, *Madkhal ilâ Nazariyyat al-Adab al-Islâmî* (Beirut: Mu'assasat al-Risâla, 1987); cImâd al-Dîn Khalîl, "Hawl Harakat al-Adab al-Islâmî al-Mucasir: Waqfa li-Murâjacat al-Hisâb," *Islâmiyyat al-Macrifa* 3 (1998): pp. 11–37; cArawî, *Jamaliyyat al-Adab al-Islâmî*. This last work deals, as well, with the entire notion of committed literature and criticizes the work of earlier critics writing on Islamic literature.

38. See, for example, Jâbir Rizq, *Muhammad cAuwâd: al-Shâcir al-Shahîd*, Nahw Adab Islâmî cAlamî, vol. 3 (al-Mansûra: Dâr al-Wafâ' lil-Tibâca wal-Nashr, 1985), a volume in the biography area; cAtiyya Zuhrî, *Fawq al-Qimma*, Nahw Adab Islâmî cAlamî, vol. 5 (al-Mansûra: Dâr al-Wafâ' lil-Tibâca wal-Nashr, 1985), a novel in the area of children's literature; Muhammad al-Hasnâwî, *cAwdat al-Ghâ'ib*, Nahw Adab Islâmî cAlamî, vol. 8 (al-Mansûra: Dâr al-Wafâ' lil-Tibâca wal-Nashr, 1988), a volume of poetry.

39. Dr. Gaber Asfour, personal communication by telephone from Cairo, July 14, 1998. Dr. Asfour is the deputy minister of culture of the Arab Republic of Egypt.

40. A glance at any catalog will testify to Mustafâ Mahmûd's extensive production. See also Hâfiz al-Maghribî and Mustafâ Bayyûmî, "Ta'sîl Tuhâwir Dr. Mustafâ Mahmûd," *al-Ta'sîl* 1 (October 1997): pp. 51–54.

41. Al-Maghribî and Bayyûmî, "Ta'sîl Tuhâwir," p. 53.

42. Al-Maghribî and Bayyûmî, "Ta'sîl Tuhâwir," p. 53.

43. Mustafâ Mahmûd, *al-Masîkh al-Dajjâl* (Cairo: Dâr al-Macârif, 1988), pp. 3–6.

44. Mahmûd, *al-Masîkh*, p. 5.

45. Yahyâ Hâjj Yahyâ, *al-Mar'a wa-Qadâyâ al-Hayât fî al-Qissa al-Islâmiyya al-Mucâsira* (Beirut: Dâr Ibn Hazm lil-Tibâca wal-Nashr wal-Tawzîc and Kuwait: Dâr Hawwâ', 1994), pp. 47–51.

46. For some recent essays on the intersection of the global and the local, see Ann Cvetkovich and Douglas Kellner, eds., *Articulating the Global and the Local: Globalization and Cultural Studies* (Boulder, Colo.: Westview Press, 1997).

47. Muhammad Mutawallî al-Shacrâwî, *Mishwâr Hayâtî*, prepared by Fâtima al-Sahrâwî (Cairo: al-Mukhtâr al-Islâmî lil-Nashr wal-Tawzîc wal-Tasdîr, 1988); Mustafâ Mahmûd, *Rihlatî min al-Shakk ilâ al-Imân* (Cairo: Dâr al-Macârif, 1991).

48. Philippe Lejeune, *Le pacte autobiographique* (Paris: Éditions du Seuil, 1975); Philippe Lejeune, "Le pacte autobiographique (bis)," *Poétique* 56 (1983): pp. 416–434.

49. See, for example, Domna C. Stanton, ed., *The Female Autograph: Theory and Practice of Autobiography from the Tenth to the Twentieth Century* (Chicago: University of Chicago Press, 1987); Sidonie Smith, *A Poetics of Women's Autobiography* (Bloomington and Indianapolis: Indiana University Press, 1987); Shari Benstock, ed., *The Private Self: Theory and Practice of Women's Autobiographical Writings* (Chapel Hill and London: The University of North Carolina Press, 1988); Bella Brodzki and Celeste Schenck, eds., *Life/Lines: Theorizing Women's Autobiography* (Ithaca and London: Cornell University Press, 1988). The above works all deal with various aspects of female autobiographies and provide wide readings of texts by women writing their selves.

50. Al-Ghazâlî, *al-Munqidh min al-Dalâl,* ed. ᶜAbd al-Halîm Mahmûd (Cairo: Dâr al-Kutub al-Hadîtha, 1965). For a discussion of the Arabic autobiographical tradition and further references, see Fedwa Malti-Douglas, *Blindness and Autobiography: Al-Ayyâm of Tâhâ Husayn* (Princeton: Princeton University Press, 1988), pp. 9 ff. See also Hilary Kilpatrick, "Autobiography and Classical Arabic Literature," *Journal of Arabic Literature* 22, part 1 (1991): pp. 1–20.

51. See, for example, Denise A. Spellberg, *Politics, Gender, and the Islamic Past: The Legacy of 'A'isha bint Abi Bakr* (New York: Columbia University Press, 1994).

52. See Malti-Douglas, *Woman's Body, Woman's Word,* which deals with this issue in a number of chapters.

53. This is something that is obvious from all the works authored by women in the Middle East and North Africa, as well as those women writing in Arabic but living outside the Middle East.

54. Zaynab al-Ghazâlî, *Ayyâm min Hayâtî* (Cairo: Dâr al-Shurûq, 1987).

55. A few examples will suffice to demonstrate this point. See, for example, Ahmed, *Women and Gender,* pp. 196 ff.; Zuhur, *Revealing Reveiling,* pp. 84 ff. See also Valerie J. Hoffman, "An Islamic Activist: Zaynab al-Ghazali," in *Women and the Family in the Middle East: New Voices of Change,* ed. Elizabeth Warnock Fernea (Austin: The University of Texas Press, 1985), pp. 233–254; Miriam Cooke, "Prisons: Egyptian Women Writers on Islam," *Religion and Literature* 20 (1988): 139–153; Timothy Mitchell, "L'expérience de l'emprisonnement dans le discours islamiste: Une lecture d'*Ayyam min Hayati* de Zaynab al-Ghazzali," in *Intellectuels et militants de l'Islam contemporain,* ed. Gilles Kepel and Yann Richard (Paris: Éditions du Seuil, 1990), 193–212; Miriam Cooke, "Zaynab al-Ghazali: Saint or Subversive?" *Die Welt des Islams* 34 (1994): pp. 1–20; Miriam Cooke, "*Ayyam min hayati:* The Prison Memoirs of a Muslim Sister," in *The Postcolonial Crescent: Islam's Impact on Contemporary Literature,* ed. John C. Hawley (New York: Peter Lang, 1998), pp. 121–139. Cooke's studies on Zaynab al-Ghazâlî overlap.

56. For Arab women and their prison narratives, see, for example, Nawâl al-Saᶜdâwî, *Mudhakkirâtî fî Sijn al-Nisâ'* (Cairo: Dâr al-Mustaqbal al-ᶜArabî, 1984); translated as Nawal el-Sa'adawi, *Memoirs from the Women's Prison,* trans. Marilyn Booth (London: The Women's Press, 1983); Farîda al-Naqqâsh, *al-Sijn: Damᶜatân wa-Warda* (Cairo: Dâr al-Mustaqbal al-ᶜArabî, 1985); Sâfî Nâz Kâzim, *ᶜAn al-Sijn wal-Hurriyya* (Cairo: al-Zahrâ' lil-Iᶜlâm al-ᶜArabî,

1986). On the critical literature dealing with some of these texts, see, for example, Marilyn Booth, "Women's Prison Memoirs in Egypt and Elsewhere: Prison, Gender, Praxis," *Middle East Report*, no. 149 (November–December 1987): pp. 35–41; Barbara Harlow, *Resistance Literature* (New York: Methuen, 1987); Barbara Harlow, *Barred: Women, Writing, and Political Detention* (Hanover, N.H.: Wesleyan University Press, 1992); Malti-Douglas, *Men, Women, and God(s)*.

57. See Shams al-Bârûdî, *Rihlatî min al-Zalamât ilâ al-Nûr* (al-Mansûra: Dâr al-Wafâ' lil-Tibâ‘a wal-Nashr wal-Tawzî‘, 1988). This text has been reprinted in Sa‘îd Sirâj al-Dîn, *Awrâq Shams al-Bârûdî* (Cairo: Maktabat Ihyâ' al-Kutub al-Islâmîyya, 1993).

58. See Hamza, *Rihlatî;* ‘Abd al-Hamîd Kishk, *Qissat Ayyâmî: Mudhakkirât al-Shaykh Kishk* (Cairo: Dâr al-Mukhtâr al-Islâmî, [1987? 1988?]). See Fedwa Malti-Douglas, *A Woman and Her Sûfîs* (Georgetown University: Center for Contemporary Arab Studies Occasional Papers, 1995); Fedwa Malti-Douglas, "A Literature of Islamic Revival? The Autobiography of Shaykh Kishk," in *Cultural Transitions*, pp. 116–129. In this last publication, the transliteration of my text was drastically (and hilariously) redone without my permission or knowledge. I am grateful to Dr. Peri Bearman at E. J. Brill for having released the copyright to this study. I have revised and greatly lengthened the study of Shaykh Kishk's autobiography in Fedwa Malti-Douglas, "Postmoderning the Traditional in the Autobiography of Shaykh Kishk," in *Arabic and Islamic Studies in Honor of Issa Boullata*, ed. Wael Hallaq, forthcoming.

59. See Carol L. Anway, *Daughters of Another Path: Experiences of American Women Choosing Islam* (Lee's Summit, Mo.: Yawna Publications, 1996), p. 169.

60. Valerie J. Hoffman, "Muslim Fundamentalists: Psychosocial Profiles," in *Fundamentalisms Comprehended*, ed. Martin E. Marty and R. Scott Appleby, The Fundamentalism Project, vol. 5 (Chicago and London: University of Chicago Press, 1995), pp. 199–230; the quote is on p. 220. Valerie J. Hoffman's *Sufism, Mystics, and Saints in Modern Egypt* (Columbia: University of South Carolina Press, 1995) is a firsthand study of Sufism in Egypt and contains some fascinating observations on its more popular manifestations.

61. See *Hiwâr ma‘a ‘A'ida*, prepared by Hanân ‘Atiyya (Beirut: Dâr Ibn Hazm and United Arab Emirates: Dâr al-‘Ulûm, 1995), pp. 5–6.

62. Munâ Yunûs, *Wajh bi-lâ Mâkiyâj* (Cairo: Dâr al-Tawzî‘ wal-Nashr al-Islâmiyya, 1993), p. 64.

63. See Kepel, *Le prophète*, p. 43; Hoffman, "Muslim Fundamentalists," p. 221.

64. See her own spiritual journey in al-Bârûdî, *Rihlatî*.

65. See, for example, ‘Imâd Nâsif and Amal Khudayr, *Fannânât Tâ'ibât wa-Najamât al-Ithâra* (Cairo: Matba‘at Khattâb, 1991); Mahmûd Fawzî, *al-Shaykh al-Sha‘râwî wa-Fatâwâ al-‘Asr* (Cairo: Matâbi‘ Rûz al-Yûsuf al-Jadîda, 1992), pp. 51 ff.; Majdî Kâmil, *Fannânât warâ' al-Hijâb* (Cairo: Markaz al-Râya lil-Nashr, 1993); Muhammad Hamza, *Shâti' al-Huzn al-Jamîl: Shâdiya min al-Tufûla ilâ al-Hijâb* (Cairo: Dâr al-Thaqâfa wal-Funûn lil-Tibâ‘a wal-Nashr, 1993).

66. Ibrâhîm ᶜIsâ, *al-Harb bil-Niqâb: Zâhirat Hijâb al-Fannânat, al-Islâm al-Saᶜûdî fî Misr* (Cairo: Dâr al-Shabâb al-ᶜArabî, 1993); Yâsir Farahât, *Maᶜrakat al-Hijâb: Asrâr warâ' al-Hijâb al-Madfûᶜ* (Cairo: al-Rawda lil-Nashr wal-Tawzîᶜ, 1993). See also Lila Abu-Lughod, "Finding a Place for Islam: Egyptian Television Serials and the National Interest," *Public Culture* 5 (1993): pp. 493–513; Lila Abu Lughod, "Movie Stars and Islamic Moralism in Egypt," *Social Text* 42 (1995): pp. 53–67. See, for example, Yasir Sofuoglu, *Islâm'i Secen Artistler: Hayat Hikayelerini Anlatiyor* (Istanbul: Mektup Yayinlari, 1994).

67. Nayra Atiya, *Khul-Khaal: Five Egyptian Women Tell Their Stories* (London: Virago, 1988).

68. Fatima Mernissi, *Le monde n'est pas un harem: Paroles de femmes du Maroc* (Paris: Albin Michel, 1991).

69. Wayne C. Booth, "The Rhetoric of Fundamentalist Conversion Narratives," in *Fundamentalisms Comprehended*, pp. 367–395. See also James L. Peacock and Tim Pettyjohn, "Fundamentalisms Narrated: Muslim, Christian, and Mystical," in *Fundamentalisms Comprehended*, pp. 115–134.

70. Booth, "The Rhetoric," pp. 376 ff.

71. Maryam Jameelah has written a number of works in which she addresses her spiritual transformation. Booth is dealing with Maryam Jameelah, *Islam and Western Society* (Lahore: Mohammad Yusuf Khan, 1976). See also, for example, Maryam Jameelah, *Memories of Childhood and Youth in America (1945–1962): The Story of One Western Convert's Quest for Truth* (Lahore: Muhammad Yusuf Khan, 1989); Maryam Jameelah, *Why I Embraced Islam* (Chicago: Kazi Publications, Inc., 1985).

72. See, for example, Murad Wilfried Hofmann, *Journal d'un musulman allemand,* trans. Lamine Benallal and Abdelhadi Mesdour (Rabat: Éditions La Porte, 1990); Amatullah Armstrong, *And the Sky Is Not the Limit: An Australian Woman's Spiritual Journey within the Traditions* (Kuala Lumpur: A. S. Noordeen, 1993); Jeffrey Lang, *Struggling to Surrender: Some Impressions of an American Convert to Islam,* 2nd rev. ed. (Beltsville, Maryland: amana publications, 1995). See also Laleh Bakhtiar, *Sufi Women of America: Angels in the Making* (Chicago: Kazi Publications, Inc., 1996); Anway, *Daughters of Another Path.*

73. Malti-Douglas, *A Woman and Her Sûfîs;* Malti-Douglas, "A Literature of Islamic Revival?"; Malti-Douglas, "Postmoderning the Traditional." Kepel in his *Le prophète,* pp. 169–182, perceptively discusses a sermon by Kishk but without delving fully into its roots in the Arabo-Islamic textual tradition.

74. See Fedwa Malti-Douglas, "Al-ᶜAnâsir al-Turâthiyya fî al-Adab al-ᶜArabî al-Muᶜâsir: al-Ahlâm fî Thalâth Qisas," trans. ᶜI. al-Sharqâwî, *Fusûl* 2, no. 2 (1982): pp. 21–29; Fedwa Malti-Douglas, "Blindness and Sexuality: Traditional Mentalities in Yûsuf Idrîs's 'House of Flesh,'" in *Critical Pilgrimages: Studies in the Arabic Literary Tradition,* ed. Fedwa Malti-Douglas, Literature East and West 25 (1989), pp. 70–78. This article has been reprinted in *Critical Perspectives on Yusuf Idris,* ed. Roger Allen (Colorado Springs, Colo.: Three Continents Press, 1994), pp. 89–96; Fedwa Malti-Douglas, "Mahfouz's Dreams," in *Naguib Mahfouz: From Regional Fame to Global Recognition,* ed. Michael Beard and Adnan Haydar (Syracuse: Syracuse University Press, 1992),

pp. 126–143 (text) and 183–185 (notes); Malti-Douglas, "Postmoderning the Traditional."

75. Malti-Douglas's *Men, Women, and God(s)* deals with this kind of intertextuality in El Saadawi's works, beginning with her earlier texts and continuing through her more recent works. For some of the Saadawian narratives, see, for example, Nawâl al-Saʿdâwî, *Suqût al-Imâm* (Cairo: Dâr al-Mustaqbal al-ʿArabî, 1987), translated as Nawal El Saadawi, *The Fall of the Imam,* trans. Sherif Hetata (London: Methuen, 1988); Nawâl al-Saʿdâwî, *Jannât wa-Iblîs* (Beirut: Dâr al-Adâb, 1992), translated as Nawal El Saadawi, *The Innocence of the Devil,* trans. Sherif Hetata (London: Methuen, 1994).

76. Here, again, the bibliography is enormous. In addition to works cited earlier, some noteworthy contributions include Gilles Kepel, *Les banlieues de l'Islam: Naissance d'une religion en France* (Paris: Éditions du Seuil, 1991); and Gilles Kepel, *A l'Ouest d'Allah* (Paris: Éditions du Seuil, 1994). This latter work also deals with Muslims in America and with the Rushdie affair. See also Antoine Sfeir, *Les réseaux d'Allah: Les fililères islamistes en France et en Europe* (Paris: Plon, 1997). The topic of Islam in America is yet another burgeoning field. Yvonne Yazbeck Haddad is the name currently leading this area, with numerous authored and edited works to her credit. See, in particular, Yvonne Yazbeck Haddad, ed., *The Muslims of America* (New York: Oxford University Press, 1991). See also Barbara Daly Metcalf, ed., *Making Muslim Space in North America and Europe* (Berkeley and Los Angeles: University of California Press, 1996).

77. Davis, *Women on the Margins,* especially pp. 209–212.

CHAPTER 2

1. I am very grateful to both Karîmân Hamza and her husband for the biographical information. Most of it was gathered at various meetings and conversations; however, she and I had an official time, on January 5, 1996, during which I confirmed the information gathered during unofficial conversations and social occasions. I am labeling this official communication as personal communication. See also Hamza, *Rihlatî,* pp. 193–194. Taarji, in *Les voilées,* pp. 57–62, has a short discussion of Karîmân Hamza.

2. For the novel, see Karîmân Hamza, *Nîjâr wal-Ghâba* (Beirut: Dâr al-Fath lil-Tibâʿa wal-Nashr, 1985). For the guide, see Karîmân Hamza, *Rifqan bil-Qawârîr* (Beirut: Dâr al-Fath lil-Tibâʿa wal-Nashr, 1985). Hamza has also published different series for children.

3. Karîmân Hamza, personal communication, Cairo, January 5, 1996.

4. As is the norm with critical discussions of autobiographical texts, I shall use the first name, Karîmân, to refer to the character in the text and the full name, Karîmân Hamza, to refer to the historical individual or the author.

5. Hamza, *Rihlatî.*

6. Mahmûd, *Rihlatî min al-Shakk.*

7. Muhammad ʿAtiyya Khamîs, introduction to Hamza, *Rihlatî,* pp. 5–17. On the Jamʿiyyat Shabâb Sayyidinâ Muhammad, see Shabâb Muhammad,

Diᶜâmât al-Daᶜwa: Min Tasjîlât al-Jamâᶜa (Cairo: Dâr al-Iᶜtisâm, 1978), p. 65. These are the actual documents of the Jamᶜiyya itself. Cf. Hoffman-Ladd, "Polemics," pp. 31–32, who places the break in "approximately 1939"; al-Misrî, *Khalf al-Hijâb*, p. 27.

8. Hamza, *Rihlatî*, pp. 19–20.

9. I have discussed this phenomenon elsewhere. See Malti-Douglas, *Woman's Body, Woman's Word*, pp. 162–164.

10. Khamîs, introduction to Hamza, *Rihlatî*, pp. 5–17.

11. Hamza, *Rihlatî*, pp. 21–22. The ellipses are in the original text.

12. See chapter 3.

13. *Al-Qur'ân*, Sûrat al-Nûr, verse 31; A. J. Arberry, *The Koran Interpreted*, vol. 2, (New York: Macmillan Publishing Co, 1974), p. 49. See also Malti-Douglas, *Woman's Body, Woman's Word;* Fedwa Malti-Douglas, *Men, Women, and God(s)*.

14. Hamza, *Rihlatî*, p. 19.

15. Karîmân Hamza, personal communication, Cairo, January 5, 1996.

16. Hamza, *Rihlatî*, pp. 22–23.

17. See chapter 3.

18. See chapter 3.

19. Hamza, *Rihlatî*, p. 28.

20. Hamza, *Rihlatî*, p. 29.

21. See chapter 3.

22. Hamza, *Rihlatî*, p. 30.

23. Hamza, *Rihlatî*, p. 33.

24. See chapter 3.

25. Hamza, *Rihlatî*, p. 198.

26. Hamza, *Rihlatî*, pp. 63–65.

27. Hamza, *Rihlatî*, p. 66.

28. Hamza, *Rihlatî*, pp. 66–68.

29. For a more detailed analysis of the geographical discourses, see chapter 8.

30. Hamza, *Rihlatî*, p. 67.

31. Cf. the slightly different experience in ᶜAtiyya, *Hiwâr*, p. 36.

32. Hamza, *Rihlatî*, pp. 125 ff.

33. Margaret R. Miles, *Desire and Delight: A New Reading of Augustine's Confessions* (New York: The Crossroad Publishing Company, 1992), p. 24.

34. Gérard Genette brilliantly analyzes these types of narration in his *Figures III* (Paris: Éditions du Seuil, 1972). I have applied these categories in the study of a classic of modern Arabic autobiography (see Fedwa Malti-Douglas, *Blindness and Autobiography: al-Ayyâm of Tâhâ Husayn* [Princeton: Princeton University Press, 1988], especially, pp. 173 ff).

35. Hamza, *Rihlatî*, pp. 140–141.

36. Ihsân ᶜAbd al-Quddûs, *Anâ Hurra* (Cairo: n.p., 1958); Roger Allen, *The Arabic Novel: An Historical and Critical Introduction*, 2nd ed. (Syracuse: Syracuse University Press, 1995), p. 130.

37. Hamza, *Rihlatî*, p. 27.

38. Hamza, *Rihlatî*, pp. 78–82. Ellipses in original.

39. Hamza, *Rihlatî*, p. 82.
40. Hamza, *Rihlatî*, p. 80.
41. Hamza, *Rihlatî*, p. 79.
42. Richard Klein, *Cigarettes Are Sublime* (Durham and London: Duke University Press, 1993).
43. Klein, *Cigarettes,* pp. 130, 154.
44. Klein, *Cigarettes,* p. 130.
45. Klein, *Cigarettes,* p. 117.
46. Hamza, *Rihlatî*, p. 81.
47. See, for example, Fedwa Malti-Douglas, "Blindness and Sexuality: Traditional Mentalities in Yûsuf Idrîs' 'House of Flesh,'" in *Critical Pilgrimages: Studies in the Arabic Literary Tradition,* ed. Fedwa Malti-Douglas, Literature East and West, 25 (1989), pp. 70–78; reprinted in *Critical Perspectives on Yusuf Idris,* ed. Roger Allen (Colorado Springs: Three Continents Press, 1994), pp. 89–96.
48. Yûsuf Idrîs, "Hâlat Talabbus," in Yûsuf Idrîs, *Lughat al-Ay Ay* (Cairo: Dâr Misr lil-Tibâᶜa, 1981), pp. 5–14. P. M. Kurpershoek in *The Short Stories of Yûsuf Idrîs* (Leiden: E. J. Brill, 1981), pp. 134–136, 139–140, discusses this story quite briefly, as does Sasson Somekh in *Lughat al-Qissa fî Adab Yûsuf Idrîs* (Acre: Maktabat wa-Matbaᶜat al-Sarûjî, 1984), pp. 29–30, 115–116. Neither critic is concerned with the major issues dealt with here.
49. Kurpershoek, *Short Stories,* p. 134, writes, "It simply tells. . . ."
50. Idrîs, "Hâlat," p. 5.
51. Idrîs, "Hâlat," p. 9.
52. Idrîs, "Hâlat," p. 11.
53. I am providing the simplest form of the verb for the activity itself and not specific examples. The narrator plays with verbal nouns, different forms of the verb, etc., to describe the visual activity.
54. Idrîs, "Hâlat," p. 12.
55. Idrîs, "Hâlat," p. 12. Ellipses are in original.
56. Idrîs, "Hâlat," pp. 5, 8.
57. Malti-Douglas, *Men, Women, and God(s),* discusses scopic regimes and the way a woman writer can subvert them. In that work, I borrow the notion of "scopic regime" from Martin Jay, "Scopic Regimes of Modernity," in *Vision and Visuality,* ed. Hal Foster (Seattle: Bay Press, 1988), p. 3. Jay, in fact, takes the concept from Christian Metz.
58. See chapter 1.
59. Shaykh al-Shaᶜrâwî's words are cited in ᶜIsâ, *al-Harb bil-Niqâb,* pp. 67–68. The author criticizes this conservative position on the power of the glance.
60. This is a common position in contemporary Islamist publications. See, for example, Muhammad al-Ghazâlî, *Qadâyâ al-Mar'a bayn al-Taqâlîd al-Râkida wal-Wâfida* (Cairo and Beirut: Dâr al-Shurûq, 1990), pp. 151–152, 217. See also ᶜAlî Hasan ᶜAlî ᶜAbd al-Hamîd, *Hukm al-Dîn fî al-Lihya wal-Tadkhîn* (Amman: al-Maktaba al-Islâmiyya and Beirut: Dâr Ibn Hazm, 1992).
61. Karîmân Hamza, *Khamsûn Hallan li-Khamsîn Mushkila: Akhtar Qadâyâ al-Mar'a fî Mîzân al-ᶜAql* (Cairo: Dâr al-Maᶜârif, 1995), pp. 93–94.
62. Karîmân Hamza, *al-Islâm wal-Tifl* (Cairo: Matâbiᶜ V.I.P., n.d.), pp. 56–59.

63. Hamza, *Rihlatî*, p. 80.

64. Karîmân Hamza, personal communication, Cairo, January 5, 1996.

65. Hamza, *Rihlatî*, p. 154.

66. Hamza, *Rihlatî*, p. 185.

67. Hamza, *Rihlatî*, p. 187.

68. Hamza, *Rihlatî*, p. 187.

69. *Al-Qur'ân*, Sûrat al-Duhâ, verse 11; Arberry, *The Koran*, vol. 2, p. 342.

70. *Al-Qur'ân*, Sûrat al-Nûr, verse 31; Arberry, *The Koran*, vol. 2, p. 49.

71. Hamza, *Rihlatî*, pp. 188–194.

72. Ni^cmat Sidqî, *al-Tabarruj* (Cairo: Dâr al-I^ctisâm, 1975). This 1975 printing contains a list of books by the author, in which it is said that *al-Tabarruj* was then in its nineteenth printing.

73. Rabî^c ibn Muhammad al-Sa^cûdî, *Zâd al-Musâfirîn ilâ Ghayr Bilâd al-Muslimîn* (Riyad: Dâr al-Fitya and Cairo: Dâr al-Sahwa lil-Nashr, 1988), pp. 22–23, cites this story without mentioning its source. See Fedwa Malti-Douglas, "An Anti-travel Guide: Iconography in a Muslim Revivalist Tract," *Edebiyât* n.s. 4, no. 2 (1993): pp. 205–213. On *tabarruj* and Sidqî's booklet, see Fedwa Malti-Douglas, "Faces of Sin: Corporal Geographies in Contemporary Islamist Discourse," in *Religious Reflections on the Human Body*, ed. Jane Marie Law (Bloomington: Indiana University Press, 1995), pp. 67–75.

74. *^cAwra* is a pervasive concept that forms part and parcel of the majority of Islamic discourses on women. For some of the sources, see, for example, Abdelwahab Bouhdiba, *La sexualité en Islam* (Paris: Presses Universitaires de France, 1979), pp. 51, 53; Ibn Manzûr, *Lisân al-^cArab*, vol. 6 (Cairo: al-Dâr al-Misriyya lil-Ta'lîf wal-Tarjama, n.d.), p. 296; al-Zabîdî, *Tâj al-^cArûs*, vol. 3 (Beirut: Dâr Sâdir, n.d.), pp. 439–440; Ahmad ibn Hanbal, *Ahkâm al-Nisâ'*, ed. ^cAbd al-Qâdir Ahmad ^cAtâ (Beirut: Dâr al-Kutub al-^cIlmiyya, 1986), pp. 29 ff.; Malti-Douglas, *Woman's Body, Woman's Word*, pp. 49, 90, 121–127, 173; Malti-Douglas, *Men, Women, and God(s)*, pp. 27–29, 53–54, 200.

75. Hamza, *Rifqan bil-Qawârîr*; Yusriyya Muhammad Anwar, *Mahlan . . . Yâ Sâhibat al-Qawârîr: Radd ^calâ Kitâb "Rifqan bil-Qawârîr"* (Cairo: Dâr al-I^ctisâm, n.d.).

76. Karîmân Hamza, personal communication, January 4, 1996.

77. Joanna Russ, *How to Suppress Women's Writing* (Austin: University of Texas Press, 1983). I have explored the difference between the two guides elsewhere. See Fedwa Malti-Douglas, "The Islamist Body Social" (paper read at the Conference on Law, Culture, and Human Rights: Islamic Perspectives in the Contemporary World, The Schell Center for International Human Rights, Yale University Law School, November 6, 1993).

78. See Nawâl al-Sa^cdâwî, *Mudhakkirât Tabîba* (Beirut: Dâr al-Adâb, 1980), pp. 14–15. The first chapter has been translated by Fedwa Malti-Douglas as "Growing Up Female in Egypt," in *Women and the Family in the Middle East: New Voices of Change*, ed. Elizabeth Warnock Fernea (Austin: University of Texas Press, 1985), pp. 111–120. The entire novel has been translated by Catherine Cobham as *Memoirs of a Woman Doctor* (San Francisco: City Lights Book, 1989). For a discussion, see Malti-Douglas, *Woman's Body, Woman's Word*, p. 118; Malti-Douglas, *Men, Women, and God(s)*, pp. 25 ff.

79. Hamza, *Rihlatî*, p. 29.
80. Hamza, *Rihlatî*, p. 123.
81. Hamza, *Rihlatî*, p. 30.
82. Hamza, *Rihlatî*, p. 220.
83. Hamza, *Rihlatî*, pp. 201–208.
84. Hamza, *Rihlatî*, p. 233.
85. See chapter 3.
86. Hamza, *Rihlatî*, pp. 37–39.
87. Hamza, *Rihlatî*, pp. 38–39.
88. Khamîs, introduction to Hamza, *Rihlatî*, p. 14.
89. Khamîs, introduction to Hamza, *Rihlatî*, p. 15.
90. Al-Sacdâwî, *Mudhakkirât Tabîba*, p. 14; for a discussion, see Malti-Douglas, *Woman's Body, Woman's Word*, pp. 121 ff., 173; Malti-Douglas, *Men, Women, and God(s)*, pp. 27 ff.
91. Fadwâ Tûqân, *Rihla Jabaliyya, Rihla Sacba: Sîra Dhâtiyya* (Amman: Dâr al-Shurûq lil-Nashr wal-Tawzîc, 1985), p. 37. For a discussion, see Malti-Douglas, *Woman's Body, Woman's Word*, p. 173.
92. Sunniyya Mâhir, who facilitates Karîmân's entry into the world of the electronic media, is an exception here. Hamza, *Rihlatî*, pp. 151–152.
93. For a discussion of these strains in El Saadawi's corpus, see Malti-Douglas, *Men, Women, and God(s)*.
94. I have discussed this issue at length as it relates to the influential autobiography by the Egyptian modernizer Tâhâ Husayn and the Indian writer Ved Mehta. See Malti-Douglas, *Blindness and Autobiography*, pp. 76 ff.; Fedwa Malti-Douglas, "al-cAmâ fî Mir'ât al-Tarjama al-Shakhsiyya: Tâhâ Husayn wa-Ved Mehta," *Fusûl* 3, no. 4 (1983): pp. 72–75.
95. See Hisham Sharabi, *Neopatriarchy: A Theory of Distorted Change in Arab Society* (New York: Oxford University Press, 1988).

CHAPTER 3

1. For gender and Sufism in a transnational perspective, see chapter 8.
2. See chapter 2.
3. *Al-Qur'ân*, Sûrat al-Hadîd, verse 16; Arberry, *The Koran*, vol. 2, p. 259.
4. Hamza, *Rihlatî*, pp. 23–24.
5. Hamza, *Rihlatî*, pp. 24–25.
6. Hamza, *Rihlatî*, p. 23.
7. See the discussion in Fedwa Malti-Douglas, "Mentalités and Marginality: Blindness and Mamlûk Civilization," in *The Islamic World from Classical to Modern Times: Essays in Honor of Bernard Lewis*, ed. C. E. Bosworth et al. (Princeton: Darwin Press, 1989), pp. 211–237.
8. On Karîmân's death wish, see chapter 2.
9. Hamza, *Rihlatî*, p. 30. The ellipses are in the original text.
10. See, for example, al-Hujwîrî, *Kashf al-Mahjûb*, trans. R. A. Nicholson (Lahore: Islamic Book Foundation, 1980), p. 103; Annemarie Schimmel, *Mystical Dimensions of Islam* (Chapel Hill: The University of North Carolina Press, 1975), p. 37.

11. Hamza, *Riḥlatî*, p. 25.

12. Russell Jones, "Ibrâhîm b. Adham," *Encyclopaedia of Islam*, 2nd ed. (Leiden: E. J. Brill, 1960).

13. A. J. Arberry, *Sufism: An Account of the Mystics of Islam* (New York: Harper & Row Publishers, 1970), p. 28. See also Arberry's introduction to Farîd al-Dîn ᶜAttâr, *Muslim Saints and Mystics: Episodes from the Tadhkirat al-Auliya'* (London: Penguin Arkana, 1990), p. 5.

14. Al-Qushayrî, *al-Risâla al-Qushayriyya*, eds. ᶜAbd al-Halîm Mahmûd and Mahmûd ibn al-Sharîf, vol. 1 (Cairo: Dâr al-Kutub al-Hadîtha, 1966), pp. 51–53. Additional material can be had elsewhere in *al-Risâla*.

15. In addition to al-Qushayrî, see also, for example, al-Hujwîrî, *Kashf*, pp. 103–105; ᶜAttâr, *Muslim Saints*, pp. 62–79.

16. Hamza, *Riḥlatî*, p. 24.

17. Schimmel, *Mystical Dimensions*, p. 36.

18. See al-Fudayl's biography in al-Qushayrî, *al-Risâla*, vol. 1, pp. 57–59. Additional material can be had elsewhere in *al-Risâla*. See also al-Hujwîrî, *Kashf*, pp. 97–100; Ibn Khallikân, *Wafayât al-Aᶜyân wa-Anbâ' Abnâ' al-Zamân*, ed. Ihsân ᶜAbbâs, vol. 4 (Beirut: Dâr al-Thaqâfa, n.d.), pp. 47–50; ᶜAttâr, *Muslim Saints*, pp. 52–61.

19. See chapter 2.

20. Hamza, *Riḥlatî*, p. 25.

21. See chapter 2.

22. See chapter 2.

23. Al-Qushayrî, *al-Risâla*, vol. 1, pp. 83–85. Additional material can be had elsewhere in *al-Risâla*. See also al-Hujwîrî, *Kashf*, pp. 139–140; ᶜAttâr, *Muslim Saints*, pp. 153–160.

24. See al-Hujwîrî, *Kashf*, pp. 139–140.

25. Hamza, *Riḥlatî*, pp. 187 ff.

26. Karîmân Hamza, *Anâqa wa-Hishma* (Cairo: V.I.P., n.d.). I am extremely grateful to Karîmân Hamza for providing me with copies of this catalog.

27. Hamza, *Riḥlatî*, p. 195.

28. Hamza, *Riḥlatî*, pp. 194–198.

29. See Fedwa Malti-Douglas, "Dreams, the Blind, and the Semiotics of the Biographical Notice," *Studia Islamica* 51 (1980): p. 144.

30. See, for example, al-Kirmânî, *Sahîh al-Bukhârî bi-Sharh al-Kirmânî*, vol. 24 (Beirut: Dâr Ihyâ' al-Turâth al-ᶜArabî, 1981), pp. 94–143.

31. See, for example, Toufic Fahd, *La divination arabe* (Leiden: E. J. Brill, 1966), pp. 329–363; Artémidore d'Ephèse, *Le livre des songes*, trad. arabe de Hunayn ibn Ishâq (Damascus: Institut Français de Damas, 1964); al-Nâbulusî, *Taᶜtîr al-Anâm fî Taᶜbîr al-Manâm* (Cairo: ᶜIsâ al-Bâbî al-Halabî, n.d.); Ibn Sîrîn, *Muntakhab al-Kalâm fî Tafsîr al-Ahlâm*, printed on the margins of al-Nâbulusî, *Taᶜtîr al-Anâm fî Taᶜbîr al-Manâm* (Cairo: ᶜIsâ al-Bâbî al-Halabî, n.d.); Ibn Abî al-Dunyâ, *Morality in the Guise of Dreams*, a critical edition of *Kitâb al-Manâm*, with an introduction by Leah Kinberg (Leiden: E. J. Brill, 1994). For an inventory of Islamic oneirocritical literature, see Toufic Fahd, *La divination arabe* (Leiden: E. J. Brill, 1966), pp. 329–363.

32. See, for example, Ahmad al-Sabbâhî ᶜAwad Allâh, *Tafsîr al-Ahlâm* (Cairo: Maktabat Madbûlî, [1977?]); Ibrâhîm Muhammad al-Jamal, *Ikhtartu lak min al-Turâth: Tafsîr al-Ahlâm* (Cairo: Maktabat al-Qur'ân, 1982).

33. Najîb Mahfûz, "Ra'aytu fîmâ Yarâ al-Nâ'im," in Najîb Mahfûz, *Ra'aytu fîmâ Yarâ al-Nâ'im* (Cairo: Maktabat Misr, 1982), pp. 139–173. On this story cycle, see Fedwa Malti-Douglas, "Mahfouz's Dreams," in *Naguib Mahfouz: From Regional Fame to Global Recognition,* ed. Michael Beard and Adnan Haydar (Syracuse: Syracuse University Press, 1993), pp. 126–143 (text), 183–185 (notes).

34. For the categorization of dream types see, for example, Artemidorus, *Oneirocritica,* trans. R. J. White (Park Ridge: Noyes Press, 1975), pp. 14–16; Ibn Ishâq, *Songes,* pp. 7, 10. The Greek equivalents are provided by the editor in the notes. For a discussion of these materials, see Malti-Douglas, "Dreams."

35. For some of the sexual subtext in this relationship, see chapter 2.

36. Toufic Fahd, "Les songes et leur interprétation selon l'Islam," in *Les Songes et leur Interprétation,* Sources Orientales, vol. 2 (Paris: Éditions du Seuil, 1959), pp. 140–142.

37. See chapter 2.

38. Hamza, *Rihlatî,* pp. 27–30.

39. Hamza, *Rihlatî,* pp. 158–159.

40. Hamza, *Rihlatî,* pp. 220–222. For the hadîth, see, for example, al-Dârimî, *Sunan al-Dârimî,* vol. 2 (Beirut: Dâr al-Kutub al-ᶜIlmiyya, n.d.), pp. 125–126; Ibn Mâja, *Sunan Ibn Mâja,* ed. Muhammad Fu'âd ᶜAbd al-Bâqî (Beirut: al-Maktaba al-ᶜIlmiyya, n.d.), vol. 2, pp. 1384–1385.

41. See, for example, al-Safadî, *al-Ghayth al-Musajjam fî Sharh Lâmiyyat al-ᶜAjam,* vol. 1 (Beirut: Dâr al-Kutub al-ᶜIlmiyya, 1975), pp. 244–245.

42. See chapters 5 and 6.

43. See chapter 5.

44. Hamza, *Rihlatî,* p. 228; ᶜAbd al-Halîm Mahmûd, *Ustâdh al-Sâ'irîn al-Hârith ibn Asad al-Muhâsibî,* in ᶜAbd al-Halîm Mahmûd, *al-Majmûᶜa al-Kâmila li-Mu'allafât al-Duktûr ᶜAbd al-Halîm Mahmûd,* vol. 15, subdivision of *al-Fuqahâ' wal-Muhaddithûn,* vol. 2 (Cairo and Beirut: Dâr al-Kitâb al-Misrî and Dâr al-Kitâb al-Lubnânî, 1991).

45. Hamza, *Rihlatî,* p. 230.

46. See W. Montgomery Watt, *Islamic Philosophy and Theology* (Edinburgh: Edinburgh University Press, 1962), pp. 58–90; the quote is on pp. 58–59.

47. Hamza, *Rihlatî,* pp. 231–232.

48. Arberry, *Sufism,* p. 46. See also his biography in al-Qushayrî, *al-Risâla,* vol. 1, pp. 72–73, with additional material elsewhere in *al-Risâla;* al-Hujwîrî, *Kashf,* pp. 108–109; ᶜAttâr, *Muslim Saints,* pp. 143–145.

49. Hamza, *Rihlatî,* p. 232.

50. Hamza, *Rihlatî,* p. 233.

51. The term *mudhîᶜ* (fem. *mudhîᶜa*) is applied to both radio and television announcers. In Karîmân's case, this is clearly a reference to her television work.

52. Hamza, *Rihlatî,* p. 234. The ellipses are in the original text.

53. Hamza, *Rihlatî,* p. 234. The ellipses are in the original text.

54. Hamza, *Rihlatî*, p. 235.

55. For a discussion of the states and stations on the mystical path, see, for example, Arberry, *Sufism*, pp. 74–83; the quote is on p. 75. See also Schimmel, *Mystical Dimensions*, pp. 98–186.

56. On some of this terminology, see Arberry, *Sufism*, pp. 74–79.

57. Hamza, *Rihlatî*, p. 118.

58. See Mahmûd, *Ustâdh al-Sâ'irîn*.

59. Hamza, *Rihlatî*, pp. 235–238.

60. Hamza, *Rihlatî*, p. 238. The ellipsis is in the original text.

61. See chapter 2.

62. See, for example, Richard P. Mitchell, *The Society of the Muslim Brothers* (London: Oxford University Press, 1969); Ahmad Râ'if, *Sarâdîb al-Shaytân: Safahât min Ta'rîkh al-Ikhwân al-Muslimîn* (Cairo: al-Zahrâ' lil-Iᶜlâm al-ᶜArabî, 1988). See also Esposito, *The Islamic Threat*.

63. Schimmel, *Mystical Dimensions*, p. 37.

64. Al-Qushayrî, *al-Risâla*, vol. 2, p. 496.

65. Karîmân Hamza, personal communication, Cairo, January 5, 1996.

66. Karîmân Hamza, personal communication, Cairo, January 5, 1996.

67. Karîmân Hamza, personal communication, Cairo, January 5, 1996.

68. Khamîs, introduction to Hamza, *Rihlatî*, p. 17.

69. Ibn al-Hâshimî, ed., *Al-Dâᶜiya Zaynab al-Ghazâlî* (Dubai: Dâr al-Fadîla and Cairo: Dâr al-Iᶜtisâm, 1989).

70. See chapter 2.

71. See, for example, Schimmel, *Mystical Dimensions*, pp. 67, 109, 112.

72. Hamza, *Rifqan bil-Qawârîr*, pp. 147–150. For the example, see Ibn Mâja, *Sunan*, vol. 2, pp. 1,203–1,204.

73. Al-Bukhârî, *Sahîh al-Bukhârî bi-Sharh al-Kirmânî*, vol. 21 (Beirut: Dâr Ihyâ' al-Turâth al-ᶜArabî, 1981), pp. 170–171.

74. For some contemporary renditions, see, for example, *al-Rajul al-Sâlih wal-Kalb* (Cairo: Safîr—Iᶜlâm, Diᶜâya, Nashr, 1987); ᶜAliyya Tawfîq and Kamâl Darwîsh, *Hikâyât ᶜArabiyya wa-Islâmiyya: Sâlim wal-Asîr wa-Hikâyât Ukhrâ* (Cairo: Matâbiᶜ al-Ahrâm al-Tijâriyya, 1986), pp. 6–8. For a discussion of these materials, see Douglas and Malti-Douglas, *Arab Comic Strips*, p. 96.

75. Hamza, *Rifqan bil-Qawârîr*, p. 149.

76. Hamza, *Rifqan bil-Qawârîr*, p. 149, n. 3.

77. Karîmân Hamza, personal communication, Cairo, January 5, 1996.

78. Hamza, *Rifqan bil-Qawârîr*, p. 150.

79. See al-Tirmidhî, *al-Jâmiᶜ al-Sahîh—Sunan al-Tirmidhî*, ed. Kamâl Yûsuf al-Hût, vol. 4 (Beirut: Dâr al-Kutub al-ᶜIlmiyya, 1987), p. 66.

80. Marjorie Garber, *Dog Love* (New York: Simon & Schuster, 1996).

81. On this foremost medieval Muslim female mystic, see the still important study by Margaret Smith, *Râbiᶜa the Mystic and Her Fellow-Saints in Islam* (Cambridge: Cambridge University Press, 1928). See also Schimmel, *Mystical Dimensions*, pp. 426–435.

82. Khamîs, introduction to Hamza, *Rihlatî*, pp. 7–12.

83. Muhammad ᶜAtiyya Khamîs, *Râbiᶜa al-ᶜAdawiyya* (Cairo: Dâr Karam lil-Tibâᶜa wal-Nashr, n.d.). I purchased this booklet in Morocco.

84. See, for example, Javad Nurbakhsh, *Le Mémorial des Saintes: Le Livre des Vies Merveilleuses des femmes mystiques musulmanes* (London: Editions Khaniqahi-Nimatullahi, 1991).

CHAPTER 4

1. See chapters 1 and 2.

2. Al-Hulw, *Falâ Tansa Allâh* (Casablanca: Matbaᶜat al-Najâh al-Jadîda, 1984). I shall retain the transliterated form of the name only when referring to the Arabic original. The names of the family members mentioned in the work will be spelled as they are in the French translation and not in transcription from the Arabic original.

3. Lahlou, *N'oublie pas Dieu,* trans., Mustapha El-Kasri (Casablanca: Imprimerie Najah El Jadida, 1987).

4. In its statistics, the American Cancer Society notes that some men are diagnosed with breast cancer. The American Cancer Society, cited in *Prevention,* October 1997, p. 196.

5. See chapters 1, 2, and 3.

6. Saghir and Kouhmane, *L'Islam.* See chapters 6 and 7.

7. Again, as with Karîmân, the first name, Leïla, will be used to refer to the central character of the work and the full name, Leïla Lahlou, to the historical individual and author of the work.

8. For a detailed analysis, see chapter 5.

9. Al-Hulw, *Falâ Tansa Allâh,* pp. 155–161. See chapter 5 for a full discussion.

10. Barbara Seaman, "Beyond the Halsted Radical," in *On the Issues* (Fall 1997): pp. 48 ff.; the quote is on p. 48.

11. Susan Sontag, *Illness as Metaphor and AIDS and Its Metaphors* (New York and London: Doubleday Anchor Books, 1990).

12. Joyce Wadler, *My Breast* (New York and London: Pocket Books, 1992); Elisabeth Gille, *Le crabe sur la banquete arrière* (Paris: Mercure de France, 1994).

13. ᶜAbla al-Ruwaynî, *al-Janûbî: Amal Dunqul* (Cairo: Maktabat Madbûlî, n.d.). On this work, see Malti-Douglas, *Woman's Body, Woman's Word,* pp. 144–160.

14. See Nawâl al-Saᶜdâwî, "Lâ Shay' Yafnâ," in Nawâl al-Saᶜdâwî, *Lahzat Sidq* (Beirut: Dâr al-Adâb, 1986), pp. 77–82; see Malti-Douglas, *Men, Women, and God(s),* especially pp. 20–43, for the importance of medicine in the Saadawian corpus and where this story is discussed.

15. Evelyne Accad, "My Journey with Cancer," *Al-Raida* 9 (1994): pp. 10–13.

16. Cf. the "Dossier Santé" on breast cancer in the Moroccan woman's magazine, *La Citadine,* February 1997, pp. 24–28.

17. See chapters 1, 2, and 3. This is a very common topos in contemporary revivalist materials.

18. Al-Hulw, *Falâ Tansa Allâh,* p. 27.

19. Michel Foucault, *Naissance de la clinique: Une archéologie du regard médical* (Paris: Presses Universitaires de France, 1963).

20. Kathryn Montgomery Hunter, *Doctors' Stories: The Narrative Structure of Medical Knowledge* (Princeton: Princeton University Press, 1991).

21. See Elaine Scarry, *The Body in Pain: The Making and Unmaking of the World* (New York and Oxford: Oxford University Press, 1985); Elaine Scarry, *Resisting Representation* (New York and Oxford: Oxford University Press, 1994), pp. 13–48.

22. See chapter 2.

23. See, for example, Malti-Douglas, *Men, Women, and God(s)*.

24. Al-Hulw, *Falâ Tansa Allâh,* p. 37, ellipses in original.

25. Al-Hulw, *Falâ Tansa Allâh,* p. 38.

26. See the medical documents in the appendixes in the original Arabic and in the French translation.

27. This is, in reality, the Hôpital Universitaire Brugmann. It will, however, appear here as Brugmann Hospital, since this is the way Leïla identifies it in her Arabic narration (Mustashfâ Brugmann).

28. Al-Hulw, *Falâ Tansa Allâh,* p. 46.

29. Al-Hulw, *Falâ Tansa Allâh,* p. 46.

30. Al-Hulw, *Falâ Tansa Allâh,* pp. 46–47.

31. On this important construct, see Eve Kosofsky Sedgwick, *Between Men: English Literature and Male Homosocial Desire* (New York: Columbia University Press, 1985). For the centrality of this construct in Arabo-Islamic culture, especially to the male gender, see Malti-Douglas, *Woman's Body, Woman's Word,* in its entirety. For manifestations of female homosociality, see Malti-Douglas, *Men, Women, and God(s),* pp. 159–176.

32. See chapter 5.

33. Al-Hulw, *Falâ Tansa Allâh,* p. 47.

34. See chapter 5.

35. Al-Hulw, *Falâ Tansa Allâh,* pp. 30, 38, 41.

36. Al-Hulw, *Falâ Tansa Allâh,* p. 43.

37. Sontag, *Illness and Its Metaphors,* pp. 5–87.

38. Al-Hulw, *Falâ Tansa Allâh,* p. 38.

39. The majority of physicians are referred to by their initials, sometimes only one initial, for the last name, and sometimes two, one for the last name and one for the first. "Fu," written in the Arabic with two consonants, stands for the Belgian oncologist, Vokaer. The shortened appellation will be retained, however, for two reasons. The first is to remain faithful to the onomastic interplays in Leïla's text, and the second is due to the fact that Leïla does not provide these physicians with their full names in her own narration of her corporal and spiritual journey.

40. Al-Hulw, *Falâ Tansa Allâh,* pp. 45–46.

41. Al-Hulw, *Falâ Tansa Allâh,* p. 51.

42. Al-Hulw, *Falâ Tansa Allâh,* p. 59.

43. Al-Hulw, *Falâ Tansa Allâh,* p. 116.

44. Al-Hulw, *Falâ Tansa Allâh,* p. 117.

45. Al-Hulw, *Falâ Tansa Allâh,* p. 121.

46. See chapter 5.

47. See chapter 5.

48. See chapter 5.

49. Al-Hulw, *Falâ Tansa Allâh,* p. 163. See, also, *al-Qur'ân,* Sûrat Yâ'-Sîn,

verse 82. I have translated this myself, but it is also available in Arberry, *The Koran,* vol. 2, p. 149.

50. Sandra Butler and Barbara Rosenblum, *Cancer in Two Voices,* 2nd ed. (Duluth, Minn.: Spinsters Ink, 1991).

51. The French letter from Tagnon to Yacoubi is in the appendixes to both the Arabic original and the French translation.

52. For a discussion of closure in the medical "plot," see Hunter, *Doctors' Stories,* pp. 126 ff.

53. See chapters 2, 3, and 8.

54. See chapter 5.

55. Al-Hulw, *Falâ Tansa Allâh,* p. 58.

56. See chapters 1, 2, and 3.

57. Al-Hulw, *Falâ Tansa Allâh,* p. 58.

58. Accad, "My Journey with Cancer," p. 11.

59. Audre Lorde, *The Cancer Journals,* spec. ed. (San Francisco: aunt lute books, 1997), p. 8.

60. My notions about the mutating body have benefited greatly from conversations with Elizabeth Grosz.

61. Al-Hulw, *Falâ Tansa Allâh,* pp. 60–61.

62. Al-Hulw, *Falâ Tansa Allâh,* pp. 67 ff.

63. Al-Hulw, *Falâ Tansa Allâh,* p. 68.

64. Grete Haentjens, ed., "Back from the Edge," *Prevention,* October 1997, p. 106.

65. Lorde, *The Cancer Journals,* pp. 28 ff. The quote is from p. 28.

66. Al-Hulw, *Falâ Tansa Allâh,* pp. 41.

67. Al-Hulw, *Falâ Tansa Allâh,* p. 27.

68. Al-Saʿdâwî, *Mudhakkirât Tabîba,* p. 5.

69. See chapter 5.

70. See chapter 5.

71. Al-Hulw, *Falâ Tansa Allâh,* p. 29.

72. Al-Hulw, *Falâ Tansa Allâh,* pp. 29–30.

73. The relationship between medicine and religion is not new with Lahlou, nor have conservative religious thinkers and leaders been averse to using modern medical treatment. See, for example, Nancy Elizabeth Gallagher, *Egypt's Other Wars: Epidemics and the Politics of Public Health* (Syracuse: Syracuse University Press, 1990), pp. 110 ff., in which she discusses the Muslim Brotherhood and modern medicine. Gallagher further notes rightly (p. 201 n. 72) that "An extended study of the activities of the Muslim Brotherhood and the other Islamic groups in public health and medicine is much needed."

74. See chapter 5.

75. I am grateful to Leïla Lahlou's husband, Mr. Abdelmalek Lahlou, for sharing with me this information about his wife.

CHAPTER 5

1. Al-Hulw, *Falâ Tansa Allâh,* p. 28.

2. Al-Hulw, *Falâ Tansa Allâh,* p. 29.

3. Al-Hulw, *Falâ Tansa Allâh,* p. 29.

4. Al-Hulw, *Falâ Tansa Allâh,* p. 31.

5. See chapters 7 and 8.

6. Al-Hulw, *Falâ Tansa Allâh,* pp. 78–79.

7. Al-Hulw, *Falâ Tansa Allâh,* p. 108.

8. Al-Hulw, *Falâ Tansa Allâh,* pp. 79–80.

9. Al-Hulw, *Falâ Tansa Allâh,* p. 92.

10. Al-Hulw, *Falâ Tansa Allâh,* p. 95.

11. Al-Hulw, *Falâ Tansa Allâh,* p. 96.

12. Al-Hulw, *Falâ Tansa Allâh,* pp. 91–99.

13. Al-Hulw, *Falâ Tansa Allâh,* pp. 57–58. See also chapter 4.

14. Al-Hulw, *Falâ Tansa Allâh,* p. 80.

15. Hamza, *Rihlatî,* pp. 200–201. See also chapter 3.

16. The two medieval mystics who set Karîmân on her journey were set on their own journeys by a voice. See chapters 2 and 3.

17. Al-Hulw, *Falâ Tansa Allâh,* p. 92.

18. See, for example, al-Hulw, *Falâ Tansa Allâh,* pp. 80, 94.

19. Al-Hulw, *Falâ Tansa Allâh,* p. 85.

20. Al-Hulw, *Falâ Tansa Allâh,* p. 87.

21. See chapter 4.

22. See, for example, al-Hulw, *Falâ Tansa Allâh,* pp. 78, 80, 91, 104.

23. See, for example, al-Hulw, *Falâ Tansa Allâh,* pp. 102–103.

24. Al-Hulw, *Falâ Tansa Allâh,* p. 103.

25. Al-Hulw, *Falâ Tansa Allâh,* p. 83, ellipses in original.

26. Al-Hulw, *Falâ Tansa Allâh,* p. 110.

27. Hamza, *Rihlatî,* pp. 201–203. See also chapter 3.

28. Hamza, *Rihlatî,* p. 201. See also chapter 3.

29. Hamza, *Rihlatî,* p. 201. See also chapter 3.

30. Hamza, *Rihlatî,* p. 203. See also chapter 3.

31. Al-Hulw, *Falâ Tansa Allâh,* p. 80.

32. Al-Hulw, *Falâ Tansa Allâh,* p. 80.

33. Al-Hulw, *Falâ Tansa Allâh,* p. 41. See also chapter 4.

34. Al-Hulw, *Falâ Tansa Allâh,* pp. 155–156.

35. Al-Hulw, *Falâ Tansa Allâh,* p. 157.

36. Al-Hulw, *Falâ Tansa Allâh,* p. 157.

37. Al-Hulw, *Falâ Tansa Allâh,* p. 160.

38. See chapter 3.

39. Al-Hulw, *Falâ Tansa Allâh,* p. 160.

40. Fahd, "Les Songes," pp. 140–142. See also chapter 3.

41. This would appear to be a reference to a curative practice that involves reciting the Qur'ân over an individual and which, according to my colleague Prof. A. A. Sachedina, is still practiced in the Middle East today.

42. Al-Safadî, *Nakt al-Himyân fî Nukat al-ᶜUmyân,* ed. Ahmad Zakî (Cairo: al-Matbaᶜa al-Jamâliyya, 1911), p. 312. For an in-depth discussion of this and other dreams in al-Safadî's biographical dictionary, see Malti-Douglas, "Dreams, the Blind," pp. 137–162.

43. Sidqî, *al-Tabarruj*, pp. 9–11; Malti-Douglas, "Faces of Sin."

44. Al-Hulw, *Falâ Tansa Allâh*, p. 137.

45. Al-Hulw, *Falâ Tansa Allâh*, p. 155. Ellipsis in original.

46. Al-Hulw, *Falâ Tansa Allâh*, p. 155.

47. See chapter 3.

48. Al-Hulw, *Falâ Tansa Allâh*, p. 32.

49. Al-Hulw, *Falâ Tansa Allâh*, p. 37.

50. Al-Hulw, *Falâ Tansa Allâh*, pp. 52, 57, 63.

51. Al-Hulw, *Falâ Tansa Allâh*, p. 135.

52. Al-Hulw, *Falâ Tansa Allâh*, p. 128.

53. Al-Hulw, *Falâ Tansa Allâh*, pp. 149–150.

54. Al-Hulw, *Falâ Tansa Allâh*, pp. 140–141. On the role of similar practices, see, for example, ʿAbd al-Latîf al-Shâdhilî, *al-Tasawwuf wal-Mujtamaʿ: Namâdhij min al-Qarn al-ʿAshir al-Hijrî* (Salé: Matâbiʿ Salâ, 1989), pp. 116–117.

55. Al-Hulw, *Falâ Tansa Allâh*, p. 147.

56. For references to this *hadîth* and other dream material, see chapter 3.

57. Al-Hulw, *Falâ Tansa Allâh*, p. 157.

58. Al-Hulw, *Falâ Tansa Allâh*, p. 158.

59. See, for example, al-Hulw, *Falâ Tansa Allâh*, p. 158. Cf. Foucault, *Naissance de la clinique*, pp. x-xi.

60. See chapters 2 and 3.

61. Al-Hulw, *Falâ Tansa Allâh*, pp. 87–88.

62. Al-Hulw, *Falâ Tansa Allâh*, p. 162. See, for example, Muhammad Fu'âd ʿAbd al-Bâqî, *al-Muʿjam al-Mufahras li-Alfâz al-Qur'ân al-Karîm* (Beirut: Mu'assasat Jamâl lil-Nashr, n.d.), pp. 139–140. *Bâb al-Samâ' Maftûh* ("The Gates [literally the gate] of Heaven are Open"), a 1989 film by the Moroccan Farida Ben Lyazid, also exploits this image from a woman's Islamic perspective.

63. See chapters 2 and 3.

64. Al-Mahdî bin ʿAbbûd, introduction to al-Hulw, *Falâ Tansa Allâh*, p. 5.

65. Gérard Genette, *Seuils* (Paris: Éditions du Seuil, 1987).

66. See chapter 4.

67. Al-Hulw, *Falâ Tansa Allâh*, p. 133.

68. Al-Hulw, *Falâ Tansa Allâh*, p. 133.

69. See chapter 2.

70. Al-Hulw, *Falâ Tansa Allâh*, pp. 156–175.

71. Al-Hulw, *Falâ Tansa Allâh*, p. 127.

72. See chapters 2 and 3.

73. Al-Hulw, *Falâ Tansa Allâh*, p. 98.

74. Al-Hulw, *Falâ Tansa Allâh*, p. 104.

75. Al-Hulw, *Falâ Tansa Allâh*, p. 105.

76. Al-Hulw, *Falâ Tansa Allâh*, p. 126.

77. Al-Hulw, *Falâ Tansa Allâh*, pp. 122–123.

78. Barbara Stone, *Cancer as Initiation: Surviving the Fire* (Chicago and La Salle, Illinois: Open Court, 1994).

79. Stone, *Cancer as Initiation*, p. 71.

80. Al-Hulw, *Falâ Tansa Allâh,* p. 121.

81. A. Taha, *La Médecine à la lumière du Coran et de la Sunna* (Lyon: Librarie Tawhid, 1994), p. 28.

82. See chapter 4.

83. *Al-Qur'ân,* Sûrat al-Shu'arâ', verse 80; Arberry, *The Koran,* vol. 2, p. 68.

84. For a more detailed discussion, see chapter 8.

85. Al-Hulw, *Falâ Tansa Allâh,* p. 104.

86. I am extremely grateful to Leïla Lahlou's husband, Abdelmalek Lahlou, for speaking with me about Leïla Lahlou and her life.

CHAPTER 6

1. Cheikh Mohammed Saghir and Kouhmane Sultana, *L'Islam, la femme, et l'intégrisme: Journal d'une jeune femme européenne* (Brussels: Édition Al-Imen, 1991).

2. As with the analyses of the works of Karîmân Hamza and Leïla Lahlou, so it will be with that of the Belgian Muslim writer: the first name, Sultana, refers to the central character in the text and the full name, Sultana Kouhmane, to the author of the work.

3. See chapter 7.

4. A great deal has been written on Islam outside the central Islamic lands and particularly in Europe. See, for example, Kepel, *Les banlieues;* Kepel, *À l'ouest d'Allah;* Philip Lewis, *Islamic Britain: Religion, Politics and Identity Among British Muslims* (London: I. B. Tauris & Co., 1994); Bernard Lewis and Dominique Schnapper, eds., *Muslims in Europe* (London: Pinter Publishers, 1994). See also the provocative Ahmed, *Postmodernism and Islam.*

5. The French spelling, Cheikh, will be retained here, especially since it functions almost as a title for Mohammed Saghir.

6. See chapters 4 and 5.

7. See chapter 2.

8. For these and other references on autobiography, see chapter 1. For more discussion of these problematics, see also chapter 8.

9. Saghir and Kouhmane, *L'Islam,* pp. 65–67. When referring to the work, I will retain the dual authorship for consistency of citation.

10. See, for example, Saghir and Kouhmane, *L'Islam,* pp. 11, 49, 64.

11. Imam Mohammed Saghir, *Vaccin et Traitement Islamiques Anti-SIDA* ([Brussels?]: [Edition Al-Imen?,] n.d.). Despite the fact that there are no bibliographical data on this work, nevertheless it would appear to be published by Edition Al-Imen in Brussels, which distributes the work internationally and sells it in its bookstore in Brussels.

12. Saghir, *Vaccin et Traitement,* p. 17.

13. See chapters 2, 3, 4, and 5.

14. Saghir and Kouhmane, *L'Islam,* p. 3.

15. See chapter 7.

16. Saghir and Kouhmane, *L'Islam,* p. 4.

17. Saghir and Kouhmane, *L'Islam,* p. 5.

18. Saghir and Kouhmane, *L'Islam,* pp. 3–8.

19. On the Prophet's significance in dreams, see, for example, Fahd, "Les Songes," pp. 140–142.

20. See chapters 3 and 5.

21. See Malti-Douglas, "Dreams, the Blind," pp. 137–162.

22. See chapter 3.

23. See chapters 4 and 5.

24. See chapters 2 and 3.

25. Saghir and Kouhmane, L'Islam, p. 9.

26. Saghir and Kouhmane, L'Islam, p. 4.

27. Saghir and Kouhmane, L'Islam, p. 3.

28. See chapter 2.

29. See, for example, Saghir and Kouhmane, L'Islam, p. 52.

30. Al-Safadî, al-Ghayth al-Musajjam, vol. 1, p. 244.

31. Saghir and Kouhmane, L'Islam, p. 5.

32. Al-Saᶜdâwî, Suqût al-Imâm; al-Saᶜdâwî, Jannât wa-Iblîs.

33. For a discussion of these issues in El Saadawi's fiction, see Malti-Douglas, Men, Women, and God(s), pp. 91–140.

34. Saghir and Kouhmane, L'Islam, p. 13.

35. Saghir and Kouhmane, L'Islam, p. 13. When quoting from the work, I am using the rendition of the phrase as it appears in the work.

36. Saghir and Kouhmane, L'Islam, pp. 13–14.

37. Some might wish to see in this title allusions to Christianity. While these allusions, of course, could be present, the use of this terminology in the title is by no means antithetical to Islam. The entire issue of the West in Sultana's journey will be analyzed in chapter 7.

38. This is an extremely popular anecdote that travels widely all over the Middle East and North Africa.

39. See chapters 4 and 5.

40. Saghir and Kouhmane, L'Islam, p. 15. Sultana opens the quotation marks to express what her Muslim sisters in Europe told her. But she never closes these quotation marks, though it is clear as the narrative continues that they should be closed where they have been in the above quote.

41. Saghir and Kouhmane, L'Islam, p. 15.

42. Saghir and Kouhmane, L'Islam, pp. 15–16.

43. Saghir and Kouhmane, L'Islam, p. 16.

44. Saghir and Kouhmane, L'Islam, pp. 16–17.

45. Classical Islam did recognize and try to conceptualize the problem posed by the existence of hermaphrodites. See, for example, Paula Sanders, "Gendering the Ungendered Body: Hermaphrodites in Medieval Islamic Law," in Women in Middle Eastern History: Shifting Boundaries in Sex and Gender, eds. Nikki R. Keddie and Beth Baron (New Haven: Yale University Press, 1991), pp. 74–95.

46. Saghir and Kouhmane, L'Islam, pp. 17–18.

47. Sultana uses the verb se découvrir, which can mean either to uncover or simply to bare one's head.

48. Saghir and Kouhmane, L'Islam, pp. 18–19.

49. Saghir and Kouhmane, L'Islam, pp. 15–19.

50. For more on these geographical issues, see chapter 8.

51. Saghir and Kouhmane, *L'Islam,* p. 15.

52. Saghir and Kouhmane, *L'Islam,* p. 9.

53. For an analysis of Karîmân's adventures with cigarettes and of the perception of this habit in contemporary revivalist discourses, see chapter 2.

54. See chapter 7.

55. Saghir and Kouhmane, *L'Islam,* p. 18.

56. For a more detailed comparison between the three texts, see chapter 8.

57. See chapter 5.

58. Saghir and Kouhmane, *L'Islam,* p. 16.

59. Saghir and Kouhmane, *L'Islam,* pp. 17–18.

60. See chapters 4 and 5.

61. Saghir and Kouhmane, *L'Islam,* p. 18.

62. See chapter 7.

63. Saghir and Kouhmane, *L'Islam,* p. 17.

64. For this popular *hadîth,* see, for example, Shaykh Muhammad ibn Sâlih al-ᶜUthaymîn, *Min al-Ahkâm al-Fiqhiyya fî al-Fatâwâ al-Nisâ'iyya* (Fez: Maktabat wa-Tasjîlât al-Hidâya al-Qur'âniyya, 1991), p. 79.

65. Marjorie Garber, *Vested Interests: Cross-Dressing and Cultural Anxiety* (New York: HarperCollins, 1992).

66. For a more detailed discussion of cross-dressing in a Middle Eastern context, see Malti-Douglas, *Men, Women, and God(s),* pp. 185 ff. See Nawâl al-Saᶜdâwî, *Rihlâtî fî al-ᶜAlam* (Cairo: Dâr Nashr Tadâmun al-Mar'a al-ᶜArabiyya, 1987), translated as Nawal El Saadawi, *My Travels Around the World,* trans. Shirley Eber (London: Methuen, 1991), pp. 296 ff.; Tahar Ben Jelloun, *L'enfant de sable* (Paris: Éditions du Seuil, 1985); Tahar Ben Jelloun, *La nuit sacrée* (Paris: Éditions du Seuil, 1985); Anwar, *Mahlan . . . Yâ Sâhibat al-Qawârîr,* pp. 78–79; Muhammad al-Ghazâlî, *Qadâyâ al-Mar'a bayn al-Taqâlîd al-Râkida wal-Wâfida* (Cairo: Dâr al-Shurûq, 1991), pp. 194–195; Mûsâ Sâlih Sharaf, *Fatâwâ al-Nisâ' al-ᶜAsriyya* (Beirut: Dâr al-Jîl and Cairo: Maktabat al-Turâth al-Islâmî, 1988), p. 11; al-ᶜUthaymîn, *Min al-Ahkâm al-Fiqhiyya,* pp. 79–80.

67. Saghir and Kouhmane, *L'Islam,* p. 18.

68. Saghir and Kouhmane, *L'Islam,* p. 18.

69. Saghir and Kouhmane, *L'Islam,* p. 17.

70. My goal here is not an in-depth study of Moroccan Islam but rather the immediate context in which Sultana's visit manifests itself in the Middle Atlas. Dale F. Eickelman's book, *Moroccan Islam: Tradition and Society in a Pilgrimage Center* (Austin and London: University of Texas Press, 1976), is a necessary work in which the much larger religious context can be seen. For a work that deals directly with women mystics in Morocco, see Mustafâ ᶜAbd al-Salâm al-Muhammâh, *al-Mar'a al-Maghribiyya wal-Tasawwuf fî al-Qarn al-Hâdî ᶜAshar al-Hijrî* (Casablanca: Matâbiᶜ Dâr al-Kitâb, 1978). See also the recent and fascinating book by Stefania Pandolfo, *Impasse of the Angels: Scenes from a Moroccan Space of Memory* (Chicago and London: University of Chicago Press, 1997).

71. See Malti-Douglas, *Blindness and Autobiography.*

72. On the female Sufi sacred in Morocco, see, for example, Sossie Andezian, "Femmes et religion en islam: un couple maudit?" in *Clio: Histoire, Femmes et Sociétés* 2 (1995), pp. 183–189; Mernissi, *Le monde*, pp. 175–179.

73. For a fascinating study that sheds a great deal of light on the Prophet Solomon, especially his relations with the Queen of Sheba, see Jacob Lassner, *Demonizing the Queen of Sheba: Boundaries of Gender and Culture in Postbiblical Judaism and Medieval Islam* (Chicago: University of Chicago Press, 1993).

74. I am extremely grateful to my friend Dr. Driss Ouachicha, who facilitated my visit to the sanctuary of Sidi Slimane. I am also grateful to Dr. Abdallah Malki and his wife, Amina Bouchakor, for sharing with me their personal experiences of the sanctuary of Sidi Slimane. Other Moroccan friends, who wished to remain anonymous, discussed with me their personal experiences in the shrine.

75. Saghir and Kouhmane, *L'Islam*, p. 62.

76. Saghir and Kouhmane, *L'Islam*, pp. 62–63.

77. Saghir and Kouhmane, *L'Islam*, pp. 45–48.

78. Phyllis Trible discusses the importance of naming for creating "personhood" in religious texts. See Phyllis Trible, *Texts of Terror: Literary-Feminist Readings of Biblical Narrative* (Philadelphia: Fortress Press, 1985), p. 15.

79. These pamphlets are limitless. One example will suffice: Hâshim ibn Hâmid al-Rifâ'î, *al-Kalimât fî Bayân Mahâsin Ta'addud al-Zawjât* ([Fez?]: Rasâ'il Islâh al-Mujtama', 1987). I purchased this pamphlet in an area of Fez known for its Islamist bookstores, and only after paying for it did I discover that the work was to be distributed free of charge!

80. Fawziyya al-Ghisasi, personal communication, Rabat, Morocco, March 18, 1996.

81. Saghir and Kouhmane, *L'Islam*, p. 63.

82. Saghir and Kouhmane, *L'Islam*, p. 63.

83. For an assessment of polygamy and Islamic law, see, for example, John L. Esposito, *Women in Muslim Family Law* (Syracuse: Syracuse University Press, 1982), pp. 109 ff.

84. Aihwa Ong, "Strategic Sisterhood or Sisters in Solidarity? Questions of Communitarianism and Citizenship in Asia," *Indiana Journal of Global Legal Studies* 4, no. 1 (Fall 1996): pp. 107–135; the quote is from p. 133.

85. Ong, "Strategic Sisterhood," p. 133. The correction and the *sic* are Ong's.

86. Fawziyya al-Ghisasi, personal communication, Rabat, Morocco, March 18, 1996. See also Abdelhamid Temsamani Chebagouda, *Mariage Mixte: Un Bonheur à Haut Risque* (Brussels: Édition Al-Imen, 1995), p. 73; Fedwa Malti-Douglas, "As the World (or Dare I Say the Globe?) Turns: Feminism and Transnationalism," *Indiana Journal of Global Legal Studies* 4, no. 1 (Fall 1996): pp. 137–144.

87. Saghir and Kouhmane, *L'Islam*, p. 63.

88. Saghir and Kouhmane, *L'Islam*, pp. 62–63.

89. Saghir and Kouhmane, *L'Islam*, pp. 34–35.

90. Saghir and Kouhmane, *L'Islam*, p. 34.

91. Saghir and Kouhmane, *L'Islam*, p. 35.

92. Saghir and Kouhmane, *L'Islam*, p. 45.
93. Saghir and Kouhmane, *L'Islam*, p. 46.
94. Saghir and Kouhmane, *L'Islam*, pp. 45–48.
95. Saghir and Kouhmane, *L'Islam*, p. 45.
96. Saghir and Kouhmane, *L'Islam*, p. 45.
97. Saghir and Kouhmane, *L'Islam*, pp. 45–46.
98. Saghir and Kouhmane, *L'Islam*, pp. 47.
99. Saghir, *Vaccin et Traitement Islamiques Anti-SIDA*, p. 4.
100. *SIDA: Les religions s'intérrogent* (Paris: L'Harmattan, 1994), p. 22.
101. See chapters 4 and 5.
102. Saghir, *Vaccin et Traitement Islamiques Anti-SIDA*, p. 49.
103. Saghir, *Vaccin et Traitement Islamiques Anti-SIDA*, p. 49.
104. See chapter 5.
105. Saghir and Kouhmane, *L'Islam*, p. 67.
106. I am extremely grateful to my student Tim Jon Semmerling for this information. Mr. Semmerling, at my request, went to the publisher of Sultana Kouhmana's work in Belgium, Édition Al-Imen. He interviewed the publisher on my behalf with questions I provided, on two occasions, December 21, 1996, and December 29, 1996.

CHAPTER 7

1. Tahar Ben Jelloun, *Hospitalité Française: Racisme et immigration maghrébine* (Paris: Éditions du Seuil, 1984); Tahar Ben Jelloun, *Le racisme expliqué à ma fille* (Paris: Éditions du Seuil, 1998).
2. Julia Kristeva, *Étrangers à nous-mêmes* (Paris: Librairie Arthème Fayard, 1988); Jacques Derrida, with Anne Dufourmantelle, *De l'hospitalité* (Paris: Calmann-Lévy, 1997).
3. Anti-North African bias is a leitmotif of all of Boudjellal's work. See, for example, Farid Boudjellal, *Les Soirées d'Abdulah: Ratonnade* (Paris: Futuropolis, 1985); Farid Boudjellal, *La Famille Slimani: Gags à l'Harissa* (Paris: Éditions Humanos, 1989). For a discussion of these issues in Boudjellal's work and elsewhere, see Douglas and Malti-Douglas, *Arab Comic Strips*, pp. 198–216.
4. Ben Jelloun, *Le racisme*, pp. 30–31.
5. Saghir and Kouhmane, *L'Islam*, p. 25.
6. The quote is from Saghir and Kouhmane, *L'Islam*, p. 18.
7. See chapter 8 for an analysis of memory and its uses in these texts.
8. Saghir and Kouhmane, *L'Islam*, p. 25.
9. Saghir and Kouhmane, *L'Islam*, p. 25.
10. Saghir and Kouhmane, *L'Islam*, p. 25.
11. Saghir and Kouhmane, *L'Islam*, pp. 25–26.
12. Saghir and Kouhmane, *L'Islam*, p. 26.
13. Saghir and Kouhmane, *L'Islam*, p. 26.
14. Saghir and Kouhmane, *L'Islam*, p. 26.
15. Saghir and Kouhmane, *L'Islam*, p. 26.
16. Saghir and Kouhmane, *L'Islam*, p. 25.
17. Saghir and Kouhmane, *L'Islam*, p. 25.

18. Saghir and Kouhmane, *L'Islam,* p. 26.

19. Saghir and Kouhmane, *L'Islam,* p. 27.

20. Saghir and Kouhmane, *L'Islam,* p. 28.

21. Saghir and Kouhmane, *L'Islam,* p. 29.

22. Saghir and Kouhmane, *L'Islam,* p. 30.

23. See chapter 6.

24. Saghir and Kouhmane, *L'Islam,* pp. 30–31.

25. See chapter 2.

26. See chapter 6.

27. See chapter 6.

28. See chapter 6, both for the knowledge of Lahlou's journey and for Sultana's dip in the spring.

29. Saghir and Kouhmane, *L'Islam,* pp. 15–16. See also chapter 6.

30. Saghir and Kouhmane, *L'Islam,* pp. 31–32.

31. Saghir and Kouhmane, *L'Islam,* pp. 32–33.

32. See Raymonda Hawa Tawil, *My Home, My Prison* (New York: Holt, Rinehart, and Winston, 1980); Ihsan Kamal, "A Jailhouse of My Own," trans. Wadida Wassef, rev. Lewis Hall, in *Arabic Writing Today: The Short Story,* ed. Mahmoud Manzalaoui (Cairo: American Research Center in Egypt, 1968), pp. 304–316.

33. See chapter 6.

34. Saghir and Kouhmane, *L'Islam,* p. 64.

35. Saghir and Kouhmane, *L'Islam,* p. 4.

36. See chapter 6.

37. See chapter 6.

38. Saghir and Kouhmane, *L'Islam,* p. 4.

39. The spelling of the hospital is different between the two accounts. In Sultana Kouhmane's text it is "Brugman" while in Lahlou, it is "Brugmann." Since the latter spelling is that found on the medical papers in Lahlou's text, that is how it will be rendered here. See Lahlou, *N'oublie pas Dieu,* p. 147.

40. Saghir and Kouhmane, *L'Islam,* p. 30.

41. Saghir and Kouhmane, *L'Islam,* p. 44.

CHAPTER 8

1. Carolyn G. Heilbrun, *Writing a Woman's Life* (New York: Ballantine Books, 1988), p. 11.

2. See, for example, Franz Rosenthal, "Intihâr," in *The Encyclopaedia of Islam,* 2nd ed., vol. 3 (Leiden: E. J. Brill, 1979), pp. 1246–1248.

3. On the female *Bildungsroman,* see, for example, Annis Pratt, *Archetypal Patterns in Women's Fiction* (Bloomington: Indiana University, 1981), pp. 13–37 (chapter written with Barbara White).

4. Amina Bouchakor, personal communication, March 22, 1998, Meknes, Morocco.

5. This took place following a lecture I delivered at al-Akhawayn University, Ifrane, Morocco, March 25, 1998, and in subsequent discussions with the physician in question.

6. Shams al-Bârûdî, *Rihlatî*, p. 22. Shâdiya's illness and subsequent cure after veiling is discussed by, among others, Shams al-Bârûdî's husband, Hasan Yûsuf, in Sirâj al-Dîn, *Awrâq Shams al-Bârûdî*, p. 79. See also Nâsif and Khudayr, *Fannânât Tâ'ibât*, pp. 86 ff.

7. See Tûqân, *Rihla Jabaliyya;* ᶜAbla al-Ruwaynî, *Al-Janûbî: Amal Dunqul* (Cairo: Maktabat Madbûlî, n.d.); Malti-Douglas, *Woman's Body, Woman's Word,* especially pp. 144–178.

8. See Zaynab al-Ghazâlî, introduction to Shams al-Bârûdî, *Rihlatî*, pp. 5–6.

9. Samîh al-Qasîm, introduction to Tûqân, *Rihla*, p. 5; Malti-Douglas, *Woman's Body,* pp. 162 ff. On the centrality of Tâhâ Husayn's autobiography, see Malti-Douglas, *Blindness and Autobiography.*

10. See Malti-Douglas, *Men, Women, and God(s),* which discusses this in several Saadawian texts. See, also, Fedwa Malti-Douglas, "Shahrazâd Feminist," in *The Thousand and One Nights in Arabic Literature and Society,* ed. Richard G. Hovannisian and Georges Sabagh (Cambridge: Cambridge University Press, 1997), pp. 40–55.

11. For a discussion, see Malti-Douglas, "Dreams, the Blind."

12. Shams al-Bârûdî, *Rihlatî,* pp. 24–25.

13. ᶜIsâ, *al-Harb bil-Niqâb,* pp. 95 ff.

14. Sirâj al-Dîn, *Awrâq Shams al-Bârûdî,* pp. 89 ff.

15. See Armstrong, *And the Sky,* pp. 34 ff.

16. See, for example, Ahmed, *Women and Gender,* pp. 96 ff.

17. For a discussion of some of these modalities, see Malti-Douglas, "An Anti-Travel Guide," pp. 205–213. See also al-ᶜUthaymîn, *Min al-Ahkâm al-Fiqhiyya,* pp. 22–25.

18. See, for example, Malti-Douglas, *Men, Women, and God(s),* pp. 177–197, among others.

19. See al-Saᶜûdî, *Zâd al-Musâfirîn,* pp. 22–23; Malti-Douglas, "An Anti-Travel Guide," pp. 210–211; Malti-Douglas, "Faces of Sin," p. 68.

20. See Malti-Douglas, *Woman's Body, Woman's Word,* pp. 104–105.

21. See Armstrong, *And the Sky,* pp. 34 ff.

22. See Fedwa Malti-Douglas, "Dangerous Crossings: Gender and Criticism in Arabic Literary Studies," in *Borderwork: Feminist Engagements with Comparative Literature,* ed. Margaret R. Higonnet (Ithaca and London: Cornell University Press, 1994), p. 226.

23. Benedict Anderson, *Imagined Communities: Reflections on the Origin and Spread of Nationalism* (London and New York: Verso, 1991), especially pp. 12 ff. It should be noted in passing that Anderson has misunderstood the relationship between grapheme and sound in the classical Arabic (and, hence, also classical Islamic) semiotic system (Anderson, *Imagined Communities,* p. 13). See, for example, Fedwa Malti-Douglas, "Sign Conceptions in the Islamic World," in *Semiotik = Semiotics: Ein Handbuch zu den zeichentheoretischen Grundlagen von Natur und Kultur = A Handbook on the Sign-Theoretic Foundations of Nature and Culture,* ed. Roland Posner, Klaus Robering, and Thomas A. Sebeok, vol. 2 (Berlin and New York: Walter de Gruyter, 1998), pp. 1799–1814.

24. Saghir and Kouhmane, *L'Islam,* p. 9.

25. Khamîs, introduction to Hamza, *Rihlatî,* p. 9.

26. Hamza, *Rihlatî,* p. 124.
27. Saghir and Kouhmane, *L'Islam,* p. 20.
28. See chapter 1.
29. See, for example, Saghir and Kouhmane, *L'Islam,* pp. 20–21.
30. Saghir and Kouhmane, *L'Islam,* pp. 20–21.
31. Jean-Noël Vuarnet, *Extases Féminines* (Paris: Hattier, 1991), p. 108.
32. See Mohamed Ali Gerbaoui, *Le Pont de Lumière: Récit de délire mystique* (Casablanca: Afrique Orient, 1992); Shaykh ᶜA'id ibn ᶜAbd Allâh al-Qarnî, *Shabâb ᶜAdû ilâ Allâh* (Fez: Maktabat wa-Tasjîlât al-Hidâya al-Qur'âniyya, 1991).

Index

Italic page numbers refer to illustrations.

Text: 10/13 Sabon
Display: Sabon
Composition: G&S Typesetters, Inc.
Printing and binding: Sheridan Books, Inc.
Index: Renate Wise